The Islamic
Movement
of Iraqi Shi'as

The Islamic Movement of Iraqi Shi'as

Joyce N. Wiley

Lynne Rienner Publishers · Boulder & London

Published in the United States of America in 1992 by
Lynne Rienner Publishers, Inc.
1800 30th Street, Boulder, Colorado 80301

and in the United Kingdom by
Lynne Rienner Publishers, Inc.
3 Henrietta Street, Covent Garden, London WC2E 8LU

Library of Congress Cataloging-in-Publication Data
Wiley, Joyce (Joyce N.)
   The Islamic movement of Iraqi Shi'as / by Joyce Wiley.
      p.   cm.
   Includes bibliographical references and index.
   ISBN 1-55587-272-7 (alk. paper)
   1. Shi'ah—Iraq—History—20th century. 2. Islam and politics—
Iraq. 3. Iraq—Politics and government. I. Title.
   BP192.7.I7W55   1992
   297'.82'09567—dc20   91-29921
                                                              CIP

British Cataloguing in Publication Data
A Cataloguing in Publication record for this book
is available from the British Library.

Printed and bound in the United States of America

The paper used in this publication meets the requirements
of the American National Standard for Permanence of
Paper for Printed Library Materials Z39.48-1984.

6-12-93

Contents

Tables and Figures

Tables

Figures

Acknowledgments

To those Iraqis who helped me contact principals of Iraq's Islamic movement and to those who provided me with information, I convey sincere gratitude. I thank two anonymous reviewers who made helpful suggestions, a number of which I have incorporated into the final manuscript. I am grateful to the editors at Lynne Rienner Publishers for their diligence and quality work. For any errors of commission, I take responsibility.

The Islamic
Movement
of Iraqi Shi'as

1

Introduction

In the seventh century, the Prophet Muhammad changed Arab society by means of the Islamic religion. In the twentieth century, Muslims are again wielding the requisites and concepts of Islam in an effort to change Arab society. Impelled by moral argument and the failures of existing governments, Muslim political activists seek to restructure their governments in accordance with God's will, as they perceive it to be set out in revelation. In the cause of Islam, disaffected citizens are challenging secular governments. When free or relatively free elections are allowed, political parties with Islamic agendas do well in Muslim countries. The Islamic Salvation Front won a majority of votes in the 1990 local Algerian elections, and Islamic parties have scored electoral successes in Jordan, Tunisia, and Egypt.

Even in the absence of elections, groups with Islamic agendas have managed to effect political change. In Iran the unarmed urban masses that were instrumental in bringing down the regime of the shah form the support base for an Islamic government. In other Muslim countries, groups with Islamic political agendas have resorted to direct action, even assassination, in their efforts to bring about change.[1]

There is no question of sectarianism in the Islamic movements of Iran, Jordan, and the North African countries, for the governments and their Islamic opponents belong to the same sect. The shah's government and his religiously motivated opponents were Shi'i, and the Jordanian and North African governments and their religiously motivated opponents are all Sunni.[2] Islamic political opposition in Iraq, however, has been branded as sectarian and attributed to Iranian export of revolution. In its official explanation for attacking Iran in September 1980, the Iraqi government cited the occurrence in Iraq of "terrorist acts and sabotage by infiltrators who came in from Iran, by Iranian residents in Iraq, and by other people of Iranian origin, who set about committing a large number of murders and injuries from explosions."[3] In his October 15, 1980, speech to the United Nations

1

Security Council, Sa'doun Hammadi, Iraq's minister of foreign affairs, charged "leaders of the reactionary and *sectarian* Da'wa Party" (emphasis added) with terrorism and collusion with Iran.[4]

A number of writers have followed the Iraqi government's lead, blaming Iranian export of revolution and sectarianism for both Islamic opposition to the Iraqi government and for the Iran-Iraq War: "Khomeini commenced a well-financed campaign to turn the Shiites in Iraq, who make up more than one-half of the population, against the Sunni-controlled government."[5] "The ayatollah deliberately put the war in a religious frame, a clash between Shi'ism in Persia and Sunni Islam in Iraq, when he denounced, as he still does, the Iraqis as 'atheists,' 'pagans,' and 'followers of the Omayyads.'"[6]

The existence of Islamic political movements in countries without sectarian divisions casts some doubt on the Iraqi government's charge that the Iraqi Islamic movement is sectarian in motivation and due to Iranian subversion. Likewise, the chronology of Iraq's Islamic movement tends to discredit the charge that the movement is traceable to Iran. As this study shows, the movement predated the Islamic Republic of Iran by two decades. The religious composition of Iraq's Islamic movement does, however, make the movement vulnerable to the charge of sectarianism. The majority of Iraq's Islamic activists, like the majority of Iraq's population, are Shi'i.[7]

But if Shi'i sectarianism implies anti-Sunnism or religious particularism, then Iraq's Islamic movement is not sectarian. The literature of the movement bespeaks an attempt by pious Muslims to modernize and govern Iraq within an Islamic context. Sayyid[8] Muhammad Baqir al-Sadr, founder and leader of Iraq's contemporary Islamic movement, did not propose to replace Iraq's governing Sunnis with Shi'as, nor did he propose an economic revolution in which a government of Sunni haves would give way to a government of Shi'i have-nots. Instead, he sought to exchange pious leaders for impious leaders, to unite "the virtuous rich and the virtuous poor"[9] in a defense of religion and traditional values. He expected Islamic government to facilitate people's doing good deeds and to restrain them from doing evil by implementing the acknowledged injunctions of Islam.[10] This motivation he shared with contemporary Sunni fundamentalists, as articulated by Maulana Abdul 'Ala' Mawdudi (d. 1979), founder of Pakistan's fundamentalist Jama'at-i Islami (Islamic Society): "The objective of the Islamic movement, in this world, is revolution in leadership. A leadership that has rebelled against God and His guidance and is responsible for the suffering of mankind has to be replaced by a leadership that is God-conscious, righteous, and committed to following Divine guidance."[11]

Sayyid al-Sadr sought to bring Islamic practices into congruence with change and to bring Islamic clerics into the management of change in Iraq. In pursuit of Islamic government, reformist Shi'i ulama (religious scholars) have led Shi'as to abandon their traditional political quietism and involve themselves in politics, in cooperation with virtuous Sunnis. Spokesmen for Hizb al-Da'wa al-Islamiya (Party of the Call to Islam), the largest group in the movement, told me in 1986 that 10 percent of its members were Sunni.[12]

The Ba'th government of Iraq has successfully portrayed Iraqi Islamic activism not only as sectarian but as weak and unpopular, even while using draconian means of repression against activists. Outsiders have tended to agree with the government's depiction, dismissing politicized Islam as having limited appeal to Iraqis. Militating against knowledge of, and even interest in, Iraq's Islamic movement are the obstructions both reporters and scholars encounter in a country with a highly repressive government and a frightened populace. The invisibility of Iraq's Shi'as also contributes to the government's success in portraying the movement as sectarian. Arab Shi'as are a disadvantaged population whose political history has received little scholarly attention. History records primarily the deeds of the powerful, and Shi'i Muslims have not held national-level political power anywhere but Iran since the Middle Ages.

Evaluating the proffered explanations for and evaluations of Islamic activism in Iraq requires an inquiry into the historical record of the movement. In the account that follows, I take care to specify the actors' categories and definitions and accept the validity of religious motivation. Relationships between human beings and a supernatural being figure in many human calculations, whether the social scientist shares the actors' belief in the existence of a supernatural being or not.

The political activists in Iraq's Islamic movement are fundamentalists in the sense that they reject secularism and insist Muslims be subject to Islamic law. They are fundamentalist in that they are attempting to construct the fundamentals of Islamic ideology in a modern society. They accept the appellation *fundamentalists*, interpreting it as "non-compromising Muslims,"[13] by which they mean that they reject syncretism and accept as legitimate sources of law only the Quran, the Prophet's traditions, and Islamic jurisprudence. Implicitly recognizing that scripture allows more than one interpretation, Iraq's Islamic activists do accept reformist rulings relative to traditional interpretations if those rulings come from esteemed Muslim jurisprudents. What they refuse to admit are non-Muslim sources of law.

Iraq's Islamic activists are not fundamentalists if the word implies a rejection of modernism and change. In word and deed they have striven for modern technology. Nor do they reject all change in social practices. They acknowledge the need to reform certain traditional social practices, including the "un-Islamic habits and social usages responsible for the backwardness of [Muslim] women."[14] Since the word *fundamentalist* is sometimes used to signify a rejection of all change and for some people has a threatening or disparaging implication, I call Iraq's Islamic political activists *Islamists*.

They are Islamist in that they advocate Islam both politically and religiously, insisting that Islamic people should have Islamic government.

Some Iraqi clerics date Iraq's Islamic movement to the post–World War I period, when clerics strove for a legitimate Islamic government to replace the Turkish government driven from Iraq by the British, but I view the 1919–1923 period of clerical activism as a precursor to the contemporary movement. This is because the intervening decades of the Hashimite monarchy were essentially without opposition to the existing government on behalf of Islam, and because the political movement that began in 1957–1958 differed in nature from the military campaign launched by the ulama in 1920. In both periods the ulama had the same declared goal, namely, legitimate government according to Islamic requirements as they perceived them, but the contemporary movement is religiously reformist and part of a decentralized political mobilization occurring throughout the Muslim world.

Like any social movement, Iraq's Islamic political movement has developed a literature embodying its essential ideas and principles. The literature exists in two modes: erudite and popular. Works in the erudite mode, Ayatollah al-Sadr's *Falsafatuna* (Our Philosophy) (1959) and *Iqtisaduna* (Our Economy) (1961), for example, are aimed primarily at the ulama. These books seek to ground the movement's tenets in Islam and demonstrate that the author's interpretations are faithful to Islam. Somewhat easier reading are abbreviated versions of these works, written for the laity, and articles he wrote for journals such as *Sawt al-Da'wa* (Voice of the Call). Ayatollah al-Sadr described his objective in the latter works as "adding to and simplifying" the arguments in books addressed to the ulama.[15] The tenor of the writing is didactic, in the manner of a pastor seeking to confirm and inspirit disciples, as demonstrated in the following quotation from an article he wrote for *Sawt al-Da'wa*: "In the absence of the Mahdi [Savior], mere mankind becomes responsible for the exalted mission. The members of the organization [Hizb al-Da'wa al-Islamiya] defend its cause for the glory of God. Those who issue the call to Islam [*al-da'wa*] have understood their religious obligation ahead [in time] of their Muslim brothers."[16]

The popular literature, often in the form of pamphlets and newspapers, provides news of the movement and of Iraqi government actions, including news not appearing in legal Iraqi newspapers, which, for most of the existence of the Islamic movement, have been instruments of the government. In Islamist publications, policies and tactics relative to the practical operation of the Islamic movement are explained and defended. Publications in this mode aim to mobilize believers and to strengthen the resolve of those already active. The weekly newspapers *Al-Jihad* (The Struggle) and *Al-'Amal al-Islami* (The Islamic Task), aimed at Islamists and sympathizers generally, are examples of publications in the popular vein.

Because the Islamic movement is highly decentralized, as indeed are all social movements, support for the cause is frequently a sense of affiliation rather than formal membership in an Islamic group. Believers responsive to the religious symbolism clerical leaders can evoke constitute a large pool of sympathizers, but only formal members can be given direct orders.

My information on the movement comes from the publications of Iraqi Islamists, supplemented by personal interviews conducted with leaders, members, and sympathizers of the Islamic groups. Declaratory information from the various sources is related to operational information on the actions of Iraqi Islamists and on the political forms taken by the Islamic Republic of Iran, an extension warranted by the affinity between the ulama leadership of Iran and the ulama leadership of Iraqi Islamists.

Although the religious convictions of Islamists direct them to high ethical standards and Islamists outside Iraq are not obliged to dissimulate as those inside Iraq are, literature written by activists and oral information given by activists are necessarily self-serving in some degree. The actors' interpretations may differ from mine and other outside observers', if for no other reason than the absence of shared experience. While it is necessary to know the actors' definitions of their situation in order to appreciate the subjective meaning of events to the participants, it is not necessary to accept those definitions as presented; thus I examine information about the movement for internal contradictions and an excess of idealism.

Internal contradictions exist in greater or lesser degree in any ideology and affect the prospects of a political movement deriving from the ideology. The resources a governing elite can bring to bear against a movement also affect its prospects. Just as a confluence of historical developments sets the stage for the genesis of a political movement, so the internal dynamics of a country and external resources available to protagonists affect the development of a political movement.

The historical context within which Iraq's Islamic movement emerged is drawn in the next chapter, which is followed by a chronicle of the actual development of the movement and, finally, analyses of the movement.

Notes

1. President Anwar Sadat of Egypt is the best-known victim of assassination by a group with an Islamic political agenda.
2. *Sunni* pertains to Muslim followers of the sunna, the path of tradition acknowledged by about 89 percent of Muslims. *Shi'i* pertains to the Shi'as, the other 11 percent of Muslims. Shi'as regard Imam Ali as the legitimate successor to the Prophet Muhammad. As used in this work, the term *Shi'a(s)* refers to the Ithna 'Ashari (Twelver) Shi'as, the majority group within Shi'ism. Ithna 'Ashari Shi'as form the majority population group in Iraq, Iran, and Bahrain and significant minorities in the other Gulf states, Lebanon, Pakistan, and

Afghanistan. The smaller branches of Shi'as are the Zaydis, who inhabit Yemen, and the Isma'ilis, associated in modern times with India.

3. 'Iraq, *Al-Niza' al-Iraqi al-Irani*, p. 13. (Translations of Arabic sources are by the author.)

4. Statement reprinted in Ismael, *Iran and Iraq*, p. 206. The foreign minister was referring to Hizb al-Da'wa al-Islamiya, founded in Iraq by Muhammad Baqir al-Sadr in 1957.

5. Renfrew, "Who Started the War?" p. 100.

6. Jansen, "Who Started the Gulf War?" pp. 15–16. *Ayatollah*, meaning "sign of God," is a title given to high-ranking Shi'i clerics. In this reference, Jansen is alluding to Imam Ruhullah Khomeini (1902–1989) of Iran.

7. A 1920 census conducted by the British military authorities, and reported in *Statistical Abstract for the Several British Overseas Dominions and Protectorates* (London, 1924), found the Iraqi population to be 56 percent Shi'i (cited in Tarbush, *The Role of the Military in Politics*, p. 14). For subsequent estimates of Iraq's religious composition, see Table 2.2.

8. In Iraq, descendants of the Prophet Muhammad are addressed with the title *sayyid* (fem. *sayyida*).

9. Muhammad Baqir al-Sadr, as cited in Batatu, "Shi'i Organizations in Iraq," p. 181.

10. al-Sadr, *Islamic Political System*, p. 36.

11. Mawdudi, *The Islamic Movement*, p. 71.

12. August 7, 1986, interview with Dr. Abu Ali, designated Hizb al-Da'wa spokesman in London, and Brother Ali, a member of Hizb al-Da'wa.

13. *Al-Da'wah Chronicle*, October 1981, p. 1.

14. al-Sadr, *Islamic Political System*, p. 36.

15. al-Sadr, *Contemporary Man and the Social Problem*, p. 22. In *Contemporary Man*, Ayatollah al-Sadr simplified and supplemented the critiques of capitalism and socialism presented in *Falsafatuna*.

16. al-Sadr, *Min Fikr al-Da'wa*, p. 11.

2

Historical Context

Located at the northwest end of the Persian Gulf, Iraq[1] is a crossroad where Semitic culture from the south and west has met Iranian culture from the east. Western and southwestern Iraq are geographically part of the Arabian Desert. Northeastern Iraq is composed of high mountains and steppe, the latter receiving enough rainfall for agriculture without irrigation. Between desert and steppe lies the central plain known formerly as Babylonia or Mesopotamia, the land between the two rivers, the Tigris and the Euphrates. Since ancient times people have used the river water to produce dates and wheat. Southeastern Iraq is yet a fourth distinctive area—marshlands in which little agriculture is possible.

In size Iraq is comparable to California. Its population is considerably less than that of California but is estimated to have reached 18 million by 1990.[2] Despite its location on the Gulf, Iraq has only about 26 miles of coastline. Iraq's main port, Basra, lies 60 miles from the sea, on the Shatt al-Arab, the confluence of the Tigris and Euphrates, which flow together their last 100 miles to the sea.

Not far from the confluence of the rivers developed the civilization of the ancient Sumerians, a non-Semitic people of unknown origin. In the ensuing millennia, the Sumerians and their successors in the plain were encroached upon by desert nomads from the south. Some of the Semitic people from the south, the Babylonians, the Assyrians, the Chaldeans, and the Arabs, themselves established great empires before vanishing into the ethnic multiplicity of Mesopotamia.

Conquerors also came from the east. The land of the Tigris and the Euphrates had been under Persian control for over 800 years when the Arab Muslim armies triumphed there in A.D. 637. Nevertheless, the overwhelming majority of the population adopted the Islamic religion and Arabic language of the conquerors, and maintained both thereafter despite subsequent periods of Persian and Turkish domination.

From the Arabs came the name Iraq, but to Arab geographers the term referred only to Lower Mesopotamia. Land north of modern Tikrit on the Tigris and somewhat north of Hit on the Euphrates was called Jazira, meaning "island," in this case the land between the Tigris and Euphrates. Modern Iraq, containing both Lower and Upper Mesopotamia, is at the intersection of Turkish, Persian, and Arab population groups. Iraq is bordered by Turkey on the north, Iran on the east, and four Arab countries—Kuwait, Saudi Arabia, Jordan, and Syria—on the south and west. Iraq's boundaries were fixed by agreement with the neighboring countries during its years as a British mandate, 1920 to 1932.

Iraq can be divided into three religious and ethnic zones. The southern half, from Baghdad south, is predominantly Shi'i Arab. The northern half is largely Sunni Arab in the western part and Sunni Kurd in the eastern part. Only in the 1947 census was a detailed population breakdown by religious and ethnic group made. At that time the Shi'as were 54.1 percent of the population, and about 95 percent of the Shi'as were ethnic Arabs. Table 2.1 gives the religious and ethnic breakdown for the entire population in 1947. Less detailed estimations of Iraq's religious composition over a period of years are presented in Table 2.2.

Table 2.1 Religioethnic Composition of Iraq in 1947

Religioethnic Group	Percentage in the Population
Muslims	
Shi'i Arabs	51.4
Sunni Arabs	19.7
Sunni Kurds	18.4
Shi'i Iranians	1.2
Sunni Turkomans	1.1
Shi'i Turkomans	.9
Shi'i Kurds	.6
Non-Muslims	
Christians	3.1
Jews	2.6
Yazidis and Shabaks[a]	.8
Sabeans[b]	.2
	100.0

Source: Iraqi Census of 1947 (as cited in Batatu, Old Social Classes, p. 40).

[a]Yazidis, erroneously called devil-worshipers, are a Kurdish people who embrace a syncretism of Muslim, Christian, and pagan beliefs. Shabaks are adherents of a Shi'i sect exclusive to several villages northeast of Mosul.

[b]Sabeans are members of a Manichean sect known for pacifism and a ceremonial need for running water.

Table 2.2 Successive Estimates of Iraq's Religioethnic Composition

Source	Percentage of Population			
	Shi'i	Sunni (non-Kurd)	Kurdish	Non-Muslim
British Census of 1920[a]	56	36		8
British Census of 1931[b]	55	22	14	9
Iraqi Census of 1947[c]	54	21	18	7
1982–1983	60[d](56)[e]	11(15)[e]	25[f]	4[g]

[a]Cited in Tarbush, *The Role of the Military in Politics*, p. 14.
[b]Cited in Sluglett, *Britain in Iraq*, p. 300.
[c]Cited in Batatu, *Old Social Classes*, p. 40.
[d]Official sources in the Gulf, cited by Bill, "Resurgent Islam in the Persian Gulf," p. 120. A 4 to 5 percent increase over approximately thirty-five years is credible given the ruralism of the Shi'as as compared with the Sunni and Christian populations and the tendency of rural populations to have larger families than do more prosperous urban groups. Rural-to-urban migrants are known to have retained the high rate of fertility characteristic of rural areas even in Baghdad. Through the 1960s, fertility was much higher in the shantytowns than in Baghdad's older urban districts. Cf. Lawless, "Iraq: Changing Population Patterns," pp. 97–129.
[e]If the over 1 million noncitizen Egyptians and Palestinians are included, the proportion of Shi'as drops to 56 percent and the proportion of non-Kurdish Sunni Muslims rises correspondingly.
[f]Ramazani, *Revolutionary Iran*, p. 4; *Middle East International*, December 5, 1987, p. 17.
[g]The non-Muslim population decreased substantially with the departure in 1950 and 1951 of the Iraqi Jews, who were estimated to be 2.6 percent of the population in the 1947 census.

Origin of the Shi'as

At the time of the seventh-century Muslim conquest, Iraq was religiously and ethnically diverse. The Persian ruling class was Magian in religion.[3] The peasantry was ethnically Aramean, descended from the earlier Babylonians. Most of the peasants worshiped sun, stars, fire, and water, but others had become Christians, either Nestorian or Monophysite. Among the

Aramean majority were substantial numbers of Arabs and Kurds, and smaller numbers of Syrians, Greeks, Indians, and East Africans. Society was organized not by ethnic or occupational group but by religious community. The ruling Sassanian Persians dealt with each community through its religious leaders; for example, in central Iraq the Sassanians held one Jewish official responsible for the entire Jewish community. Religious leaders themselves were given privileges. To use the Jewish community as an example again, rabbis were exempt from the poll tax paid by the general population.

The Muslim conquest prompted many peasants to convert to Islam. Most of the Persians, desirous of maintaining their positions and their property, also converted. The converts brought with them the traditions of Mesopotamia, including some of their former religious practices and much of the Persian administrative system.

Iraqi Muslims soon became party to a disagreement among the Arab conquerors over who was the rightful successor to the Prophet Muhammad, a disagreement that was to have a decisive influence on the subsequent history of Iraq. The first four caliphs (successors) were accepted, however reluctantly, by all; but a minority of the Arab Muslim community rejected the legitimacy of the Umayyad rulers who thereafter effected a hereditary succession to the caliphate (political authority accorded the Prophet's successors). The minority considered the family of Ali, Muhammad's cousin and son-in-law, to be the rightful successors. They were called *shiya'*,[4] meaning "partisans," in this instance the partisans of Ali. Shi'ism thus began as a political legitimist movement among the Arab conquerors.

Muslim converts in Iraq rallied to the Shi'i idea that the *umma* (Muslim community) was not being governed properly because it had the wrong governors. One grievance of the converts was that zakat, a wealth tax, was not collected after the reign of the third caliph, Uthman, meaning that wealthy Arabs often paid no taxes. Aware that the equality of believers is integral to Islam, many converts resented the privileged position of the Arab elite. Devout Muslims were further affronted by the mode of living in the Umayyad capital, Damascus. Belief that the Umayyads were insufficiently pious and economic discontent coalesced with partisanship for Ali. The early strongholds of Shi'ism were Kufa in southern Iraq, near modern Najaf, and Mada'in in central Iraq, near Baghdad.[5]

At Karbala, some 50 miles from Kufa, Ali's son Hussein was martyred by an Umayyad army on the tenth of the month of Muharram in the year A.H. 61[6] (October 10, 680), ending serious Shi'i contention for political power but not Shi'as' sense of rectitude. Having embraced Shi'ism, the people of southern and central Iraq maintained their beliefs through centuries of discrimination by non-Shi'i governors. Their congregation in a geographical area helped them retain group identity and encouraged the conversion to Shi'ism of Arab nomads and others who moved into the region.

The organization of the Islamic empire by religious community also contributed to the endurance of Shi'ism. Muslim governments continued the Persian practice of identifying people by their religious affiliation, religious leaders serving as liaisons between their communities and the government. Religious leaders were thus able to exercise control not only over religious doctrine but over many legal and economic matters as well, providing clerics leverage over the lives of their coreligionists. Citizens turned to religious leaders when they needed someone to intervene with the government on their behalf.

Ithna 'Ashari Shi'as asserted a divinely inspired series of twelve Imams, religious leaders invested with political authority, from the Prophet Muhammad's family. Of them, only the First Imam, Ali, the Prophet's son-in-law, ever exercised political power, but Shi'as assigned religious authority to all twelve. After Ali came Ali's son Hasan; third was Hasan's brother Hussein. Then came Imam Hussein's son, and so on. Each Imam designated his successor, usually his oldest son. The tombs of Ali and Hussein and four of the other Twelve Imams are in the holy cities of Iraq—Najaf, Karbala, Kazymiya, and Samarra.

Through the centuries, pilgrims from Persia and other Shi'i communities came to Iraq to visit the holy cities. The devout were even transported to Najaf, where Ali is buried, for their own burials. Shi'i pilgrims and deceased Shi'as were thus valued sources of revenue for both Iraqi Shi'as and the Iraqi government. After the eleventh-century establishment of Shi'i theological schools in the holy cities, Najaf in particular, students and religious scholars were attracted to Iraq, further strengthening Shi'ism in the Iraqi population.

Occasional Shi'i political ascendance also helped maintain Shi'ism. The Buwayhis, who ruled an area including southern Iraq from A.D. 945 to 1055, took the oath of allegiance to the Sunni caliph in Baghdad but were themselves Shi'i.[7] At other times there were less powerful Shi'i dynasties in Baghdad, Basra, and Hilla, a Shi'i city in south central Iraq, near the site of ancient Babylon. For most of Iraq's history, however, Shi'as were not part of the government.

From Capital of the Islamic Empire to Ottoman Backwater

In A.D. 750 the Sunni Umayyad rulers of the Islamic empire were replaced by the Sunni Abbasid dynasty. Baghdad replaced Damascus as the capital of the empire. The early years of the Abbasids were a time of opulence in Baghdad, but succession to the caliphate and ways of financing the government and army were always problematic. Successions were usually bloody, and the government raised money through *iqta'*, a system of tax farming. The taxpayers who owned and worked the land were assigned to concessionaires whose interest was in getting the most they could out of the land before they lost the concession. Since most of the farmers were Shi'i, citizens who recognized the danger in *iqta'* and the accompanying corruption were liable to, and inhibited by, accusations of Shi'i sympathies. Caravan trade between Europe and Asia expanded rapidly during the Abbasid era, but no new tax was inaugurated to give the prosperous urban traders a share of the tax burden. Continued tax farming increased regionalism by decreasing central government control over and interest in outlying areas.

In approximately the ninth century, Iraq began what was to become a thousand-year decline. Population decreased from several million in the eighth century to barely 1 million in 1800.[8] The most ominous failure of the government was its neglect of the irrigation system. Without an intricate irrigation system, southern and central Iraq is just a red clay desert, incapable of sustaining agriculture. Individual cultivators and landowners could not maintain the system by themselves, for the necessary maintenance entailed large expenditures and the implementation of coordinated plans across extensive areas. Barrages were required to raise the level of the rivers, dikes to prevent floods, and drainage channels to prevent salinization. In the absence of constant effort to remove sediment from the channels, they silted up and the rivers changed courses, damaging rural areas. Arab tribes encroached on the settled area from the south, and Turkish and Mongol tribes threatened the eastern frontier.

Until the eleventh century, the Abbasids were strong enough in Iran and Afghanistan to force the Turkic tribes to turn northward, but once the Abbasid line of defense at the Oxus River was breached, there was nothing to stop the Asiatic tribes from pouring into Islamic lands. In A.D. 1258 the Mongols attacked Baghdad, ending the Abbasid dynasty and what was left of Islamic unity. The Mongol conquest brought the complete collapse of the irrigation system in Iraq. Wars over succession and wars among the various tribes afflicted Iraq for the next two centuries.

At the beginning of the sixteenth century, the Shi'i Safavids came to power in Iran. The Safavids obliged their subjects to adopt Shi'ism, thereby differentiating their Persian empire from the Sunni Ottoman empire to the west and the Sunni Mughal empire to the east. Differences between Sunnism and Shi'ism were widened by the Safavids, with Sunni[9] persecution of *ahl al-bayt* (the family of the Prophet) becoming a central theme. The Safavids promoted Karbala as a pilgrimage site, Mecca being under Ottoman control. To help them convert their empire, the Safavids brought Shi'i ulama from Lebanon and Iraq to Iran.[10]

The struggle for control of Iraq was then between Sunni Turks and Shi'i

Persians, with the rivalry framed in religious terms, Sunnis versus Shi'as, and the people of Iraq prominent among the victims. In 1534, Ottoman Turks gained ascendance in Iraq. They ruled until 1917, sending pashas from Istanbul to administer Iraq as a province of their empire. The Turkish administrators developed a tacit alliance with local Sunni notables, intermarrying with them to form an Iraqi-Ottoman elite. Rivalry between the Ottoman Empire and the Safavid Persian Empire continued, impeding commerce in Iraq and fueling Ottoman suspicions about Shi'i loyalty to the state. Not until 1639 did a treaty between the Ottomans and Safavids bring a period of increased security to Iraq.

The people of Iraq were not necessarily convinced that they should side with their foreign coreligionists against each other. The fighting of 1802 is the only known time in which the sides clearly involved Iraqi Shi'i Muslims versus Iraqi Sunni Muslims.[11] Against that are several documented instances of the local population groups helping one another. During a massacre committed by a Safavid army in 1621, for example, the lives of many Sunni Iraqis were saved when the guardian of the Shi'i shrine of Karbala listed them as Shi'i.[12]

Ottoman government in Iraq was not service-rendering. The Ottomans conceived of government as being for the benefit of the rulers, not of the ruled. They made no effort to incorporate the tribes or the Shi'as into the state, to equalize taxes, build roads, or repair the irrigation system. The inevitable consequence of centuries of governmental neglect was flooding and famine, which in turn facilitated the spread of plague. In the eighteenth and nineteenth centuries, both famine and plague were recurrent in Iraq.

Within Ottoman Iraq, each community was dominated by a few families, among them the families of religious leaders. Christian, Jewish, and Muslim religious leaders served as mediators between their respective communities and governmental authorities, whose Turkish language most Iraqis did not comprehend. Although not as powerful as the political and economic elites, the religious aristocracy was more stable.[13] The Ottomans continued the Abbasid practice of appointing a *naqib* (pl. *nuqaba'*, principal leader) from a renowned family to be the head of every religious community. Each large city had its own *naqib*, with the position tending to be hereditary. The *nuqaba'* of Baghdad, Basra, and Mosul participated in government ceremonies and, along with members of their families, were exempt from military service. Other high-ranking religious personnel were the ulama, imams (prayer leaders in charge of mosques), and qadis (judges in religious courts). "The religious establishment was narrow in its recruitment. Positions were granted through political appointment, auction, or inheritance."[14] Loyal adherence to Ottoman rule was the policy of the Arab Sunni clerics as a group. The Shi'i and Kurdish clergy also complied, but not so reliably.

In Iraqi towns, both Sunni and Shi'i, quranic schools continued a long tradition of oral education, their curricula in some places supplemented with reading and writing. A man who became a village teacher, called mulla in the Shi'i villages and shaikh[15] in Sunni villages, was opting for a life of poverty. The impoverishment of the rural areas, particularly the Shi'i and Kurdish areas, meant there was little for the village teacher other than the high regard people had for men of learning and piety. In communities too poor or small to have a trained teacher, an individual with some religious education became religious leader by an informal process. Religionaries were paid by the people for services rendered. Observant Shi'as paid their religious taxes to the mujtahids (high-ranking ulama authorized to make binding interpretations of Islamic law). The mujtahids disbursed the money for charity and Islamic education, without governmental supervision.

Under the Ottomans, the Shi'as enjoyed religious freedom in their holy cities but not elsewhere. According to Carsten Niebuhr, who traveled through Iraq in 1764 and 1765, the Shi'as were allowed a degree of religious freedom because of the pilgrimage revenues they brought to Iraq.[16] Trade patterns also helped the Shi'i community maintain relative independence under the Ottomans. Most of Iraq's trade was with Persia and was conducted by Shi'i and Jewish families with branches in both Iraq and Persia.

During the eighteenth century, Iraq, athwart the route to India, became important to the British. By the middle of the nineteenth century, it had become a British sphere of interest. Under pressure from an expansionist Europe, the Ottoman government in Istanbul began in 1839 to institute a number of modernizing reforms; but Iraq, considered a place of exile by the Ottomans, did not receive its first reformer, Midhat Pasha, until 1869. In Midhat Pasha's brief three years in Iraq, he implemented the Ottoman Land Law (1858) and the Ottoman Law of Vilayets (1864). The latter created a provincial administrative system of the European type, and the former assigned individuals title to land previously regarded as common tribal property. Religious and commercial urban notables who knew when land was being offered and what the value of title would be were the main beneficiaries of the land reform law. The farmers themselves either did not know what was being offered or, if they knew, did not take advantage of the opportunity because they feared conscription would result from having their names registered with the government.[17]

Among other late Ottoman reforms were the opening of several Turkish-language primary schools and the expansion of civil law. "The monopoly over the country's legal institutions held by a few religious families, who possessed vast wealth, land, and political power, sustained by their religious authority" was curtailed.[18] The religious elite was unsuccessful in its attempt to resist the Ottoman reforms, but the families in the Sunni religious elite did attain compensation in the form of membership in newly established governing councils and appointments to high bureaucratic positions.[19] The

Shi'i clergy succeeded in preventing Shi'as from attending the government schools.

Along with secularizing reforms, the Turks sought to strengthen the center of their empire by conscripting more men and extracting more revenue from the provinces. For the year 1911, the Ottoman bank estimated the state received 30 percent of the grain of the irrigated area of Iraq while the cultivators received only 54 percent. The other 16 percent went to landlords who were often absentee. Malnutrition was the lot of four-fifths of the population.[20]

At the same time, the forces of modernization and some of the reforms were benefiting Iraq. Because of the new Turkish schools and missionary activities, literacy went from about .5 percent in 1850 to 5–10 percent in 1900. As part of their plan to centralize authority, the Turks asserted control in tribal areas, improving security in Iraq. Steamships greatly reduced the sailing time between Baghdad and Basra, contributing to an eightfold increase in Iraq's trade between 1870 and 1914. With improved conditions, population grew.

Critical political changes were also occurring. The secular thrust of the Young Turks who gained ascendance in Istanbul in 1908 destroyed the only legitimating connection between Turks and Arabs, namely, the religious connection. In Iraq, Basra took the lead in an Arab nationalist movement seeking independence. In 1913, under the leadership of Sayyid Talib Naqib, eldest son of the Sunni *naqib* of Basra, the people of Basra, mostly Shi'i, signed a demand for independence. In the Ottoman army, secret societies of Arab nationalists, many of them Iraqis, were formed.

British Dominance, 1917–1958

World War I brought profound changes to Iraq. As soon as the war began, the British invaded Iraq from the Gulf. The Shi'i ulama declared jihad,[21] and even clergymen (including Sayyid Muhsin al-Hakim, who later became the leading Shi'i authority in Iraq) went to the front. Of more military significance, the call for jihad led thousands of Arab tribesmen to join the Turkish effort to repel the invasion. Called *mujahidin* (fighters for Islam), the tribesmen were not paid, armed, or fed by the Turks.[22] Indeed, many were not even friendly to the Turks. The British made rapid initial progress despite the "joint" defensive effort, but at Kut they were caught in a devastating siege, with the Arab population of the city and surrounding area helping the Turks. Only after reinforcements arrived were the British able to occupy Baghdad. Mosul was not taken until after the international armistice, but with the fall of Mosul, the British were in control of all three of the Ottoman vilayets that made up Iraq: Basra, Baghdad, and Mosul.

For continued control, the British elected to rely on indigenous elites as the most economical means. In order to get elite cooperation, the British recognized one tribal leader for each rural area. In some regions, such as Amara, complete ownership of huge areas was assigned to tribal shaikhs who collected revenue from the tribes for the government and were given a share of what they collected.[23] Shaikhs who had been responsible to their tribes for their positions became responsible to the government, which supported their claims against their tribespeople and rivals. The designated shaikhs, both Shi'i and Sunni, became rich as a result of the British system of control. Most other Iraqis had to pay more taxes under British rule than they had under the Ottomans, partly because the British were better able to collect the taxes assessed than the Ottomans had been.[24]

Since the meaning and essence of *Muslim* is "one who submits to God's revealed law," Iraqi Muslims found it difficult to reconcile Islamic ideology with submission to government by the non-Muslim British. A variety of pro-independence groups were organized, including a Shi'i-Sunni group called Haras al-Istiqlal (Guards of Independence), which was supported by leading Shi'i ulama. The leader of Haras al-Istiqlal was Sayyid Muhammad Hasan al-Sadr, an alim (Islamic scholar) from a leading Shi'i clerical family of Kazymiya. Other prominent members included Ali al-Bazirgan, a Sunni of Turkish origin; Jalal Baban, a Sunni Kurd; and Shakir Mahmoud, an Arab Sunni of Baghdad. The constitution of the party included among its objectives the elimination of religious factionalism in Iraq and the appointment of one of the sons of Sharif Hussein (a Sunni Muslim) as king of Iraq.

Sharif Hussein of Mecca was a descendant of the Prophet Muhammad and a member of the Prophet's clan, the Banu Hashim; hence he and his family are called Hashimites and honored for their lineage: "From the early days of Islam, there was a group of Muslims sympathetic to the claims of the Banu Hashim in general and of the *ahl al-bayt* in particular, which propounded and looked forward to the leadership of a perfect man and was always eager to attribute such heightened characteristics to their leaders among the Banu Hashim."[25]

Imam Muhammad Taqi Shirazi, who became the foremost Shi'i mujtahid in 1919, issued a *fatwa* (pl. *fatawin*, authoritative religious opinion) declaring that "none but Muslims have any right to rule over Muslims."[26] In response to the *fatwa*, the notables of Karbala circulated a petition in June favoring "a Muslim Arab government headed by one of the sons of our Sayyid the Sharif [Hussein] and a national representative assembly for the people of Iraq."[27] The British arrested and deported six of the notables responsible for the petition.

Undeterred, Imam Shirazi wrote to Sharif Hussein regarding the establishment of an Arab kingdom in Iraq. The letter was secretly circulated to the mid-Euphrates tribes for the signatures of tribal leaders and then personally delivered to the sharif by Imam Shirazi's emissary, Shaikh Muhammad Riza al-Shabibi. In the Shi'i city of Kazymiya, the leading ulama lent their weight to the effort by drafting a petition calling for an "independent constitutional Arab Islamic government presided over by one of the sons of the Sharif."[28]

In May 1920, joint Shi'i-Sunni religious ceremonies celebrating *mawlid al-nabiy* (the birthday of the Prophet) were held in both Sunni and Shi'i mosques. The ceremonies were followed by political speeches and patriotic poetry. Prominent among the Sunni initiators of the alliance between Sunnis and Shi'as were Ahmad Dawud, an alim from East Baghdad; Yusuf al-Suwaidi, a former shari'a (Islamic law) judge from al-Karkh; and Ali al-Bazirgan, a layman from Haras al-Istiqlal. Joining Sayyid Muhammad al-Sadr in organizing the Shi'as was Ja'far Abu al-Timman,[29] a wealthy lawyer from Kazymiya.

In spring 1920, at San Remo, Iraq was declared a British mandate, convincing Iraqis that they would not get independence without fighting. In June, ten of Karbala's ulama were arrested for circulating a letter urging defense of Iraq against the "infidels." Yusuf al-Suwaidi failed to raise a military force in Baghdad by offering men £6 per month, but the Shi'i clerics of Najaf were successful in their efforts to arouse the tribes.[30] In July, the tribes of the mid-Euphrates rebelled against the British mandate.

During the revolt, Yusuf al-Suwaidi and Muhammad Hasan al-Sadr solicited tribal pledges to the provisional government that set up administrative units in Najaf, Karbala, and other liberated towns. Most Sunni tribes did not join the revolt, in part because of greatly increased British subsidies to their tribal leaders.[31] The revolt was confined to about one-third of the country and lasted three months, costing the British £40 million and 426 lives. Iraqi losses were well over 9,000 casualties, with British air power being the decisive ingredient in the defeat of the revolt.

Determined to cut the cost of administering Iraq and to prevent another rebellion, the British set up an Arab government with Faisal, son of Sharif Hussein of Mecca, as king. Each Arab minister in the new government had a British adviser without whose approval the minister could not act. For the first election of a national assembly, the mutasarrifs (provincial governors) were informed that all candidates had to be willing to ratify a treaty recognizing British "rights" in Iraq;[32] thus Iraq's experiment in democracy got off to a somewhat undemocratic start.

Once Faisal became the British candidate to head a government that was *not* independent, the Shi'i ulama lost some of their enthusiasm for him. Adding to their disenchantment was an administration that contained no Shi'as among the ten mutasarrifs, thirty-five *qa'imaqam* (district administrators), and eighty-five *mudirun* (local officials), except in the holy cities.[33] The most powerful group of Iraqis in the new government consisted of the ex-Ottoman officers who dominated King Faisal's cabinets. Like him, they were Sunni. They tended to be from Baghdad and from modest backgrounds.[34] Along with the ex-Ottoman officers, the early cabinets usually contained a Jew as minister of finance and, after a period of lobbying by the Shi'as, a Shi'a as minister of education. Parliament, which had little power, was dominated by the landowning shaikhs, most of whom were Sunni.

Sati al-Husri (1880–1968), theoretician of secular Arab nationalism, was brought to Iraq by King Faisal in 1921. In Iraq, al-Husri set up an educational system that sought to instill in students "the sentiments needed to achieve Arab unity."[35] Al-Husri was very critical of the traditional religious instructors and, as director of education from 1923 to 1927, did not hesitate to bring in Arab teachers from outside Iraq. His entire program of government schools promoting Arab nationalism was problematic for the Shi'i ulama, and they responded by trying to keep government schools out of Shi'i areas, thereby adding to their reputation for obscurantism. Although Arab nationalism is based on common language rather than race or religion and would not necessarily exclude Iraqi Shi'as even if they were non-Arab in origin, Arab nationalism is secular and inconsonant with the religious identity that for centuries helped maintain Shi'ism in Iraq.

Unlike Shi'ism in Iran and Sunnism in Iraq, Shi'ism in Iraq has rarely had a government sponsor. This plus the extreme poverty of rural Iraq has resulted in a paucity of clergy in rural areas. Although some observers have assumed that this shortage means religion sits lightly with Iraqi peasants, peasant exposure to religion is greater than the small number of rural clergy would suggest. Traditionally, Iraqi Shi'as have gone to the clergy in the holy cities, as opposed to clerics' coming to the people by taking up residence in nonurban areas.

Many observers have noted an uncommon obedience among Iraqi Shi'as. Sir Arnold Wilson, a British official in Iraq from 1914 to 1921 and high commissioner from 1918 to 1920, marveled at the great influence the "arch-conservative" mujtahids had over the Shi'i community. Thomas Lyell, another British administrator in Iraq in the 1920s, recorded that the lives of Shi'as were absolutely regulated by Islamic law, as interpreted by the mujtahids. Sayyids enjoyed prestige and often power in Shi'i villages. Itinerant holy men from the seminaries of Najaf periodically toured southern villages, staying in the shaikhs' guest houses. Rural shaikhs are reported to have given as much as 25 percent of their after-tax income to religious institutions and to the sayyids, compared to 20 percent expended on their immediate families.[36] V. H. W. Dowson, an agricultural expert who studied ways to improve date production in southern Iraq in the early 1920s, reported that not only were Iraqi date cultivators devout and fairly regular in their religious observances, but they even enjoyed long hours discussing theological niceties.[37]

As leaders of the Shi'i community, the ulama were highly devoted to their concept of duty. Despite being defeated in the 1920 revolt, they continued their campaign for independence from the non-Muslim British. In April 1922, with the mujtahid Mahdi al-Khalisi of Kazymiya taking a leading role, 200 Shi'i notables held a conference in Karbala at which they agreed on the following demands: (1) complete political independence as opposed to mandate status, (2) immediate convocation of a national assembly, (3) half of the cabinet to be Shi'i, (4) half of government officials to be Shi'i, and (5) jihad against the Wahhabis.[38]

In November 1922 and again in June 1923, the ulama issued *fatawin* prohibiting participation in the election of a constituent assembly to approve Iraq's mandatory relationship with Great Britain.[39] In response to the *fatawin*, the British banished Shaikh Mahdi al-Khalisi and his son, Shaikh Muhammad al-Khalisi, along with Sayyid Muhammad Hasan al-Sadr, all of whom were Kazmawis (natives of Kazymiya). Their exile led the two highly respected mujtahids in Karbala, Ayatollah Muhammad Hussein Na'ini (1860–1936) and Sayyid Abu al-Hasan al-Isfahani (d. 1945), and several other leading ulama to leave Iraq for Persia.[40] In Tehran, some of the Iraqi ulama set up the Higher Organization of the Representatives of Iraq, known also as the Jam'iyat Bain al-Nahrain (Association of Mesopotamia), to work for Iraq's independence. The British, however, were in firm control of Iraq, and the ulama were obliged to come to terms with that fact. Some of the expatriate ulama signed pledges to abstain from politics and were allowed by the British to return to Iraq in 1924.

With the Shi'i ulama sidelined by deportations and their promises to abstain from politics, the government set up a Department of Awqaf (pious endowments) to administer the charitable funds previously administered by the ulama. An increasing number of personal status matters formerly dealt with by shari'a courts were referred to civil courts. The number of schools with government financing and government-approved curricula expanded steadily. In the period between 1921 and 1930, the number of government primary and secondary schools grew from 84 to 306,[41] not a large increase given the size of the country but an ominous one for the Muslim religious schools. In 1929 the government established a girls' school in Najaf, a major departure from tradition. The various changes moved Iraq toward both modernization and secularization, substituting governmental services for the welfare, legal, and educational functions hitherto performed by clerics.

After their failure to defeat the mandate in Iraq, high mujtahids such as Ayatollah Muhammad Hussein Na'ini ceased their opposition to governments.[42] In the holy cities, where Shi'i religious institutions were congregated, clerics continued to have access to the revolving congregation of tribesmen and villagers making visits to the shrines, and the mujtahids did on occasion support the government; for example, in 1924 both the Sunni and Shi'i religious authorities backed the transfer of the caliphate to Sharif Hussein, thereby endorsing the rule of his son, King Faisal, in Iraq.[43]

Among the Shi'i clergy, the ranking cleric was the one responsible for the theological colleges in Najaf. In the early 1920s, Najaf had some twenty theological colleges and around 6,000 students. Entering the seminaries at about age fifteen, students proceeded through three levels of study at their own pace. The first level, taught by senior students, was the *muqaddamat* (preliminaries), in which students had to become highly proficient in the Arabic language. In the second level, *al-sutuh* (the externals), the teachers were new mujtahids, and the subjects taught were *fiqh* (Islamic jurisprudence) and *usul al-fiqh* (principles of jurisprudence). The third level, *dars al-kharij* (graduation classes), was taught by the principal mujtahids and dealt with the specialized knowledge each student needed for writing his treatise. Modern sciences were not included in the curricula of the seminaries, and religious teachings were suffused with superstition.[44] The average student completed his studies in fifteen years, although forty-year-old students were not uncommon. A successful scholar received an *ijaza* (authorization to be a mujtahid) and was incorporated by his sponsoring alim into the ulama community. Clerics who achieved less could stay on as students, earning money by reading prayers over the dead, or they could take positions as teachers in villages.

The Shi'as of the mandate period were divided in political opinion. One point of view was represented by the Watani (Nationalist) Party, which advocated giving priority to cooperation with Sunni Iraqis in order to get rid of the British. A second view was represented by the Nahda (Awakening) Party, which advocated pressuring the existing Sunni government for Shi'i representation and jobs. King Faisal, for his part, acknowledged there could be no viable, independent Iraq unless the Shi'as were integrated into the system, and he worked to move Shi'as into the government. The king maintained communication with the Shi'i community through a special Shi'i liaison, Sayyid Baqir Ahmad al-Hasani, known in the Shi'i community as Baqir al-Balat (Baqir of the Palace).[45]

As Shi'as moved up the educational and economic ladders, intermarriage between Shi'as and Sunnis began to occur. Iraq's Sunni Arabs have some feelings of superiority, consequent to centuries of political and economic advantage, but hostility between the Iraqi sects has been slight. Theological differences were not such as to prevent intermarriage.[46]

Politically, one of the most problematic issues between the government and the Shi'as was conscription. King Faisal and his ex-Ottoman officers believed that a strong army was necessary to independence[47] and that conscription was the necessary means to a strong army. Conscription, however, was strenuously opposed by both Shi'as and Kurds in the knowledge that they would be the common soldiers serving under Arab Sunni officers. The British took the position that the government could have conscription if it could enforce it without British help—which of course it could not.

Throughout the mandate period, government practices reflected the government's narrow base of support within the country. British airplanes, with their ability to monitor and attack from the air, were frequently required to keep recalcitrant tribes under control and paying their taxes. Elections were always rigged by the government. Rarely was a second nominee allowed for any seat. Numerous "political parties" were formed, but they revolved around the personalities of notables and lacked organization at the local level.

Although most Iraqis remained wretchedly poor, material progress did occur during the mandate period. Testifying to improved conditions, population slightly more than doubled between 1905 and 1947. Shi'as were involved with the government as they had not been under the Ottomans. Whereas no Shi'a had served in the Ottoman parliament, the Iraqi Parliament of 1928 included twenty-six Shi'as among its eighty-eight members.

In 1930, as a condition for acquiring independent status, the government signed a twenty-five-year treaty of preferential alliance with Great Britain. In 1932 Iraq was admitted to the League of Nations as an independent country. British influence continued through the presence of the Royal Air Force, in the persons of British advisers to each government ministry, and through British control of the Iraq Petroleum Company, a major source of government revenue. In matters not apposite to British interests, however, Iraq's political elite was able to determine outcomes. Thus when Sir Ernest Dowson, a British land tenure expert, recommended land reform as the only way to alleviate the severe rural poverty, the influence of the landlords in the Iraqi government prevented action on his recommendation.

In 1933 King Faisal died, and without his conciliating influence, conflicts grew sharper. The government passed a law preventing cultivators from moving from one farm to another if they were in debt—which virtually all were. Agricultural production declined, partly because peasants escaped their new bondage by fleeing to the cities.

In 1934 conscription was introduced, leading to a doubling of the size of the army between 1932 and 1936.[48] In the military college, cadets were taught that Atatürk and the shah of Iran had got rid of foreign control by means of their armies, the message being that Iraq should do likewise. The political and military elite worked together to prevent the developing middle class and the reformist party, the Sunni-Shi'i Ikha (Brotherliness) Party, from breaking into the government.

Throughout 1935 in tribal areas there were sporadic protests against the big landlords and conscription. Shi'i demands were parliamentary representation in proportion to their numbers in the population, free elections, freedom of the press, and reduced taxes.[49] In 1935 and 1936 the mid-Euphrates tribes again rebelled, although on a smaller scale than in 1920. This time it was an Iraqi general, the Kurd Baqir Sidqi, who ordered planes to bomb the tribespeople.

The ulama refrained from opposing the government. The country was nominally independent, and the Hashimite monarchy met their standards for legitimate government. Nonresistance accorded with their traditional tendency to acquiesce to any government that formally recognizes Islamic law and does not interfere with Islamic social institutions. Ayatollah Abu al-Hasan Isfahani, the senior mujtahid in Najaf, earned praise for his eschewal of politics and his regular program of welfare for the poor. His refusal to allow any changes in the seminary curriculum while he was chief mujtahid abetted secularization by encouraging even pious Shi'i families to send their sons to secular schools, where they could acquire the skills necessary to the modern middle class. Within the clerical establishment, there were those who advocated modernizing religious education in order to compete with government schools,[50] but extreme traditionalism prevailed.

Strict adherence to age-old religious and social practices inevitably rendered the ulama less relevant to society. Even their religious functions were diminished as expanded literacy made the Quran available to people who had formerly relied upon the ministrations of clerics. Among the educated young, the influence of the Shi'i religious establishment declined as the new ideologies of Arab nationalism and communism spread in urban areas. The Iraqi Communist Party (ICP), formed in 1934, showed itself able to recruit successfully in the Shi'i community, even attracting young men from prominent clerical families. Also competing with the ulama for leadership of the Shi'i community were the patriarchs of landowning tribal families represented in the legislature and, increasingly, Shi'as with modern educations.[51]

In 1948 the British insisted the Iraqi government ratify the Portsmouth treaty extending Iraq's 1930 defense treaty with Britain. Hoping to acquire Shi'i support for the treaty, which guaranteed Britain military bases in Iraq, the government installed Iraq's first Shi'i prime minister, Salih Jabr. The ploy was unsuccessful in that neither he nor a second Shi'i prime minister, Sayyid Muhammad Hasan al-Sadr, could make the treaty palatable to Iraqis. Faced with violent street demonstrations against the treaty, the government finally had to leave it unratified.

When the state of Israel was proclaimed in 1948, the Iraqi government was obliged to declare martial law. Although Shi'as had never taken the interest in Palestine that the Sunni nationalists had, both groups were offended by the loss of a land that had been an eminent part of the Muslim *umma* for centuries. Iraqi troops were sent to aid Jordan's Arab Legion in Palestine but failed to make a difference. The loss of Palestine reflected badly on the Hashimite family, which ruled in Iraq and Jordan, and discredited the Iraqi establishment generally. Many Iraqis concluded that Iraq's alliance with Britain was meaningless when the issue was one of concern to Iraq.

After Ayatollah Isfahani's death, Shi'i religious authority was transferred to Sayyid Muhammad Burujirdi, who resided in Qumm, Iran. Ensuring that the ulama would continue to refrain from political involvement, a 1950 conference convened by Ayatollah Burujirdi in Qumm adopted a prohibition on political activity by ulama and agreed to withdraw clerical status from offenders.[52]

Some laypeople, however, did interfuse politics and religion. As early as the 1950s, observers noted that young Iraqis were expressing their hostility to Britain in particular and to the West in general by a self-conscious assertion of Muslim identity.[53] The Ikhwan al-Muslimin (Muslim Brotherhood), which in Iraq showed concern for Shi'i sensibilities, was particularly strong among the Sunni Arabs of Mosul. Connected with the Ikhwan was a Sunni fundamentalist party, Hizb al-Tahrir al-Islami (Islamic Liberation Party), which advocated a unitary Islamic state and distributed literature against both communism and the Iraqi government. Among the Iraqi leaders of Hizb al-Tahrir was Shaikh Abd al-Aziz al-Badri (d.1969), who developed a close working relationship with the Shi'i clergy.[54]

Since elections to parliament usually offered voters only one candidate, who had been approved by the government, street demonstrations were a major means by which people expressed political opposition. In November 1952 the political opposition initiated an *intifada* (unarmed uprising) in the streets. A series of strikes by oil, transportation, and cigarette workers followed in 1953.

In the belief that Communists were organizing the political opposition, the government sought to enlist the ulama against communism. The British ambassador went to Najaf on October 6, 1953, to meet with Iraq's ranking Shi'i clergyman, Muhammad Hussein Kashif al-Ghita. The two agreed that they should combine their weight to combat communism.[55] The Quran directs Muslims to "fight those who have not faith in God and the hereafter" (Sura 9, verse 29), a directive that would seem to apply to Communists, even though some Iraqi Communists were ideologically inconsistent enough to be believing Muslims. The danger of communism to Islam had been emphasized a decade earlier by Sayyid Qutb (1906–1966), ideologist of the Egyptian Muslim Brotherhood:

> We may go the Islamic way, or we may go the communist way; one of these two we must inevitably follow in the end. Or there are also Europeans and Americans; we may adopt their social systems and choose these in preference to our own Islamic social system. But finally these

systems also run out into communism, over a short or a long period,
because their doctrines are by nature the same as those of communism,
their philosophy of life is the same, and any differences are superficial
rather than real.[56]

The British brought back to Iraq the blind mujtahid of Kazymiya, Shaikh
Muhammad al-Khalisi, who, from his exile in Iran, had in 1951 published a
strident refutation of Communist criticisms of religion. In Iraq, Shaikh al-
Khalisi lived up to his reputation for fervent anticommunism.[57]

Village society in the 1950s continued to be "molded by the system of
ultimate goods and evils," with piety necessary for a good reputation.[58]
Southern villagers and tribespeople aspired to visit Najaf and Karbala and to
be buried in Najaf. On Ashura (the tenth day of the month of Muharram and
the anniversary of Imam Hussein's death), ritualized funeral processions were
held for Imam Hussein. Each year villagers solicited funds to send some of
their men to Karbala to participate in the *ta'ziya*, a ritual of condolence held
forty days after Ashura. During Ramadan (the month of obligatory fasting)
and Muharram, religious readings were held in local mosques, often made of
mud brick and hardly distinguishable from the *sara' if* (mud huts) of the
peasants. Women mullas, who earned their livings and considerable respect
for their knowledge of the Quran and Islamic tradition, conducted readings for
women in private homes.[59] Fully trained clergymen continued to be scarce in
rural areas, likely affecting the depth of peasant knowledge about Islam but
not necessarily the degree of commitment.

Despite a 1954 government ban on political parties, political opposition
continued in Baghdad. The idea of an Arab nation, free from foreign control,
commanded an enthusiastic following among students and educated Iraqis.
British participation in the 1956 invasion of Suez completed the discrediting
of the Iraqi government, connected as it was with the British. Large, angry
crowds demonstrated in Baghdad, Najaf, and Mosul and lesser ones in Kut,
Samawa, and Kirkuk. Evidence that they were losing their power to influence
even the residents of the holy cities was thrust upon the ulama when they
agreed to a government request to calm the demonstrators and discovered they
could not. Day after day, crowds returned to the streets of Najaf and other
cities to protest the attack on Egypt.

Faced with widespread opposition, the governing elite sought a
progressive image. Among the steps taken were the 1957 establishment of
the coeducational University of Baghdad and a March 1958 constitutional
amendment granting women with at least primary education full political
rights. While such measures may have placated some, they were insufficient
for others and inflammatory to traditionalists. After months of incubation, on
July 14, 1958, a military coup brought down the Iraqi government. Except
for light resistance at the home of Prime Minister Nuri Sa'id, no one tried to
defend the British-installed monarchy.

Summary

Primarily because of political disagreements among its seventh-century Muslim conquerors, Iraq became a religiously divided province of the Islamic empire. The rural areas, containing the majority of the population, became Shi'i. The ruling class, residing in the cities, was Sunni. For centuries, during which the government's reach was circumscribed by a lack of technology and financial wherewithal, and communal interaction was minimal due to population distribution and poor transportation, the sects existed with little friction. The Sunni community maintained itself through association with the various governments, and the Shi'as, although very poor as a group, preserved conviction and community through the force of tradition and the communication each local community had with the Shi'i holy cities.

After Iraq was occupied by the British during World War I, the ulama of the two religious communities cooperated with each other and with Arab nationalists in an attempt to rid Iraq of foreign domination. The government ultimately established by the British was a secular Arab nationalist government consisting almost exclusively of Sunni urbanites; but once independent, it met the Shi'i ulama's requirements for legitimate government because it was headed by a practicing Muslim who was a descendant of the Prophet Muhammad.

The forty-odd years of British domination were years of extensive changes in Iraqi society. Population more than doubled, increasing from less than 3 million when the British arrived to 6,339,960 in 1957.[60] Government policies and the extreme poverty of the rural areas pushed large numbers of peasants to the cities, where they congregated in make-do slums. Tribal shaikhs, too, moved to the cities, where they directed their sons into the professions. Government wherewithal developed with the increasingly educated populace and oil income. The growth of education and government services expanded the modern middle class and decreased the functions of the ulama. Increased education and urbanization modified parochialism and, along with the triumph of a secular Arab nationalist ideology in the Arabic-speaking world as a whole, contributed to a decline in the influence of religion and the number of religionaries. Within this context of social change and political ferment, Iraq's Islamic movement developed.

Notes

1. I do not purport to give a history of Iraq. The objective in this chapter is to convey the religious and political background of Iraqi Shi'as.

2. The population estimate of 18 million is the commonly accepted Western estimate and very likely includes noncitizen Egyptians and other

expatriates. The Iraqi population in 1980 was only 13,214,000, according to the Iraqi government's *Annual Abstract of Statistics* for 1984, p. 48 (cited in Farouk-Sluglett and Sluglett, *Iraq Since 1958*, p. 246). Population figures for the 1980s have not been released by the Iraqi government itself.

3. Details of the early history are after Morony, *Iraq After the Muslim Conquest*.

4. Since the singular form *Shi'a* has come into English, the plural is anglicized to *Shi'as* in this study.

5. For a brief, informative account of·the historical development of Shi'ism, see Hodgson, "How Did the Early Shi'a Become Sectarian?" pp. 1–13. I have relied primarily on Shaban, *Islamic History*, for economic aspects of early Shi'i history.

6. A.H., Anno Hegirae, is the year after the emigration of Muhammad from Mecca to Medina, which took place in A.D. 622. Muharram is the first month in the Islamic calendar, which, being lunar, has 12 months of 29 or 30 days each, for a total of 354 days.

7. Buwayhi (also known as Buyid) allegiance to the Sunni caliph was politic because doing otherwise would likely have aroused Sunni animosity. The allegiance was tenable because the caliph was in no position to exert political control over the Buwayhis. For an engaging account of Buwayhi society, see Mottahedeh, *Loyalty and Leadership in an Early Islamic Society*.

8. Nieuwenhuis, *Early Modern Iraq*, p. 1.

9. The non-Shi'i Muslim majority had by this time come to be called *Sunni*.

10. Esposito, *Islam*, pp. 64–65.

11. Nieuwenhuis, *Early Modern Iraq*, p. 195n.

12. The basic source used for Iraqi history during the Ottoman period is Longrigg, *Four Centuries of Modern Iraq*.

13. Political and economic elites tended to discontinuity because of the Ottoman practices of frequently transferring political power and confiscating property.

14. Walid Khadduri, "Social Background," p. 269.

15. The use of the word *shaikh* for both leaders of tribes and clerics reflects the root sense of the word, "an elderly, venerable gentleman." In recent years, *shaikh* has become the customary title for Shi'i clerics as well as Sunni clerics.

16. Niebuhr was the only survivor of a scientific expedition sent to the Arab world by the king of Denmark in 1760.

17. Military service in the Turkish army was commonly prolonged beyond the legal three-year period and was likely to lead to a grave in Yemen or southeastern Europe, as noted in Longrigg, *Iraq, 1900–1950*, p. 38.

18. Walid Khadduri, "Social Background," p. 72.

19. A leading member of the Sunni religious establishment, Abd al-Rahman al-Gaylani, subsequently became the first prime minister of Iraq. Another member of the same family, Rashid Ali al-Gaylani, was prime minister in 1941.

20. Details of the economic history of this period are after Issawi, *The Economic History of the Middle East*.

21. Jihad literally means "struggle" and can apply to struggling against evil in society and individual souls. In this case, the ulama were calling for military struggle against the invaders.

22. Cf. al-Nafeesi, "The Role of the Shi'ah," p. 141.

23. Foster, *Iraq*, p. 66.

24. Among the sources utilized for twentieth-century Shi'i history are:

Haldane, *The Insurrection in Mesopotamia, 1920*; Bell, *The Letters of Gertrude Bell*, vol. 2; Ireland, *Iraq*; Burgoyne, *Gertrude Bell*; Sluglett, *Britain in Iraq*; and Batatu, *Old Social Classes*.

25. Sachedina, *Islamic Messianism*, p. 136.

26. Vinogradov, "The 1920 Revolt in Iraq," pp. 135–136.

27. Cited in al-Nafeesi, "The Role of the Shi'ah," p. 197.

28. Ibid., p. 201. Calling for a constitutional Islamic government headed by a monarch was not a departure for the ulama. The Iranian constitution of 1907, supported by many Shi'i ulama, provided for a government limited by a constitution and by ulama authority to oversee legislation and government policies.

29. Translated literally, *Abu Timman* means "father of rice," a name given the family because they were large-scale rice merchants. *Abu* (father [of]) is frequently used with a noteworthy trait to identify a person or family in Iraq.

30. Gertrude Bell, one of the British administrators in Iraq before and during the revolt, gives numerous instances in which lower-ranking Sunni ulama worked with the Shi'i ulama. She also reveals how the British in effect co-opted high-ranking Sunni ulama. See Bell, *The Letters of Gertrude Bell*, vol. 2; and Burgoyne, *Gertrude Bell*. For an account in English of political activity by Iraq's Shi'i ulama, see Hairi, *Shi'ism*.

31. al-Nafeesi, "The Role of the Shi'ah," p. 242. British subsidies to the Dulaim, a large Sunni tribe on the upper Euphrates, increased from £3,750 in 1919 to £21,000 in 1920.

32. al-Adhami, "Elections for the Assembly," p. 18.

33. Marr, *History of Iraq*, p. 45.

34. Pool, "The Transformation of Iraqi Political Leadership," pp. 63–87. Baghdad had one of the few military preparatory schools in the Ottoman provinces. The school provided an opportunity for advancement unavailable to most Arabs in the Ottoman Empire. Those who took the opportunity were generally from Baghdad because it was not a boarding school, and they were generally from families of modest means because wealthy Iraqis had other options for their sons.

35. Cleveland, *The Making of an Arab Nationalist*, p. xiii.

36. The information on expenditures by rural shaikhs is from Walid Khadduri, "Social Background," p. 128. For non-Iraqi observations of the Shi'i community of this era, see Arnold Wilson, "Mesopotamia, 1914–1921," pp. 144–161, and Lyell, *Mesopotamia*.

37. Dowson, "Date Cultivators of Basra," pp. 247–260.

38. Sluglett, *Britain in Iraq*, p. 306. The fifth demand, jihad, was in response to a perceived threat from followers of the Arabian Peninsula's Shaikh Muhammad Ibn Abd al-Wahhab. Shaikh Abd al-Wahhab and his Wahhabis, or Ikhwan (Brotherhood) as they called themselves, sought to purify Islam of *bida'* (innovation). Fierce desert warriors, the Ikhwan had sacked Karbala in 1801, causing considerable loss of life. In 1922 they were again threatening the Shi'i areas of Iraq.

39. A *fatwa* is binding only on the followers of the mujtahid making the ruling. In a coordinated clerical campaign, a number of mujtahids issue essentially the same ruling.

40. High-ranking Shi'i clerics have historically relocated from Iraq to Iran and vice versa in response to disputes between themselves and the Iraqi and Iranian governments.

41. Foster, *Iraq*, p. 260.

42. Ayatollah Na'ini and a number of other mujtahids had aided the constitutional movement (1905–1911) in Iran as well as the anti-British movement in Iraq and were disappointed with both efforts. Cf. Hairi, *Shi'ism*, p. 126 and passim.

43. Majid Khadduri, *The Gulf War*, p. 25.

44. Details on Shi'i seminaries are from Jamali, "The Theological Colleges of Najaf," pp. 15–22; from Lyell, *Mesopotamia*; and from Momen, *Shi'i Islam*, pp. 200–203.

45. Sayyid Baqir is called Sayyid Bakir Wahid al-'Ain (Baqir [son of] One-eye) by Batatu, *Old Social Classes*, p. 1160, and Sayyid Baqir Ibn Sayyid Ahmad Baqir al-'Ain (Baqir son of Sayyid Ahmad Baqir One-eye) by Sluglett, *Britain in Iraq*, p. 78. The reason for the name is that Sayyid Ahmad was blind in one eye.

46. Scholars disagree on the import of theological differences between Sunnism and Shi'ism. Among those who hold the differences to be minor are Abbas Kelidar and Hamid Algar. Cf. Kelidar, "The Shii Imami Community," p. 3, and Algar, *The Roots of the Islamic Revolution*, pp. 55–57. There is general agreement that the most significant difference is the Shi'i doctrine of the imamate, the belief that God has at all times provided humans an infallible guide to govern their affairs. Given the Shi'i concept of rightful rulers whose religious authority entitles them to political authority and the Sunni tradition of caliphate, according religious authority to political rulers, there could theoretically be a Sunni caliph vying with a Shi'i imam for the right to be the political and religious successor to the Prophet. In actuality, neither Sunnis nor Shi'as have a living candidate to put forward as the Prophet's successor, thus scholars such as Hamid Algar argue that this most significant of the differences is largely moot.

47. Faisal had been told by Winston Churchill at the Cairo Conference of 1921 that he could be a full sovereign when he could maintain peace and order unaided. Cf. Klieman, *British Policy in the Arab World*, p. 163.

48. Hemphill, "The Formation of the Iraqi Army, 1921–1933," pp. 88–110.

49. Majid Khadduri, *Independent Iraq*, p. 55n.

50. Among the advocates of educational reform was Shaikh Muhammad Rida al-Muzaffar, who was responsible for establishing in Najaf the Kulliya al-Fiqh (College of Jurisprudence) in 1936. Cf. al-Asafi, "Shaikh Muhammad Rida al-Muzaffar," pp. 83–86.

51. The first Shi'i college graduate, Sa'ad Talib, completed his education at the Baghdad Law School in 1921. Cf. Walid Khadduri, "Social Background," p. 286.

52. Some 2,000 clerics attended the conference. Within Iran, Ayatollah Burujirdi was never able to prevent Ayatollah Kashani from engaging in political activity, but high-ranking Iraqi clergy did abide by the prohibition.

53. Harris, *Iraq*, p. 88.

54. Information on the activities of Hizb al-Tahrir in Iraq is from al-Adib, "Taghyir Ijtima'i." Hizb al-Tahrir was founded on the West Bank by a Palestinian alim, Ahmad Taqi al-Din al-Nabhami, around 1951. Members of Hizb al-Tahrir expected that a unitary Islamic state would be able to liberate Palestine. The party's platform called for an elected ruler, but leaders accepted the use of violence to the extent "necessary" for establishing a society based on Islamic principles. In 1952 Jordan refused to allow Hizb al-Tahrir to function legally within its territories. Cf. Sahliyeh, "The West Bank and the Gaza Strip," pp. 88–100.

55. Batatu, *Old Social Classes*, p. 694, mentions the visit Ambassador Troutback made to Najaf to see Ayatollah Kashif al-Ghita. The meeting is discussed in some detail in Abu Malik, "Al-Qadiya al-'Iraqiya," p. 8.

56. *Social Justice in Islam*, p. 280. Sayyid Qutb's preceding argument indicates that European and American social systems are the same as Communist systems in that all of them are materialistic in principle.

57. Shaikh al-Khalisi took a leadership role in the 1963 killings of suspected Communists in Kazymiya, as noted in Chapter 3.

58. Quint, "An Iraqi Village," pp. 376–378.

59. For reports of rural religiosity, see Fernea, *Guests of the Sheikh*; Quint, "An Iraqi Village"; and Thesiger, *The Marsh Arabs*.

60. Iraq, *Abstract of Statistics 1968*, p. 63.

3

Da'wa, the Call to Islam

In its religious sense, *da'wa* is an invitation to humans to believe in the true religion, Islam. In its political sense, *da'wa* is an invitation to adopt the cause of Islam. In the late 1950s, Iraqi ulama began to issue *da'wa* in both senses. The ulama considered Islam to be imperiled and knew themselves to be a declining social group, their historical position undermined by secularism. Arab nationalism and communism had attracted large numbers of Iraqis.[1] Both ideologies were secular, part of their essence being the separation of religion from government and the rejection of clerical involvement in politics. Arab nationalism stood against the universalism of Islam; communism threatened religion itself.

Faced with the choice of clinging to traditions rendered obsolete by events or developing new patterns better able to stem defections from traditional beliefs, a group of Najaf's young ulama began in late 1957 to meet in the home of a prestigious young alim, Sayyid Muhammad Baqir al-Sadr (1931–1980), to discuss possible corrective measures.[2] In the belief that God promised Muslims they would be victorious if they followed his religion, the ulama considered the series of failures[3] in the Islamic world to be proof that a return to Islam was needed. Influenced by the ideas of the Egyptian Muslim Brotherhood, particularly Hasan al-Banna, they focused on the quranic verse that says "God changes not the condition of a people until they change that which is in themselves" (Sura 13, verse 11).[4] The young ulama reasoned that an ethical transformation of individuals had to precede any ethical transformation of society. Young Muslims had to affirm their own intellectual identity and be made aware of the dangers in foreign influences before any reform of society could occur.[5]

Sayyid al-Sadr believed that the practice of Islam had deviated in the past, making it necessary "to separate religion from the customs and apprise the people of the true nature of religion and its role in life."[6] The mujtahids could correct deviations in traditional interpretation and practice through *ijtihad* (authoritative interpretation of Islamic law), thereby helping educated young

Muslims reconcile their faith on a rational basis. Sayyid al-Sadr stressed the need to exercise *ijtihad* properly, incorporating modern social and political possibilities and harmonizing the world of faith with scientific knowledge.

Sayyid al-Sadr and the other reformist ulama sought a means by which they could reach out to modern, educated laymen in order to enlist this important group in the cause of Islam. Reaching out required adopting more assertive methods and a language meaningful to educated young Muslims. The reformist clerics organized study circles, first among the ulama and then among the laity. Sayyid al-Sadr revolutionized thinking in Najaf by the respect he showed for the ability of educated laypeople to understand religious law and by his acceptance of nonseminarians in his classes.[7] Young people embraced his idea that they could be religious scholars even though they were not turbaned clerics.[8] As one Islamic movement newspaper reported,

> the Sayyid [al-Sadr] wrote a large number of books heralding changes in both the teaching methods at the seminaries of Najaf and in the method of presentation of the vast amount of research being conducted at these colleges. Within a short space of time he was able to relate to a wide spectrum of young people in the country.[9]

According to a special edition of *Al-Jihad* (the weekly newspaper of the Islamic movement of Iraq), Hizb al-Da'wa al-Islamiya was organized in the month of Rabia' al-Awwali A.H. 1377,[10] a date that fell in October 1957. A thirty-nine-page pamphlet containing several articles written by Sayyid al-Sadr for *Sawt al-Da'wa*, one of the main publications of the Da'wa Party, dates the establishment of Hizb al-Da'wa to "early 1958."[11] After the revolution of July 14, 1958, Hizb al-Da'wa received the support of Ayatollah Muhsin al-Hakim, the chief religious authority in Iraq;[12] thus "after the 1958 revolution" is sometimes given as the date of its founding. The various dates correspond to stages in the party's organizational formation. Plans for the party were made by ulama in Sayyid al-Sadr's home in 1957. Shaikh Murtada al-'Askari assumed responsibility for organizing the educated young laymen willing to call their brothers to Islam, and the laymen who became the organization's "hands" were invited to meet with the ulama in early 1958.[13] Official religious sanction was given later that year.

In an article written for *Sawt al-Da'wa*, Sayyid al-Sadr explained his choice of name for the organization, saying *da'wa* accurately expresses the group's mission of "calling the people to Islam" and "instructing the largest number of people possible in Islam."[14] Sayyid al-Sadr described the study circles as part of the first stage of the call to Islam, the two goals of this stage being "preparing the faithful and mobilizing [*ta'bi'a*] the *umma* spiritually and intellectually."[15] The instrumental acts by which the Da'wa party was to prepare and mobilize the *umma* were "publishing pamphlets, obligating each member and supervisor to attend cell meetings, reading, establishing celebrations, building libraries and schools, and attending scientific discussions and lessons in jurisprudence."[16]

Ayatollah al-Hakim backed the reform effort by establishing new libraries and religious centers. In his words, "There are a great number of points in common usage among students and the general public which have no foundation in religion."[17] Ayatollah al-Hakim's move to activism was decided by the 1958 military takeover of the Iraqi government. While less than a complete revolution, the change of government was more than a military coup. Not only was the Hashimite monarchy for which the ulama campaigned in 1919 and 1920 swept away, but the new government headed by General Abd al-Karim Qasim (1914–1963) allied itself with the ICP and enacted a land reform program that limited the amount of land any one individual could own, thereby breaking the economic and political power of the Iraqi landlords, major backers of the clerical establishment. In support of General Qasim or the ICP or both, thousands of Iraq's poor became politically active for the first time, a sea change in Iraq's political system.

Four of Ayatollah al-Hakim's sons, including his eldest son, Muhammad Yusuf al-Hakim, responded to the land reform law by sending telegrams to the prime minister. They declared that land reform, because it involved confiscation of private property, violated Islamic law. Possibly influenced by their protests, the government compensated owners and required recipients of land to make relatively high payments to the government, but the land reform program went forward. By July 1959, 6 million donums[18] had been taken over for distribution. Some wealthy Shi'i families were prompted by their loss of political and economic power to take their personal property and move to Great Britain or elsewhere. Those who stayed in Iraq settled into a middle-class existence. For the Shi'i religious establishment, the shrinking of its support base was profoundly disturbing.

Nor was diminished financial support the only serious problem confronting the ulama. Educated young Shi'as were becoming available for politicization and were responding to any political leader whose rhetoric could convey a vision of modernization and success for the country. Secular parties campaigned for and attracted the support of these young Shi'as. Although there is doubt that the ICP was actually responsible, the party was blamed for using its freedom under Qasim to disrupt prayer services and circulate anti-God pamphlets, even posting leaflets on the pillars of Rashid Street, the main street of downtown Baghdad.[19] The ulama discovered to their chagrin that some Iraqis could not distinguish between *shi'i* (pertaining to Shi'as) and *shuyu'i* (Communist) and believed that support for the Communists was support for Shi'ism.[20]

The ulama reacted by organizing themselves to combat "communism" more effectively. In 1958 Ayatollah al-Hakim authorized the formation of

Jama'at al-'Ulama' (Society of Religious Scholars) "to establish bridges between Islam and various segments of the *umma*, especially the educated strata and students."[21] Shaikh Murtada al-Yasin, maternal uncle of Muhammad Baqir al-Sadr, became the first leader of the Jama'at. (A partial listing of the members is contained in Appendix 1.) Mujtahids accepted assignments to write reinterpretations or explications of religious law on given subjects. Jama'at al-'Ulama' established a variety of health, welfare, and educational institutions in the manner of the Egyptian Muslim Brotherhood (see Table 3.1).

An early undertaking of the reformist ulama was the publication of Islamic periodicals and books, aimed at both converting other ulama to activism and filling the void created in religious education by the demise of traditional Islamic schools. (See Appendix 2 for a listing of the publications and their authors.) Among the periodicals was *Al-Adwa' al-Islamiya* (Islamic Lights), published by the steering committee of Jama'at al-'Ulama'. A regular feature of *Al-Adwa'* was "Risalatna" (Our Message), written by Muhammad Baqir al-Sadr. Sayyid al-Sadr also wrote a series of books critiquing non-Islamic ideologies and setting forth what is required of Muslims. In his books, he sought to expose the shortcomings of democratic capitalism, communism, and socialism and to offer reasoned arguments for the superiority of Islamic ideology over all other ideologies.

The possibility of an alliance between Iraq's Islamist Sunnis and the Shi'i ulama, directed against Qasim and for Islamic government, became more likely in 1959 when Shaikh Mahmud Shaltut, rector of Cairo's al-Azhar University, the most prestigious center of Sunni scholarship, officially declared that those Shi'as known as Ja'faris[22] do follow the sunna of the Prophet Muhammad: "The difference between the Ja'fari and Sunni schools is not greater than the difference among the Sunni schools themselves. They [the Ja'faris] believe in the fundamental principles of Islam."[23] As an authoritative Sunni recognition, Shaikh Shaltut's *fatwa* authorizing instruction in Shi'i jurisprudence strengthened the Ja'fari claim to be a fifth madhab (school of Islamic law).

General Qasim, in the meantime, was pursuing policies of benefit to Shi'as. In Karbala, the government built low-income houses and a water system, and between Karbala and Najaf a long-needed road was constructed. Shi'as in the bureaucracy and the army were promoted. *Sara'if* outside Baghdad were replaced with public housing.

The government also made changes in personal-status laws. Law number 188 of December 1959 abolished polygyny and gave women equal rights with men in inheritance. Both changes were contrary to tradition and were opposed by the clergy, but the law against polygyny did not arouse strong opposition. Tribal leaders were essentially the only Iraqis sufficiently well-to-do and so little touched by changed standards that they practiced polygyny in

---

Table 3.1 Institutions Founded by Jama'at al-Ulama

Jam'iyat al-Sunduq al-Khairi al-Islami (Islamic Benevolent Fund):
Founded in the early 1960s by Jama'at al-'Ulama' of Baghdad and Kazymiya, the
  fund was administered according to strict shari'a regulations.[a]

  Committees:
      To found small clinics and hospitals for the medical treatment of the sick
      To found a home for orphans and institutes for the blind and physically
          handicapped
      To found a shelter for the infirm
      To provide assistance for the poor

Religious Primary and Secondary Schools:
    Madrasa Baghdad al-Jadida (School of New Baghdad)
    Rauda al-Zahra' lil-Atfal (al-Zahra' Nursery School) in Baghdad
    Markaz Ta'lim al-Banat al-Rashida (Instruction Center for Rightly Guided Girls)
        in Baghdad (late afternoon attendance)
    Madrasa al-Zahra' (daytime school for girls) in Baghdad
    Madrasa al-Imam al-Sadiq Lil-Banat (primary school for girls) in Basra
    Markaz Ta'lim al-Rajal al-Rashidin (Instruction Center for Rightly Guided Men)
        in Basra
    Markaz Ta'lim al-Banat al-Rashida (Instruction Center for Rightly Guided Girls)
        in Basra
    al-Imam al-Baqir Secondary School for Boys in Hilla (an evening school)
    Markaz Ta'lim al-Banat al-Rashida (Instruction Center for Rightly Guided Girls)
        in Na'maniya

Kulliya Usul al-Din (College of Religious Principles) in Baghdad[b] was founded by
Sayyid Murtada al-'Askari and Hujja Mahdi al-Hakim. Along with traditional
theological subjects, innovative courses such as Islamic economics were taught.

Source: al-Khatib Ibn al-Najaf, *Tarikh al-Harakat al-Islamiya al-Mu'asira*, pp. 78–82.
[a]Provincial administrators: in Basra—Sayyid Muhammad Abd al-Hakim, in Diwaniya—Hujja
Muhammad Baqir al-Hakim, in Na'maniya—Ayatullah Qasim Shubbar, in Hilla—"one of the
faithful."
[b]The goal of Jama'at al-'Ulama' was to make the College of Religious Principles the center of a
modern Islamic university patterned on al-Azhar in Cairo.

---

the 1950s, and tribal leaders were already antagonistic to the government
because of the land reform law. The change in inheritance law, however,
affected virtually all families with property and did engender determined
opposition.[24]

Pressure on Qasim had led him to promise to allow political parties to form and function legally as of January 1960, and he did as promised. In response to the opportunity for an open political contest, two parties with religious platforms applied for licenses on February 2, 1960: the Sunni Hizb al-Tahrir al-Islami and the Islamic Party, the latter newly formed by Iraqi Shi'as. Both parties envisioned a state ordered according to the precepts of Islam, and both were denied licenses by the minister of interior.

Shi'i ability to oppose the Iraqi government was strengthened in February 1960 when Ayatollah Burujirdi of Qumm, the *marji' al-taqlid al-mutlaq* (supreme religious authority whom Shi'as should imitate), issued a letter against land reform, thereby altering his own stand against ulama participation in politics.[25] Although his letter and a subsequent letter by another Iranian ayatollah, Muhammad Mosavi Bahbahani, were prompted by developments in Iran, they enabled the Iraqi ulama to move into the political arena. Immediately after Burujirdi openly opposed land reform, Ayatollah al-Hakim took forceful action against the ICP, issuing the following proclamation: "Any connection with the Communist Party is unlawful. Such a connection is in the nature of disbelief and infidelity, or it is supportive to disbelief and infidelity."[26] The proclamation reportedly generated letters of penitence from many Shi'as who had been favorably disposed to the ICP.

Considering communism's promise of social justice to be fundamental to its appeal to Iraqis, the ulama moved to accentuate Islam's promise of social justice. Shi'i publications, which previously concentrated on attacking communism and nationalism, began to project Islam as a positive alternative.[27] Sayyid al-Sadr's stress on Islam's requirement of economic justice is an example of the ulama's more positive approach in the competition for young minds.

Leaders of Hizb al-Da'wa contacted leaders of the Iraqi Ikhwan al-Muslimin, and the two groups agreed that an Islamic state should be set up in Iraq by means of Shi'i-Sunni cooperation and the creation of an Islamic awareness among the people.[28] After a period of lobbying by proponents of the Islamic parties, the Court of Cassation overruled the government's refusal to license a religious party, and the Islamic Party, now an amalgam of the two parties that had previously applied, was granted a license in April 1960. Ayatollah al-Hakim was the party's sponsor or guarantor and Nu'man Abd al-Razzaq al-Samarra'i, a Sunni layman, was its acting leader. The party's professed objective was to oppose "atheism and materialism."

The Islamic Party's application for a newspaper permit, the paper to be called *Al-Jihad*, was denied by the government, but other newspapers presented the party's views, which were highly critical of the government. The ulama themselves attacked the ICP through a barrage of *fatawin*. In April, Shaikh Murtada al-Yasin delivered a *fatwa* declaring adherence to the Communist Party to be one of the greatest sins, and Mirza Mahdi Shirazi opined that the prayers and fasting of Muslims who had embraced communism were unacceptable to God. In June Shaikh Shirazi ruled that Muslims could not buy meat from a Communist butcher, nor could a Communist son inherit from a Muslim father. The Islamic Party also submitted a memorandum to General Qasim asking him to authorize a review of Iraq's laws to bring them closer to the "spirit of Islam."

In 1960 Qasim began to withdraw his protection from the ICP. Over a period of months, several thousand Communists and suspected Communists in the Sunni cities of Mosul, Kirkuk, and Ramadi and some Sunni districts of Baghdad were murdered or forced to flee their homes. The perpetrators appeared to be conservative army officers associated with the Islamic Party. Opinion in the Shi'i community was that Ayatollah al-Hakim's political naivete had led him to associate his name with a party over which he had no control.

Disagreements waxed among the Shi'i ulama, the sides divided generally according to age. The younger ulama were led by Sayyid al-Sadr, who contended that the necessary course was to continue their reforms, exercising more control over the political groups of laypeople being mobilized. The older, more conservative ulama decried all political activity on the part of the ulama and observant Shi'as. Sayyid al-Sadr's writings and his reformist deductions were attacked as distortions of Islam, an accusation that pained him: "A movement which wants to reconstruct society is faced with prejudice and severe opposition. All activities aimed at revolutionizing society are resented by the masses, who in the fight against the new values and conceptions use the weapon of religion."[29]

On October 15, 1960, the Hilla weekly *Al-Fayha'*, in the name of the Islamic Party, severely castigated the government for a number of failings, including "atheistic concepts such as the equality of women."[30] On October 19, eleven members of the administrative committee of the party were arrested, and in November the Mosul branch of the party was ordered disbanded. Even so, the Islamic Party won 40 percent of the votes in the February 1961 Teachers Union elections in the Sunni Arab province of Ramadi, the only elections in which it presented a list of candidates.[31] Shortly thereafter, all political parties and their newspapers were declared illegal.

Later in 1961 the Islamic Task Organization (Munazzamat al-'Amal al-Islami) was formed by ulama in Karbala.[32] The "Islamic Task" referred to in the group's name is the mobilization of the Shi'i community in the pursuit of Islamic government. Subsequently, other city-based Islamist groups were formed, with the common purpose "to oppose the Communist expansion and to work to establish God's government in the future."[33] In 1962 Jama'at al-Ansar al-Da'wa (Society of Followers of the Call), also known as al-Ansar (the Followers), was organized to assist in the call to Islam.[34] Members of al-Ansar were devoted Muslims of considerably less education than members of Hizb al-Da'wa.

Recruitment

In 1962 and 1963 the activist clerical establishment engaged in a camouflaged series of conferences and lectures for the purpose of recruiting pious young laymen to the movement. Most of the meetings took place in Najaf, but the Husainiya[35] Al Yasin in Kazymiya and Husainiya Al Mubaraka in East Karada (Baghdad) were also sites for meetings.[36] Potential recruits were known personally by the one who would "call" them to Islam, that is, recruitment was along lines of established interaction. Callers recruited family members, classmates, and fellow soldiers; only practicing Muslims were considered for recruitment. Along with religious literature, callers offered potential recruits respect; giving them to realize that they and their families, as practicing Muslims, were highly esteemed. The need for Muslims to meet the intellectual challenges of managing social change in congruence with Islamic beliefs was stressed, as was religious obligation.

The organizational efforts to expand Hizb al-Da'wa beyond Najaf were delegated to specific disciples. Abd al-Sahib Dakhil (Abu 'Isam) (d. 1972) carried the responsibility for organizing Da'wa in the universities. Shaikh Arif al-Basri (d. 1974) became clerical guide to Da'wa members in Baghdad. Females were included in the new ministry by means of Sayyid al-Sadr's sister, Bint al-Huda (Daughter of the Righteous Path), a recognized and respected 'alima (female religious scholar) who organized study circles for pious young women. Sayyid Mahdi al-Hakim (d. 1988) served as the means of communication between the clerical authorities in Najaf and the callers in Baghdad.[37]

Agitation via pamphlets and from pulpits functioned to arouse believers to question Iraq's political and economic situation and to intensify and direct existing tensions. Recruits developed an esprit de corps through reference to religious symbols and the promotion of intimacy and feelings of belonging. Idealistic young people who might have joined secular parties cemented their bonds with the community of believers. The Islamic groups served to channel the energies of those who joined them, making members feel part of something important, something larger than themselves. Group solidarity was augmented by slogans with sentimental significance. Male activists grew beards in imitation of Muslims of the Prophet's time. Some of the activist young women donned the scarves and loose coats associated with Sunni Islamists in Egypt and elsewhere, the traditional Iraqi 'abaya' (black cloak that covers all but the face of a woman) being ill-suited to any job requiring the use of two hands.

Morale, necessary to overcome future adversities, was fostered by depicting the mission as sacred and success as inevitable. The belief that the movement's success would usher in a virtual millennium overvalued the goal but contributed to morale. The goals of Islamizing society and eventually establishing God's government on earth were congruent with the upbringing of Iraqis from pious families. By rejecting the standards of Iraq's new political and economic elites and punctiliously embracing Islamic prohibitions, recruits placed themselves on a higher moral plane than that of Iraq's political and economic elites.

Opposition to the Movement

First to attribute the heightened religious activity in Iraq to an Islamic movement was the ICP. In 1962 an internal ICP report in Basra discussed the necessity of combating "a reactionary organization linked to the ulama of Najaf." A publication of the Lebanese Communist Party even referred to "a new Iraqi party by the name of Hizb al-Da'wa al-Islamiya."[38]

Opposition came also from Arab nationalists. Iraq's religious movement and its campaign against socialism collided with the ascendancy of Egyptian President Gamal Abdul Nasser, whose Arab nationalism incorporated a variety of socialism. Within Najaf, young supporters of Sayyid al-Sadr engaged in fistfights and shouting matches with Arab nationalists. During 1962 and 1963, Sayyid al-Sadr was verbally attacked by nationalist members of his own *hawza* (center of religious studies), Hussein al-Safi in particular.[39]

Early in 1963, the Qasim era came to an end. On February 8, the Ba'th Party and Arab nationalists in the army initiated a coup. The Ba'th Party was a small political group organized in Syria in the mid-1940s and in Iraq in the late 1940s. Its slogan of "unity, freedom, socialism" referred to Arab unity and freedom from foreign domination, popular causes among Iraqi army officers and students. Various sources have asserted that coup participants had assistance from the U.S. Central Intelligence Agency (CIA); for example, King Hussein of Jordan was quoted in *Al-Ahram*, Egypt's official newspaper, as saying that prior to the 1963 coup in Iraq, "Numerous meetings were held between the Ba'th Party and American Intelligence, the more important meetings taking place in Kuwait."[40] Radio transmissions, reportedly from the CIA, were used to give the Ba'thists names and addresses of Communists to be arrested and executed.

Two days of intense fighting followed the coup, as Communists and other beneficiaries of Qasim's policies took to the streets to support him. Many of the Shi'i districts of Baghdad joined the resistance to the coup, but the army's tanks ultimately won the battle.

With the Ba'th Party in control of the new government, nine months of Communist-hunting followed. One of the Ba'th torturers was Saddam Tikriti, later to become president of Iraq as Saddam Hussein. Some 10,000 suspected Communists were arrested and hundreds were killed without benefit of trial.[41] Shaikh Muhammad al-Khalisi, the blind mujtahid whom the British had brought back to Iraq after the *intifada* of 1952, terrorized the residents of Kazymiya with his *sha'latiya* (a colloquialism meaning "executioners"), branding as Communist anyone who had supported Qasim.[42]

Perhaps referring to Hizb al-Da'wa, the Ba'thists claimed to know of a reactionary, sectarian party called Hizb al-Fatimi (Fatimid Party). Islamic publications assert that no such party existed and that the name was a Ba'thist fabrication intended to discredit the Islamic movement as sectarian, as the term *Fatimi* implies Shi'i. Islamists note that, in fact, Sunni clerics like Shaikh Amjad al-Zahawi and Shaikh Abd al-Aziz al-Badri were writing regularly in Islamic movement publications in the 1960s.[43]

In November 1963, Arab nationalists in the army intervened to oust the Ba'thist government. With a view to creating one Arab nation in the future, the new regime, which was headed by Abd al-Salam Arif, undertook measures to bring Iraq's governmental and economic systems into alignment with those of Egypt. On July 14, 1964, the government nationalized all banks and insurance companies, plus thirty-two private manufacturing and trading companies. The nationalizations reduced private fortunes, a major source of *awqaf*, leading to a further decline in ulama income.

Islamic movement clergymen strongly opposed the nationalizations. The outspoken Sunni clergyman Shaikh al-Badri published a book condemning socialism and calling for Islamic government. The Shi'i ulama sent the government telegrams protesting the confiscation of private property. To the ulama, the "Arab socialism" espoused by President Arif and Egypt's President Nasser equaled communism. Ayatollah al-Hakim declined an invitation to a conference at al-Azhar, the highly respected Islamic university in Cairo, giving as his reason the fact that al-Azhar had issued "a verdict in favor of communism as being not antagonistic to Islam . . . rather as being perfectly in consonance with Islam." This, he stated, in his telegram to the Egyptian ambassador, was a "vitiation of Islam."[44] Of course it was socialism that al-Azhar, at President Nasser's request, had declared consonant with Islam. Some years later, Ayatollah al-Hakim's son Mahdi stated the belief succinctly in a letter to the Pakistan Shi'ah Mutalbat Committee, "Socialism and communism are synonymous. . . . Socialism is the first stage to the establishment of communism."[45]

In 1963 and 1964, clerics and lay members of Hizb al-Da'wa stepped up their efforts to bring religious awareness to Madinat al-Thawra (City of the Revolution), the suburb for Baghdad's poor built during Qasim's regime. Their activities brought them to the attention of the Arif government, which then formed the Second Branch, a special department in the Directorate of Public Security, to combat underground Shi'i groups.

In October 1965 the Arif government allowed the exiled Iranian ayatollah, Ruhullah Khomeini, to come to Iraq to live and teach. Ayatollah Khomeini attempted to woo Najaf's senior ulama into political action against the shah of Iran but got a frosty response from Ayatollah al-Hakim and hence from other Iraqi ulama.[46] Iraqi Islamists adhered resolutely to their strategy for achieving an Islamic society through gradual and peaceful tactics, relying on education and the persuasion of individuals. From early in the Islamic movement, Islamists had wanted to establish a modern university for the pious laity, and the plan came to fruition with the establishment of Kufa University in Najaf. Financing was provided by the ulama and prominent Shi'i families such as the Shubbars.

In April 1966 President Abd al-Salam Arif was killed in a mysterious helicopter crash. He was succeeded as president by his older brother, Abd al-Rahman Arif, whose government faced a major crisis when Israel occupied Jerusalem and the West Bank, the Egyptian Sinai, and the Syrian Golan Heights in June of the following year. The Arab world and all its governments were discredited. Jama'at al-'Ulama' of Baghdad and Kazymiya directed appeals for Israeli withdrawal to the secretary general of the United Nations and to other organizations. To the same end, the Jama'at sent a delegation consisting of two Sunnis and two Shi'as on a mission to every Muslim capital from Iran to Malaysia.[47] The members of the delegation were Shaikh Abd al-Aziz al-Badri, Muhandis (Engineer) Abd al-Ghani Shandala, Dr. Jalil Ibn Sayyid Dawud al-'Attar, and Sayyid Adnan al-Bika'.

Within Iraq, competition between Islamists and secular political groups continued. In September 1967 the ICP/Central Command (ICP/CC) split off from the ICP and launched a guerrilla operation in southern Iraq. For months the ICP/CC continued its armed challenge to the government, receiving passive support from the peasants. Since the second Arif government was too weak to control the Communists and was widely believed to lack the necessary support to stay in power, the ulama began encouraging demonstrations and strikes in Baghdad to try to influence the direction of political change. Islamists were joined in the demonstrations by Ba'thists who "portrayed themselves as friends of the Muslims and enemies of communism."[48]

In July 1968 several Arif associates, including Colonel Ibrahim al-Dawud, who was said to be under "clerical influence,"[49] joined with Ba'thist officers to seize power. This "clerical influence" was presumably Sunni because al-Dawud was Sunni, and it was very likely the Muslim Brotherhood, for the Sunni clerical establishment itself is not known to have opposed the Arif governments. The leader of the Muslim Brotherhood, Abd al-Karim Zaidan, was given a place in the new, short-lived cabinet. Two weeks later, the Ba'thists ousted their temporary allies and took complete control of the government.

Notes

1. With Gamal Abdul Nasser's 1952 rise to power in Egypt, Arab nationalism surged in popularity in Iraq. Arab nationalists organized in the Iraqi army and were instrumental in bringing down the Iraqi monarchy in 1958. The Communist Party, small in actual members according to Batatu, was nonetheless able to organize large urban demonstrations in the late 1950s. Cf. Batatu, *Old Social Classes*, p. 1000.

2. Preface to al-Sadr, *Rituals*, p. 9. The name 'Muhammad' is sometimes omitted from Sayyid al-Sadr's name, as he was called by his second name, Baqir. If all Iraqi boys *named* "Muhammad" were *called* "Muhammad," confusion would reign in clerical families, which may give all their sons the first name "Muhammad." The name is especially dear to Shi'as because the Mahdi is to be named "Muhammad."

3. The failure of the Muslim community to maintain its territorial integrity, to achieve genuine self-government, and to develop economically have been viewed as evidence of God's displeasure.

4. All quranic quotations are from *The Meaning of the Glorious Quran* in two volumes, translated from the Arabic by Abdullah Yousuf Ali.

5. al-Sadr, *Islamic Political System*, p. 98.

6. Ibid., p. 35.

7. August 7, 1986, interview in London with Dr. Abu Ali and Brother Ali.

8. Shi'i religionaries are identifiable by the turbans they wear.

9. *Crescent International* of May 16–31, 1981, cited in Siddiqui, *Islamic Movement 1980–1981*, p. 319.

10. *Al-Jihad*, November 24, 1986, p. 1.

11. al-Sadr, *Min Fikr al-Da'wa*, p. 5.

12. August 6, 1986, interview with Hujja Mahdi al-Hakim, son of Ayatollah Muhsin al-Hakim. Ayatollah al-Hakim's sponsorship of Hizb al-Da'wa in 1958 is corroborated by Salih al-Adib in *Al-Jihad*, February 8, 1986, p. 7. *Hujja*, the reduced form of *Hujjat al-Islam* (proof of Islam), is the title of a mujtahid who ranks just below an ayatollah.

13. al-Adib, "Taghyir Ijtima'i." The reference to laypeople becoming the "hands" of *da'wa* conveys their submission to clerical authority.

14. al-Sadr, *Min Fikr al-Da'wa*, p. 9.

15. Ibid., p. 26.

16. Ibid. The means by which Sayyid al-Sadr sought to mobilize the *umma* are almost word for word the means more recently used by the Hujatiyah Society of Iran to propagate Islam. Cf. Schahgaldian, *The Clerical Establishment*, p. 64n. Schahgaldian believes Hujatiyah's constitution was published in 1982, which would be about twenty-five years after Sayyid al-Sadr wrote of Da'wa's strategy. Both Hujatiyah and Sayyid al-Sadr may have drawn on previously established guidelines for proselytization within the Islamic community, or Hujatiyah may have drawn on Sayyid al-Sadr.

17. *Hayat-e-Hakeem*, p. 29.

18. Each donum is .62 of an acre.

19. Penrose and Penrose, *Iraq*, p. 200.

20. al-Khatib Ibn al-Najaf, *Al-Harakat*, p. 14.

21. Ibid., p. 16. Al-Khatib Ibn al-Najaf's 1958 date for the organization of Jama'at al-'Ulama' was also given to me by Hujja Mahdi al-Hakim.

22. Ithna 'Ashari Shi'as follow the teachings of the Sixth Imam, Ja'far al-Sadiq, and are therefore sometimes called Ja'faris.

23. Statement of Shaikh Shaltut on July 7, 1959, cited in Chirri, *Shiites Under Attack*, p. 109. The four Sunni schools of law (Hanafi, Shafi'i, Maliki, and Hanbali) agree on fundamental dogma but differ in their interpretations of the Quran and in their application of the law.

24. The social function of various inheritance laws has not, to my knowledge, been scientifically evaluated. It may be that equal inheritance undermines patriarchy by capacitating dissatisfied women to be more independent of male relatives. No evidence is available from the Iraqi experiment, for one of the very first actions of the Ba'th government that replaced General Qasim was to amend the personal-status law of 1959 so that male heirs would again receive a double share.

25. Floor, "Character of the Iranian Ulama," p. 504. Landlords in Iran had appealed to Burujirdi and other religious leaders to try to prevent the shah's proposed land reform bill. The Iranian government did then delete from the bill those passages the ulama deemed against Islam, rendering the bill relatively useless as a reform.

As noted in Chapter 2, Ayatollah Burujirdi had in 1950 engineered a binding prohibition on clerical involvement in politics.

26. *Hayat-e-Hakeem*, pp. 49–50.

27. Arjomand, "Ideological Revolution in Shi'ism," p. 189.

28. Mahdi al-Hakim, cited in "Iraq on Simmer," pp. 5–6.

29. al-Sadr, *Islamic Political System*, p. 35.

30. Dann, *Iraq under Kassem*, p. 302.

31. Ibid., pp. 301–302.

32. March 13, 1988, telephone interview with an imam from a prominent clerical family of Karbala. He was working in Karbala when the Islamic Task Organization was formed but is unwilling to let his name be used because his nonagenarian father is, or was at the time of the interview, in an Iraqi prison. Around 1969, nonclerical members were admitted to the organization.

33. al-Katib, *Tajribat al-Thawra*, p. 172.

34. August 6, 1986, interview with Sayyid Mahdi al-Hakim in London.

35. A *husainiya* (pl. *husainiyat*) is a religious studies center for the male Shi'i population.

36. al-Khatib Ibn al-Najaf, *Al-Harakat*, pp. 21–22.

37. al-Adib, "Taghyir Ijtima'i," and *Sawt al-'Iraq al-Tha'ir*, July 1988, pp. 1 and 10.

38. al-Adib, "Al-Hizb al-Fatimi."

39. Hasan, *Al-Shahid al-Sadr*, p. 33. Hussein al-Safi, a Najafi (native of Najaf), joined the Ba'th party after it came to power in 1963. He rose to become a minister in the second Ba'th government but was ultimately executed by that same government.

40. *Al-Ahram* (Cairo), September 27, 1963, as cited in Batatu, *Old Social Classes*, pp. 985–986.

41. Batatu, *Old Social Classes*, pp. 988–990.

42. I have not seen any written reference to Shaikh al-Khalisi's role in the bloodbath of 1963, but it was common knowledge in Kazymiya during my residence in Iraq in the late 1960s and early 1970s. Many Shi'as were appalled at

the killings and attributed Khalisi's actions to his being either a CIA accomplice or mentally unstable. As evidence for the first supposition, they cited visits to him by several Americans. As evidence for the second explanation, they cited examples of irrationality in his behavior. He once waged a three-month campaign against eating rabbit meat, something the Muslims of Kazymiya did not do, and could not do, given that there were no rabbits available.

43. al-Adib, "Hizb al-Fatimi." The name Fatimi is associated with Shi'ism because Shi'as are devoted to the Prophet Muhammad's daughter, Fatima, through whom *ahl al-bayt* is descended, and because a Shi'i dynasty, the Fatimids, governed Egypt in medieval times.

44. *Hayat-e-Hakeem*, p. 54.

45. Ibid., pp. A-41 and A-42.

46. Hamid Rouhani, *A Study and Analysis of Imam Khomeini's Movement* (originally published in Persian as *Barrasi va Tahlili Nehzat-e Imam Khomeini*), as excerpted in *Crescent International*, October 16–31, 1987, pp. 9 and 11. Sayyid Rouhani, a Persian, was with Ayatollah Khomeini in Najaf during his exile there. His book is considered to be an official history of the Iranian revolution.

47. al-Khatib Ibn al-Najaf, *Al-Harakat*, p. 70. Shaikh al-Badri and the layman Shandala were Sunnis.

48. al-Katib, *Tajribat al-Thawra*, p. 186.

49. Batatu, *Old Social Classes*, p. 1074. When exiled from Iraq, Colonel al-Dawud took up residence in Saudi Arabia. In 1990 he was reportedly advanced by the Saudis as a possible replacement for Saddam Hussein.

4

State Violence

The supreme legislative and executive body of the Ba'th government was the Revolutionary Command Council (RCC), which from 1968 to 1977 consisted entirely of Sunni Ba'thists. All cabinet ministers and governors of the eighteen provinces were appointed by the RCC, chaired by Saddam Hussein (then known as Saddam Tikriti), a young man who had risen meteorically in Iraqi politics and proceeded to dominate the country.

Saddam was born in a Sunni Arab village near Tikrit in 1937. Part of his early life was spent in village poverty with his mother and stepfather, who reportedly abused him. At the age of nine, he was sent to Baghdad to live with his mother's brother, an army officer. There he was allowed to enter school for the first time. When he completed the ninth grade, in approximately 1956, he tried to get into the military school but was rejected because of poor grades.[1] Saddam became known for a willingness to kill Communists and may have become a CIA asset.[2] His willingness to kill led to his recruitment into the Ba'th Party in connection with the 1959 Ba'thist attempt to assassinate Qasim. Saddam worked as a torturer in the first Ba'th government (February to November 1963) and was imprisoned by the Abd al-Salam Arif government in 1964. After getting out of prison under mysterious circumstances in 1966, Saddam went to Egypt, where he attended school, reportedly in desultory fashion.

When the Ba'th returned to power in 1968, Saddam reappeared as vice-president of the country, with responsibility for developing the Ba'th Party among civilians. Although one of his kinsmen, Ahmad Hasan al-Bakr, the ranking military man in the Ba'th Party, was president, from early on Saddam was considered the strongman in the government.

The Shi'i ulama found themselves confronted by a new government strategy, one far more inimical to their welfare than had been the secularization of the British or the leftist policies of Qasim. Within weeks of taking power, the Ba'th government began the periodic purges that were to characterize its rule.[3] In October the government made public "evidence" of a

45

pro-Israeli spy ring, and on January 5, 1969, it hanged fourteen "spies," some of them from Iraq's small Jewish community. In spring 1969, the government engaged with the shah of Iran in a contest of diplomatic one-upmanship that had dire consequences for Iraqi Shi'as. Among the moves was an Iraqi government message to the Iranian ambassador in Baghdad on April 15, notifying Iran that Iranian navy personnel would no longer be allowed on Iranian vessels in the Shatt al-Arab.[4] On April 19, Iran abrogated the 1937 treaty that set the border on the Iranian side of the Shatt and announced it would cease to pay Iraqi tolls and to fly the Iraqi flag in the Shatt.

The Iraqi president, Ahmad Hasan al-Bakr, visited Ayatollah al-Hakim, requesting that he condemn the Iranian government. When Ayatollah al-Hakim declined to jeopardize the access of Iranian pilgrims to Iraq's holy cities by condemning the shah, the Iraqi government arrested the Iranian seminarians in Najaf. Salih Mahdi Ammash, the minister of the interior, ordered the closure of Kufa University in Najaf and confiscated the university's operating and endowment funds. Strict censorship was placed on religious publications.

After intervention on the seminarians' behalf by Ayatollah al-Hakim, the government "allowed" them to leave Iraq, but other Shi'as accused of being Iranian, some 20,000 in all, were picked up and dumped at the Iranian border. At the beginning of June, Ayatollah al-Hakim led a motor procession of ulama and merchants from Najaf to Baghdad to protest the government's actions.[5] During his extended stay in Baghdad, thousands of Shi'as came to pay homage to him.

The government responded by arresting and torturing the ayatollah's son Mahdi and then publicly accusing Sayyid Mahdi of being an Israeli spy. This charge was used to prevent people from visiting the ayatollah. Sayyid Hasan Shirazi (1934–1980), who made a speech critical of the government's actions at Husainiya Tehraniya in Karbala, was imprisoned for nine months, tortured, and then exiled. Shaikh Abd al-Aziz al-Badri, who spoke in Sayyid Mahdi's defense from the minbar (pulpit) of a major Sunni mosque, was arrested and killed in prison, becoming the first martyr of the contemporary Islamic movement in Iraq. Shaikh al-Badri's death was considered a message to Sunnis inclined to join forces with Shi'as, for his tortured body was deposited at the door of his home.[6]

A number of Shi'i scholars, including Sayyid Mahdi al-Hakim, addressed a letter to the government, dated 21 Rabia' al-Awwali A.H. 1389 (June 1969), demanding that:

1. The censorship which has been imposed under the state laws on Islamic publications, for the suppression of Islamic ideals, should be withdrawn at once.
2. . . . permission should be given to start a daily newspaper which should uphold the Islamic view of life and expression of Islamic belief.
3. We demand, therefore, that there should be no confiscation of property,

no false accusations of espionage, and no leveling of false charges on the basis of difference of political views. Such harassment should cease. There should be no victimization of such persons, on the basis of unreliable evidence, or on the basis of confessions extracted by torturing such persons. Such sentences are barbarous.

4. . . . the Iraqi students . . . in this Centre of Learning should not be forced to conscription in the army until their graduation. . . . The students hailing from other Muslim lands who come here for the purpose of study should be permitted by law to stay here as long as their courses of studies require.

5. The law should also provide that every Muslim, to whatever sect he may belong, should be permitted to stay in any of the holy places, in accordance with his religious belief.[7]

The government proceeded to confiscate religious endowments in Najaf and ban religious processions. Islamic schools were abolished, recitation of the Quran on radio and television was terminated, and instruction in Islam was removed from government schools.[8] Representatives and associates of Ayatollah al-Hakim were arrested. The Shi'i community responded with antigovernment demonstrations in Najaf and other Shi'i cities, including Basra, where the demonstrations lasted three days. A group of Shi'as inclined to answer the government's violence with violence of their own formed an organization called Jund al-Imam (Soldiers of the [Twelfth] Imam).[9] Ayatollah al-Hakim forbade membership in the Ba'th Party and sent his son Mahdi to advise Shi'as around the country of the prohibition. Sayyid Mahdi then fled into exile before a death sentence against him could be implemented. In late 1969 government forces raided the homes of lay members of Islamic groups. Their books were confiscated or burned; they were arrested and tortured.[10] Doubts about the religious acceptability of using violence against a government that acknowledged Islam and a realization that their position was weak relative to that of the government led to a decision to allow Jund al-Imam to lapse.

On January 20, 1970, the government announced it had uncovered a conspiracy involving the shah of Iran and a group of Iraqi army officers. Some forty-four people were executed within twenty-four hours of the announcement of the plot, including at least three who were sympathetic to the Islamic movement: Mahdi al-Tammimi, director of Shi'i schools in Baghdad; the retired general Muhsin al-Jannabi; and General Muhammad Faraj.[11]

The next move came from Ayatollah Khomeini and gave answer to a rising belief that there was no way to reform either the Iranian government or the Iraqi government. Between January 21 and February 8, 1970, Ayatollah Khomeini delivered a series of seminal lectures in Najaf. In the lectures, published in English under the title *Islamic Government* (1985), he called for direct hierocratic rule and asserted that the faqihs (Muslim jurisprudents) have a duty to establish an Islamic state. He rebuked the quietist faqihs for restricting themselves to prayers and discussing points with one another. He also expressed a peculiar optimism regarding the efficacy of protest: "If a collective protest were made against the oppressors who commit an improper act or crime . . . they certainly would desist. They are cowardly and they retreat very quickly."[12]

On June 2, 1970, Ayatollah al-Hakim died. Refusing government transport, a large crowd accompanied his bier the 110 miles from Baghdad back to Najaf.[13] After a short period during which consensus was reached, Ayatollah al-Hakim's followers transferred their allegiance to Sayyid Muhammad Baqir al-Sadr and to Ayatollah Abu al-Qasim Khu'i. With Sayyid al-Sadr becoming Ayatollah al-Sadr, there continued to be one Arab *marji'* (pl. *maraji'*, religious authority consulted by other mujtahids). Politically, Ayatollah al-Sadr represented a middle ground between the other two *maraji'* in Najaf, between Ayatollah Khomeini's advocacy of clerical rule and the avoidance of politics endorsed by Ayatollah Khu'i.

The Ba'th government gave itself a new constitution on July 16, 1970. The new constitution referred to Islam only in the statement that "Islam is the religion of the state." Law 117 (1970) reduced the amount of agricultural land one owner could hold and eliminated compensation to landowners for confiscated land. The government sought to excavate and glorify Iraq's pre-Islamic history as a way of uniting Iraqis. Costumes, plays, and geographic sites from Iraq's ancient past were expressly publicized, and the names of the Iraqi liwas (administrative districts or provinces) were changed to pre-Islamic names, such as Babylon.[14]

The ulama perceived the government's promotion of Iraq's pagan past as a further attack on Islam. Believing in Islamic brotherhood, the ulama were not keen on Arab nationalism, but Arabism at least acknowledged its debt to Islam as the ideology that enabled the Arabs to unite and to the Quran as the means by which the integrity of the Arabic language had been maintained. To the clergy, paganism had no redeeming value whatever.

In 1971 the government began curtailing the visas of all non-Arab seminarians, greatly reducing the number of students in Najaf. In September the government expelled to Iran about 40,000 Fayliya Kurds, the only Kurds who are Shi'i. Even though the Fayliya Kurds had for centuries occupied the area east of Baghdad, where Iraq's Sunni Kurdish north meets its Shi'i Arab south, the government claimed they were Iranian. Like many Iraqis, the Fayliya Kurds may have come from Iran at some time in history, but they had been in Iraq for generations and had intermarried with other Iraqis.

As many as 2 million Iraqis, which would be around 20 percent of Iraqi Shi'as, are designated "of Iranian origin" on their citizenship documents.[15] Some of these families came from Iran centuries ago; others are only a generation or two removed from Iran. As for actual Iranians in Iraq, shortly before the Ba'thist accession to power, Iraqi sources had estimated that 22,860 people living in Iraq in 1968 had Iranian passports.[16] Nevertheless,

60,000 more "Iranians" were expelled to Iran in November 1971 after Iran occupied three Persian Gulf islands belonging to the United Arab Emirates. Because many of these *muhajirin* (expellees) did not know the Persian language and failed to adjust to Iranian society, they left Iran and formed refugee camps in Syria along the Iraqi border or moved into the Sitt Zaynab district of Damascus. The properties of *muhajirin* were confiscated and sold by the government.[17] Relations between Iran and Iraq were severed, and from 1971 to 1976 Iranian pilgrims were not allowed to visit the Shi'i shrines in Iraq, depriving Najaf and Karbala of their main source of income.[18]

In early 1972, presumably in response to information extracted from Abd al-Sahib al-Dakhil, a Da'wa leader who had been arrested in 1970, the government briefly imprisoned Ayatollah al-Sadr and Shaikh Muhammad Baqir al-Hakim, one of the sons of Ayatollah al-Hakim. Abd al-Sahib Dakhil died a grisly death in prison in 1972,[19] his fate a harbinger of the state violence the Ba'thists would increasingly use against their political opponents. The government moved to require that civil servants in responsible jobs be members of the Ba'th Party. Highly placed individuals who were unwilling to join the party were retired from government service.

The Ba'th government accompanied its iron fist against educated, observant Shi'as with social programs of benefit or potential benefit to the poor. Health insurance was introduced and electricity extended to villages. The minimum wage was raised in 1973, 1974, and 1977. Additional workers were included under the social security program.[20] Yet what the government gave, it could also take away. When it nationalized the Iraq Petroleum Company in June 1972, salaries of government employees were cut to help the government withstand an expected marketing boycott of Iraqi oil by the international oil companies. The nationalization was popular nonetheless, politically active Iraqis having campaigned for it for at least two decades. The government took advantage of the popularity of the nationalization to conduct "mass" arrests of Islamic activists. Many Iraqis cited the government's strength and courage in standing up to imperialism as justification for overlooking its domestic excesses, although the extent of those excesses was not fully known.[21] The oil industry nationalization and the friendship treaty with the Soviet Union that preceded it belied the belief that Saddam was the CIA's man, since both acts implied that the government was not subject to Western control.

Toward Totalitarianism

In 1973 the government reorganized and recast its security forces. From the East Germans and the KGB, the Soviet secret police, the Ba'thists received organizational recommendations, training, and sophisticated equipment for surveillance and "interrogation."[22] Then in March 1974 the government launched a determined effort to subjugate the Iraqi Kurds. As funerals of young soldiers multiplied in Shi'i mosques, the ulama again had the temerity to make representations to the government. When this was to no avail, the ulama included public protest against the war in the 1974 Ashura observances. On July 18 the government arrested thirty Shi'i leaders. Five of them (a leader of Hizb al-Da'wa, Shaikh Arif al-Basri, and four of his students) were eventually executed.[23] In an effort to protect his students, Ayatollah al-Sadr issued a *fatwa* forbidding membership in Hizb al-Da'wa. To forestall arrest, Islamists sought jobs in the West, Lebanon, and the Arab Gulf states.

In a move galling to the Shi'i community, which had seen so many native-born Shi'i Iraqis expelled or frightened into leaving, the RCC in January 1975 promised Iraqi nationality to any non-Palestinian Arab of good character. Economic pressures on non-Ba'thists were increased when the government guaranteed state positions to all Ba'th Party members who were university graduates.[24] Given the ban on Iranian pilgrims and the requirement of Ba'th party membership to hold decisionmaking positions in the governmental bureaucracy, the economic situation of many families forced them to join the party or leave the country. According to Ayatollah al-Sadr, "The tyrants . . . have monopolized the government on a tribal basis. They have closed the income sources of all the people except those who accepted humiliation and disgrace, sold their dignity and became slaves."[25] The educational system was included in the push toward total government control. As a Ba'th Party report described the changes made in education, "The Party has insisted on radical change in this sector, including the removal of persons of reactionary and bourgeois views from all levels of education, from nursery schools to university, [and] the provision of new books and syllabuses which conform to the principles of the Party and Revolution."[26]

Rising prices compounded the difficulties of families whose income was reduced by forced retirement from government service. High government expenditures in the 1974–1978 period pushed the economy over its maximum production boundaries, creating shortages that led to inflation, officially estimated at 16 percent per annum between 1968 and 1975 and 25 percent between 1975 and 1980.[27] Engineers, teachers, lawyers, and other civil servants were unable to afford private housing and were obliged to remain unmarried unless they were willing to live with the husband's parents. In Baghdad especially, housing was extremely expensive.

In March 1975 the government signed the Algiers agreement with the shah of Iran, setting the Iran-Iraq border at the Thalweg line in the Shatt al-Arab rather than on the Iranian side of the Shatt, where a 1937 treaty had placed it. In return, the shah withdrew his support from the Iraqi Kurds. Within two weeks, the Kurdish resistance collapsed. Early in 1976, the government deported 200,000 people, mostly Kurds, from the northern border areas to the Shi'i south of Iraq. Numerous arrests of Iraqi Shi'as and Shi'i pilgrims in Iraq occurred in 1976.[28]

The government's method of control was costly not only for Shi'as and Kurds but for the economy as well. Labor productivity in Iraqi industry was low, leading in 1976 to a series of seminars involving members of the RCC. Three reasons for the low productivity were ultimately cited: tension between workers and managers, poor coordination, and political discontent. Saddam Hussein responded without addressing any of these factors: "No increase in wages if there is no increase in productivity."[29] Individual freedoms decreased as, from 1976 on, Ba'th Party members were assigned responsibility for their neighborhoods and required to report on the activities of their neighbors.

Problems comparable to those in industry existed in the inefficient and inhibiting Iraqi bureaucracy. Bureaucratic power, which logically depends on expert knowledge, in Iraq depended on political reliability. The Economist Intelligence Unit reported in 1980 that the Iraqi civil service was short of adequately trained staff, had a rapid turnover in positions of authority, and had standards that deteriorated incrementally the further the office was from Baghdad.[30] The forced retirement of highly placed Shi'as played its part in the bureaucracy's poor performance.

Although mass gatherings were banned, some 30,000 Shi'as, many of them obligated by religious vows, set out on February 5, 1977, to make their annual pilgrimage from Najaf to Karbala to honor the martyred Imam Hussein. Called the Safar *intifada*, the march was carefully organized by clerics in Najaf.[31] Marchers were arranged by *husainiya*, with contingents coming from areas throughout southern and central Iraq. Leaflets announcing the pilgrimage were printed by hand to avoid alerting the government for as long as possible. Three large banners and a number of smaller ones were made. The pilgrims left Najaf on Friday, the Muslim holy day, chanting such slogans as:

> All the people are against you.
> Oh Ba'th, we don't accept you.
>
> Najaf has offered four martyrs.
> Tell Bakr each of their fingers is a hundred.[32]

The procession was led by men carrying a large banner in green, the color of Islam. On it was the hand of God over the hands of men, an obvious message for the Ba'th government. The ulama say they hoped that force would not be used against such a large group or, if it was, that it would provoke personnel or policy shifts within the government.

Between Najaf and Karbala the procession was intercepted by the army and attacked from the air by army helicopters.[33] Over the next two days, army tanks flushed out those who had fled into the city of Karbala. Although some soldiers deserted to the demonstrators, the army killed sixteen and arrested about 2,000. Another eight were sentenced to death on February 25. To the extent the *intifada* was reported internationally, it was termed a "riot," leading to speculation that the pilgrims were well armed, perhaps having acquired weapons from Kurds who had been deported south.[34] In fact, few in Iraq, other than the government and some Kurds in the north, had weapons in 1977. The displaced Kurds were picked up without notice and trucked south by the government.

If the government did not know of the ulama's leadership role in the Islamic movement before the Safar *intifada*, it knew afterward. Those arrested were asked which mujtahid they followed and what their relationship to Ayatollah al-Sadr was.[35] After the interrogations, Shi'i study circles were curbed, and many Islamic movement leaders fled Iraq.[36] On November 23, Ayatollah Khomeini's eldest son was assassinated in Iraq, for which the ayatollah publicly blamed the shah. By this time, 20 percent of all Iraqi government employees were working for the security services.[37]

In 1978 it was again the Communists' turn for government accusations and purge. Lured from the underground in 1974, individual Communists had been identified by the government, making it possible for the government to eliminate virtually the entire ICP in one fell swoop. Only those few who were tipped off by friends or relatives in the police managed to escape capture by leaving the country or hying into the Kurdish mountains the day the arrest orders went out.

The government increased its efforts to make Ba'thism the dominant ideology in Iraq. In 1978, when attendance in literacy classes was made compulsory for all illiterate Iraqis between the ages of fifteen and forty-five, Ba'thist ideology was made mandatory in the literacy classes. The religious traditionalism of local communities was disturbed as the government punished rural families who resisted sending their women to the literacy schools. Refusing to join the Ba'th Party when asked became grounds for imprisonment.

Ayatollah Khomeini was placed under virtual house arrest in September and, at the request of the shah, was "allowed" to leave for France in October. There he could communicate more readily with his followers in Iran than he had been able to from Iraq. As the shah's opposition gathered momentum, the Iraqi government took steps to decapitate its own Islamic opposition.

On June 12, 1979, Ayatollah al-Sadr was put under a closely guarded house arrest that lasted until March 1980, the month before his execution. On June 13, his supporters staged the Rajab *intifada* at his home in Najaf.[38] Large groups of men arrived successively from Baghdad, Basra, Nasriya, Kirkuk, Diwaniya, al-Samawa, Diyala, and elsewhere to proclaim their allegiance to him as *marji'*. Among the demonstrators were clerics, university professors and students, workers, fellahin (sharecroppers), and members of the air force. Their chants were: "In the name of Khomeini and Sadr, Islam is always victorious. Long live, long live, long live Sadr. Islam is always victorious." Demonstrations also took place in Karbala, Kufa, and Madinat al-Thawra. The government response was to send armored army units against the demonstrators, killing scores of them.

From confinement, Ayatollah al-Sadr issued a *fatwa* declaring that believing Muslims were obliged to struggle against the Ba'th Party. In al-Thawra, the party organization collapsed, raising doubts about the party loyalty of other Shi'i Ba'thists. The government escalated its repression, arresting some 3,000 Shi'as and executing a number of those arrested. Among the arrestees were twenty-two Shi'i clerics and three Sunni clerics in whose behalf Amnesty International contacted President Ahmad Hasan al-Bakr on July 3.[39] (President al-Bakr himself had been put under house arrest in June 1979, but his arrest was not public knowledge at the time Amnesty International contacted the Iraqi government.)

In June and July 1979 a large number of clergymen were executed, including Hujja Qasim al-Mubarqi',[40] whose mosque was the center of Islamic activity in Madinat al-Thawra, and Shaikh Qasim Shubbar, a nonagenarian who was long since retired. (Appendix 3 gives the names and duty assignments, plus the dates of death, for other clergymen executed by the Ba'th government.) Fifteen clergymen were expelled, including Sayyid Muhammad Shirazi, elder brother of Ayatollah Hasan Shirazi, who had been forced into exile a decade earlier.

Revolutionary Da'wa

Any possibility of a reformist integration between Islam and Ba'thism disappeared in July 1979 when Saddam Hussein purged the upper ranks of the Ba'th Party, executing twenty-one top-ranking Ba'thists. Ex-president Ahmad Hasan al-Bakr subsequently died under mysterious circumstances in his home. Several Shi'as were brought up from the lower ranks of the Ba'th Party to serve in the new government, but thousands of other Shi'as were expelled from the country. Nearly all power moved into the hands of Saddam Hussein. Confirming the reduced significance of the RCC, the National Assembly Law of 1980 officially granted the president far-reaching powers at the expense of the RCC. People said of Saddam Hussein as Leon Trotsky said of Stalin, "The Party has become its Central Committee, and the Central Committee has become its Secretary-General. Thus the Party has become one man."[41]

Leaders of the Islamic movement concluded they would have to abandon mass demonstrations in favor of nonpeaceful means of protest, an option made possible by the triumph of the Islamic revolution in Iran. Ayatollah al-Sadr wrote for *Sawt al-Da'wa*:

> In the present situation, Islam needs not reform, but revolution. The reformative calls that built religious schools and published books are now peripheral, although they served a good purpose. The main battle that Islam is fighting now is against its enemies. The schools and their curricula, the newspapers and the magazines with their aims, and the radio stations, are all tools in the hands of the authorities. The only way to change the propaganda is to change the rulers. So our *da'wa* is a revolutionary one, an uprising to save the *umma* from its present corrupt situation.[42]

From his house arrest, Ayatollah al-Sadr tape-recorded messages dispatched to the faithful throughout Iraq. The messages were addressed to Arabs and Kurds, Sunnis and Shi'as. They stressed the brotherhood of all Muslims and the need for military struggle. In the words of the so-called last message, the best known of the series, "It is necessary to assume a fighting position. . . . I have spent this existence for the sake of Shi'i and Sunni equally in that I defended the message that united them and the creed that embraced them in a body."[43]

On July 31, the newly formed Islamic Liberation Movement, a coalition of the main Iraqi Islamic parties, issued a statement to the press outside Iraq. The statement pledged support for Ayatollah al-Sadr and announced that Iraqi Islamists were adopting violent methods as a result of government violence against them. (See Appendix 4 for the text of the statement.) The press release said the government was holding more than 10,000 detainees, that 36 had died under torture, and that 100, mostly clergy, were under sentence of death.

With the adoption of militant tactics, the Islamic groups divided into civilian and military wings. The civilian branches continued to concentrate on raising Islamic consciousness; the military wings added *mujahid* (fighter) to their names and undertook guerrilla actions. (See Appendix 5 for a list of groups formed after the adoption of militant tactics.) The *mujahidin* are combatant members of the various Islamic groups, not a group with its own ideology.[44] Willing to sacrifice their lives rather than submit to unjust authority, they pattern themselves after Imam Hussein, who "fought against the heretics, sacrificing himself for the principles of the Prophet."[45] Jund al-Imam revived; the Islamic Task Organization became militant.

Hizb al-Da'wa, which had previously acquired its members by individual recruitment, reportedly found itself inundated with Iraqis seeking to enlist. The identification of the Ba'th Party in general and Saddam Hussein in particular as the unscrupulous enemies of Islam had been confirmed for many believers. Polarization between religion and Ba'thism facilitated recruitment by Islamic groups, despite the dire consequences of political opposition in Iraq. Many young people, both the educated and the urban poor, were sufficiently encouraged by the success of the Iranian Revolution and affronted by the Iraqi government's methods of violent coercion to join the Islamic groups.

The Islamic Task Organization came to public attention in mid-1979 when it carried out a number of guerrilla actions in Baghdad. Then in August 1979, a *mujahid* member of Da'wa, Dr. Ghazi al-Hariri, attempted to assassinate Saddam Hussein at Karama Hospital in Baghdad by hiding explosives under his clothes. The attempt was foiled by Saddam's security men, who found the explosives.[46]

On September 18, Dr. Hussein Shahristani, director of research at the Iraqi Atomic Energy Authority and a practicing Muslim, was arrested.[47] In the wake of his arrest, several more scientists, including Sa'id Malik al-Ali, one of Iraq's top irrigation engineers; Abd al-Halim Naji Abd al-Fatah al-Rawi, chief engineer in the Ministry of Irrigation; and Karani Rafiq Tawfiq al-Daougramaji, an agronomist, were arrested, presumably because they protested Shahristani's arrest.[48]

Early in October, Jama'at al-'Ulama' officially declared its support for the change to violent tactics. In a *fatwa* issued on the first of Du al-Qa'da (the eleventh month of the Muslim year), Jama'at al-'Ulama' called on Iraqi Muslims, especially educated young men, to "move to a new phase on the path of struggle for right and honor."[49] Near the end of 1979, Da'wa's military force, subsequently called the Shahid al-Sadr (Martyr al-Sadr) Force, was formed.[50] During Ashura, in November 1979, a Shi'a named Talib Alwan al-Alili, also known as Jabbar, opened fire on government security forces monitoring a Shi'i religious ceremony in Karbala.[51] Four security agents were killed before the *mujahid* was captured by other government agents. Afterward, an expansion of government security forces was announced, and arrests of Islamic activists escalated. (See Table 4.1 for information on activists who died in custody during this period.)

In March 1980, ninety-six members of Da'wa were reportedly executed. On March 31, RCC Resolution 461 made membership in Hizb al-Da'wa al-Islamiya a capital offense, retroactively. The next day Samir Nur Ali, a *mujahid* in the Islamic Task Organization, attempted to kill Deputy Prime Minister Tariq Aziz at Mustansariya University in Baghdad. Ayatollah al-Sadr and his sister, Bint al-Huda, were executed on April 8. Over 30,000 Shi'as were expelled to Iran in the month of April. On May 2, Ayatollah Hasan Shirazi was assassinated at his place of exile in Lebanon. By Saddam Hussein's account, the government executed 500 Shi'i activists between 1974 and 1980.[52]

According to government sources, Da'wa activists are vertically

Table 4.1 Islamists Who Died in Government Custody Between December 1979 and
         Mid-February 1980

	Occupation	Place of Origin
1.	Lawyer, Postal Service	Kamaliya
2.	?	Madinat al-Thawra
3.	Cleric	Madinat al-Thawra
4.	Warrant officer	Madinat al-Thawra
5.	Taxi mechanic	Baghdad
6.	Student, College of Technology	?
7.	Cleric and scholar	Madinat al-Thawra[a]
8.	Student, College of Technology	Madinat al-Thawra
9.	Warrant Officer, Habiniya Air Base	Madinat al-Thawra
10.	Warrant Officer, Military College	Kamaliya[b]
11.	Student, Mustansariya University	Kamaliya
12.	Employee, Ministry of Justice	Kamaliya
13.	Teacher	Basra
14.	Worker	Madinat al-Thawra
15.	Student, secondary school	Kut
16.	Accountant, Audit Department	Kut-residing in Baghdad
17.	Merchant of food	Najaf
18.	Soldier	?
19.	?[c]	?
20.	Engineer, Cable Office	Kut
21.	Student, middle school	Khalis
22.	Graduate of law school, Audit Department (Kazymiya section)	Basra
23.	Flight engineer	Kharnabat
24.	Certified teacher	Kufa
25.	Engineer	?
26.	*Ustadh* (probably a writer)	Madinat al-Thawra
27.	Military captain	?
28.	?	Kazymiya

(continues)

Table 4.1 (continued)

	Occupation	Place of Origin
29.	Instructor, College of Agriculture	Madinat al-Thawra
30.	Employee, Ministry of Justice	Madinat al-Thawra
31.	Warrant officer	al-Rifa'i
32.	Military officer	al-Rifa'i

Source: Al-Mujahidun, April 1, 1980, pp. 11–12. (Names of the activists are given in the source but omitted here.)
[a]Activists 7, 8, and 9 are from one family, the al-Malikis.
[b]Activists 10, 11, and 12 are from the al-Sudani family.
[c]Only the name, the date of death, and the fact of torture are given.

organized, with members of one cell not knowing members of other cells.[53] Vertical linkages mean that one of the linked groups is subordinate to the other and that groups at the same level cannot communicate with each other directly. Only the center is fully acquainted with all the facts of the organization. Discipline and security benefit from the absence of horizontal linkages, but Islamists often recognize each other by dress, demonstrated knowledge of Islamic publications, and positions taken on religious issues.

Mujahidin cells are called by the names of martyrs whose deaths they seek to avenge. Thus, after Samir Nur Ali was killed for trying to assassinate Tariq Aziz, the Samir Nur Ali group attacked the Iraqi embassy in Rome on June 6, 1980. The leader of the operation, *mujahid* Muzaffar Baqir, was injured in the attack and ultimately died in the hospital. The Muzaffar group then attacked government officials at a photographic exhibit in Baghdad on July 14, 1980.[54] And so on.

Ayatollah Khu'i, the senior cleric in Najaf, applied to leave Iraq immediately after the execution of Ayatollah al-Sadr. Permission was denied, and his personal funds as well as religious funds in his care (the latter amounting to 780,000 Iraqi dinars, somewhat over $2 million) were confiscated from Rafidain Bank.[55] His telephone was cut off, his students arrested, and some of his students and assistants executed. The government's treatment of Ayatollah Khu'i further embittered Iraqi Muslims who had thought Ayatollah Khu'i's avoidance of politics, his advanced age, and his position as *marji'* for many Shi'as in Pakistan, India, and Afghanistan would protect him.

In May 1980 Iraq notified the secretary general of the United Nations that

Da'wa had met with Iranians in Qumm and drawn up plans to bring down the Iraqi government.[56] The source of the government's information was said to be a captured Da'wa member, Amir Hamid al-Mansuri (number 13 in Table 4.1). On June 6, 1980, Iraqi airmen led by a Da'wa member, Flight Engineer Ghalib Ibrahim Tahir, attempted to assassinate Saddam Hussein by shelling an air force reviewing stand.

The government continued its ongoing program of expelling Shi'as, forcing 23,672 to walk into one northern district of Iran between July 1980 and June 1982. (See Table 4.2 for specific dates and numbers.) At this point, Jama'at al-'Ulama' al-Mujahidin (Society of Militant Ulama) was formed outside Iraq to provide the movement with coordination and leadership formerly provided by Ayatollah al-Sadr. Shaikh Muhammad Baqir al-Hakim became the society's *amin 'amm* (secretary general). Imam Khomeini[57] called for the removal of Najaf's seminaries to Qumm, in Iran, but "Yusuf Sayyid Muhsin Tabataba'i," the oldest son of Ayatollah Muhsin al-Hakim, rejected the call in August 1980.[58]

In September 1980 Iraq invaded Iran. In the early months of the war, neither the superpowers nor international organizations condemned the invasion, an omission interpreted by members of the Islamic movement to indicate powerful international support for Iraq's government. Kuwait became Iraq's de facto ally, its port serving as Iraq's main port. Saudi Arabia, Kuwait, and the other Arab Gulf states extended financial and logistic support to Iraq.

Isolated with one supporter, Iran, and reeling from the loss of Ayatollah al-Sadr and the government's increased repression, Islamic activists made another tactical change, this time a withdrawal from Iraq. Some went to Iran to continue their jihad as part of Iranian military units. Others, whose cells had not been penetrated by arrests, remained in Iraq in a state of dormancy. Contrary to the contention in various Western publications, martyrdom is not intrinsically appealing to many Shi'as. In the absence of directives from duly recognized group leaders, many waited.

On April 15, 1981, the government issued a decree offering from 2,500 to 4,000 Iraqi dinars (approximately $8,000 to $10,000) to Iraqi men who got rid of their "Iranian" wives, presumably meaning wives whose citizenship documents indicate Iranian origin. The reason for the decree seemed to be a government desire to divide and create resentments within the Shi'i community. Regulations on places of worship, appointments to the clergy, and content of sermons were promulgated by the government, blocking the only means of public communication within religious communities. Shi'i ulama, like the Sunni ulama, were to receive their salaries from the government. Shi'i shrines and mosques were to be administered by the government, depriving the Shi'i ulama of the financial autonomy that had made political activity possible for them.

Table 4.2 Iraqis Expelled Across the Border into the Bakhtiran District of Iran During a Two-Year Period

Date	Number of Expellees	Circumstances
July 24, 1980	4,088	?
March 3, 1981	1,240	Temperature was minus 11°C. Eight girls and young women died en route.
January 29, 1982	3,058	Six died from the cold.
January 30, 1982	2,832	Eight died en route.
March 4, 1982	8,084	Four died from mines; three died from the cold. Many others required medical treatment.
March 7, 1982	4,270	Temperature was minus 10°C. A baby died, as did a sixty-year-old shaikh.
June 9, 1982	100	Expellees were common criminals.
	Total 23,672	

Source: Official files of Bakhtiran District, as reported by Dr. Abd al-Wahab al-Hakim in *At-Tayar al-Jadeed*, November 1988, p. 2. Translation from Arabic is by the author.

Readers of the Iraqi government press, the only legal press in Iraq, would not have known Iraq had any Islamic militants; and non-Iraqi media lacked access to news sources other than the government. To supply themselves with news of the movement, Islamists outside Iraq therefore set up presses in Beirut, Tehran, and London and organized underground transmission networks. (See Appendix 6 for a partial listing of publications by expatriate Iraqi Islamists.) Along with news, Islamist publications contained a myriad of writings conveying the superior qualities of Ayatollah al-Sadr and other leaders and martyrs of the movement. In fact, a saint cult has developed around Ayatollah al-Sadr, serving to bolster morale and confirm to members that God's blessed martyrs are identified with the movement.

Senior Shi'i officers in the military were reported—perhaps hyperbolically—to have made five attempts on the life of Saddam Hussein in the first six months of 1981.[59] Twelve officers and 200 other ranks were executed on July 27 in connection with the alleged attempts. Forty civilians linked to the officers were arrested after weapons were found in Kazymiya, Madinat al-Hurriya, and Miriya, all of which are Shi'i suburbs of Baghdad. Government executions of Shi'as and Kurds proceeded ad nauseam. Hizb al-Da'wa reported that 166 of its members and supporters were executed early in 1982.[60] In mid-1982, an air force pilot attempted to assassinate Saddam Hussein by strafing the Unknown Soldier Monument in Baghdad, while Saddam was taking part in a ceremony there.[61]

At Dujayl, a planned agricultural community 40 miles northeast of Baghdad, Da'wa *mujahidin* staged a major armed attack against Saddam Hussein and his body guards in July 1982. About 150 people were killed during the engagement. Afterward, the government virtually razed the town. Some 300 persons were arrested, including family members of those killed in the battle.[62] Smaller actions included the bombing of the Ministry of Planning on August 1.

Muhammad Baqir al-Hakim has said that Ayatollah al-Sadr designated him and three other ulama to assume overall leadership of Iraq's Islamic movement in the event of his death, but four organizational efforts to authorize new leadership failed for lack of recognition by Imam Khomeini, upon whose favor the leaders were dependent after their withdrawal from Iraq.[63] Finally, on November 17, 1982, Muhammad Baqir al-Hakim announced from Tehran the formation of al-Majlis al-A'la lil Thawra al-Islamiya fi al-'Iraq (the Supreme Assembly of the Islamic Revolution of Iraq), hereafter referred to as the Majlis (Assembly). The organization described itself as representing "all the Muslim people of Iraq, Sunnis as well as Shi'as" and the Islamic Republic of Iran as "the foundation (and the prime mover) of the World Islamic Revolution."[64]

The formation of the Majlis was preparation for a transitional Iraqi government that could assume responsibility if Iran captured Basra, Iraq's second-largest city. Although Iran failed to capture Basra, the Majlis continued to coordinate the activities of Iraq's Islamic groups. The organization's central committee, which originally had sixteen members, has met with some regularity under the chairmanship of Hujja Muhammad Baqir al-Hakim. (See Table 4.3 for names and titles of Majlis leaders.) The Majlis as a whole has no regular meetings but has in fact met about once per year. The organization publishes a weekly newspaper called *Al-Shahada* (Martyrdom).

In May 1983 over 100 male members of the al-Hakim family were arrested by the Iraqi government. Six of them were executed immediately.[65] Seventy-year-old Sayyid Hussein al-Hakim, who witnessed the hangings, was dispatched to Tehran to warn Muhammad Baqir al-Hakim to desist from opposing the Iraqi government. In the same month, changing its antireligion

Table 4.3 Leadership of al-Majlis al-A'la lil Thawra al-Islamiya fi al-'Iraq
(Supreme Assembly of the Islamic Revolution of Iraq, or Majlis
[Assembly])

Hujja Muhammad Baqir al-Hakim, chairman[a]
Hujja Mahmud Hashimi,[a] chief spokesman[b]
Sayyid Muhammad Baqir al-Nasri, director of public relations[b]
Abu Thar al-Hasan, executive director (until January 1988, when he died of chemical
wounds received at Hajj Umran in November 1987)[c]

Members of the central committee:
  Shaikh Muhammad Khalid Barazan (Kurdish)[d]
  Shaikh Muhammad Mahdi al-Asafi[a]
  Shaikh Muhammad al-Haidari[d]
  Shaikh Abu Zahir[d]
  Shaikh Abu Maythum al-Khafaji, commander of *basij* forces[d]
  Sayyid Abd al-Aziz al-Hakim[a]
  Sayyid Kazim al-Ha'iri[a]
  Shaikh Abbas al-Muhri[a]
  Sayyid Muhammad Taqi al-Mudarrisi,[a] leader of the Islamic Task Organization

[a]One of the original sixteen members of the central committee, as reported in *Crescent
International*, November 1–15, 1982 (cited in Kalim Siddiqui, *Issues in the Islamic Movement,
1982–1983*, p. 91).
[b]Iraqi Islamic Association in America, *Nashra I'lamia* (Information pamphlet), pp. 5–6.
[c]*Kayhan International*, January 30, 1988, p. 8.
[d]*Kayhan al-'Arabi*, January 9, 1988, p. 4.

stance, the Iraqi government convened an Islamic conference in Baghdad. The
Iraqi delegation was headed by Ali Kashif al-Ghita, a Shi'i cleric who had
accepted government employment before the Ba'thists came to power.[66] The
government began addressing political rhetoric to Islamic issues, and the
media began to devote more time to religious programming.

In 1983 the Majlis established its own military force of about 200
volunteers, set up a base at Hajj Umran in the part of Iraqi Kurdistan captured
by the Iranian army, and called upon Iraqi Muslim combatants to report there.
At the time, the coalition of Islamic groups had three types of military units:
special forces, reserve forces, and *basij* forces. The special forces, named Badr,
carried out guerrilla operations inside Iraq but also participated in Iranian
military operations. Included in Badr was the special Hamza force of Iraqi
prisoners of war who had volunteered to join the Islamic opposition forces.
Basij units consisted of volunteers who received elementary military training
and light weapons but no pay. Within Iraq, the Majlis helped to supply

independent Islamic groups, as well as its own *mujahidin*.[67] Two Iraqi
Kurdish groups became members of the Majlis: al-Harakat al-Rabitat al-
Islamiya fi Kurdistan (Kurdish Islamic Movement or KIM), led by Shaikh
Abd al-Rahman Nurasi and Mulla Uthman Abd al-Aziz; and the Kurdish
Hizbullah (Party of God), commanded by Muhammad Khalid Barazan.
Hizbullah is comparable to al-Ansar al-Da'wa in that its members are devoted
Muslims of considerably less education than members of Da'wa. Hizbullah
differs from al-Ansar in that al-Ansar was formed at a time when the Islamic
movement was reformative in both goals and methods and led by Ayatollah
al-Sadr. Hizbullah formed after the movement became revolutionary.

Islamist women organized the League of Muslim Women. A *mujahida*
(pl. *mujahidat*, female fighter) named Um Karar planted the explosives that
blew up the government building for intelligence operations. *Mujahidat* are
reported to (1) organize cells, (2) write and distribute pamphlets that "expose
the authorities and their practices," (3) counter government propaganda, (4)
transport weapons and ammunition, and (5) communicate information to and
from *mujahidin*.[68] A number of the *akhawat* (sisters) have died in prison,
nineteen-year-old Maysun Ghazi, for one.[69]

In 1984 a group of Kurdish ulama, including suspected leaders of KIM,
were executed by the government.[70] Ten more of the al-Hakims who
remained in prison were executed in February and March 1985.[71] When the
government confirmed its execution of al-Hakim family members, it said
they were killed for having formed the Iraqi *mujahidin*, whose original leader
is reported to have been Ayatollah al-Hakim's youngest son, Sayyid Abd al-
Aziz al-Hakim. The government accused the *mujahidin* of treason and of
helping Iraqi soldiers flee the war fronts.

In response to Kuwait's financial and logistical support for the Iraqi
government's war effort, *mujahidin* attacked several sites in Kuwait,
including the U.S. embassy, in December 1983. In April 1985 there was an
attempt on the life of the amir of Kuwait. Two relatives of the al-Hakim
family, 'Ala' Muhammad Rida al-Atrash and Wadi' Abd al-Hussein al-Atrash
were among those accused in the Kuwaiti incidents.

In June 1985, 599 Iraqis were reported executed, among them an
undetermined number of Islamic activists. Sayyid Muhammad Ali al-Hakim
was in the group, as were a number of Kurdish ulama, including Shaikh Isam
Arif of Sulaimaniya and Shaikh Rami Tuskharmatu'i of Kirkuk.[72] In
November 1985, Amnesty International reported that sixty Iraqi prisoners,
including Da'wa members, were put to death.

Estimates of the total number of Islamic activists killed by the
government are inexact, but taking the 500 Da'wa members Saddam Hussein
acknowledged having executed by 1980 and adding those affirmed by
Amnesty International and those killed at Dujayl adds up to about 1,000
deaths reported in Western sources. Chibli Mallat refers to Iraqi sources that

indicate that between 5,000 and 10,000 Islamists had been killed by the mid-1980s.[73] Mallat's figures come from scholarly Islamic sources, not the popular press, and are probably as close to accurate as is possible. The opposition groups themselves do not know how many of their members, not to mention sympathizers, have been executed. As their publications phrase it, "Only God knows how many believing Muslims the Ba'th government has executed." In 1986 *At-Tayar Al-Jadeed*, not a fundamentalist publication, put the number of disappeared and executed Iraqis of all political persuasions at 30,000.[74]

On April 9, 1987, the Da'wa cell, Shahid al-Sadr, staged an armed attack on Saddam's motorcade in Mosul.[75] Saddam escaped but is said to have shed tears to learn he was hated even in Mosul, in the Sunni Arab heartland near Tikrit. During the Iran-Iraq War, Iraqi activists had hopes for a military coup in Iraq. Da'wa spokesmen told me in August 1986 that they had reason to believe that an Islamic government could come about as a result of elections allowed by a transitional military government in Baghdad. The coup did not occur, or at least did not succeed.

In June 1987 the commander of Iran's Revolutionary Guards announced plans to increase the military role of popular forces inside Iraq. Kamal Kharazi, spokesman for Iran's war propaganda office, told the Iranian press that the war should be continued by Iraqis themselves. Iraqis who had been fighting as part of Iranian military units were formed into all-Iraqi units. Imam Khomeini directed that Hizbullah brigades be established inside Iraq.[76] At approximately the same time, Iraqi opposition groups reported that the Iraqi government had attacked Islamic guerrilla forces in Iraq's southern marshes with chemical weapons.[77] The geographic location of the marshes, in conjunction with heavily armed Iraqi troops along the border, made it impossible for people injured there to escape Iraq; thus the attacks, assuming they occurred, were not reported in the international press.

On September 7, 1987, foreign diplomats witnessed an armed attack on the reviewing stand of a military parade in Ba'quba, a city northeast of Baghdad. Fifty to 100 people were reportedly killed. Actions by guerrillas within Iraq are not disclosed in the Iraqi press, nor are they usually covered by the international press, but after the Ba'quba incident, it was reported that "evidence of internal unrest is growing."[78] Bombing incidents occurred throughout the fall, leading the government to place Madinat al-Thawra, called Saddam City after October 1982, under a virtual curfew. In November, the government used chemical weapons against resistance forces at Hajj Umran in northern Iraq. Abu Thar al-Hasan, executive director of the Majlis, was one of those receiving severe chemical wounds in the government's attack against Hajj Umran.[79]

Da'wa reported taking the lead in organizing Hizbullah cells within Iraq. A Da'wa leader, Abu Mujahid, explained to an international gathering of

Islamic movement leaders in December 1987 that Hizbullah is not a party but a means of strengthening existing Islamic parties,[80] the implication being that members of Hizbullah honor the leadership of Da'wa and the ulama. At the sixth meeting of the Majlis in January 1988, Hujja Muhammad Ali Rahmani, commander of exile mobilization and an official of the Iranian Revolutionary Guards, was among the speakers reporting on progress made "heeding the Imam's [Khomeini's] directive to organize Hizbullah cells inside Iraq." (See Appendix 7 for the names and titles of those who spoke at the meeting.) At least during the life of Khomeini, Iraqi Hizbullah units received directives and funding from the Iranian government.

In 1988, Kurdish and Islamic resistance groups increased their operations out of the sizable area under their control in northern Iraq. The Majlis military forces were headed by Muhammad Taki Maula and reportedly consisted of 40,000 men, some located in the north and others in the marshes of southern Iraq. The Badr Corps had been reorganized into an infantry division, an artillery division, an armored division, and a guerrilla unit.[81] The two Kurdish Islamic groups had an estimated 4,000 *mujahidin*, a relatively small part of overall Kurdish armed strength,[82] but the Islamic forces enjoyed the support of substantial numbers of Kurdish civilians. The Iraqi government used chemical weapons against resistance forces and Kurdish civilians in Halabja in August 1988. Unlike the alleged June 1987 attacks in the southern marshes and the November 1987 attack at Hajj Umran, the chemical attacks at Halabja were widely reported. Fleeing Kurdish civilians were able to cross into Iran and Turkey, where they were examined by international physicians who confirmed the source of their injuries.

Showing a "democratic" face to the world, Saddam Hussein announced on November 27, 1988, that the formation of political parties would be permitted, although "militant" Shi'i groups, would be excluded.[83] Except for Kurdish groups in the northeast, Shi'i groups were very likely the only organized opposition groups in Iraq at the time. In any case, no move toward democracy resulted from the offer.

In furtherance of its resolve to continue to resist, the Majlis opened an office in Damascus. Iraqi terrain, much of which is red clay desert without so much as a tree for camouflage, works against a strategy of armed resistance, but some actions continued to occur. In January 1989, *Al-'Amal al-Islami* reported attacks on two sites in Baghdad, a nightclub in Karada and the Hotel Jundiyan in Baghdad proper, both of which Islamists deemed settings for immoral activities.

In January and February 1989, government forces used helicopters to attack "Muslim dissidents" in southern Iraq.[84] The government's willingness to kill civilians in areas from which guerrillas operate worked against a strategy of armed resistance, but given the enmity between Muslims and Saddam Hussein, resistance continued. In a June 1990 communiqué, prompted by the exchange of letters between Iran and Iraq with regard to a formal peace, the Majlis issued a statement reviewing Iraqi Islamic opposition to the Ba'th government, beginning with the confrontation between Ahmad Hasan al-Bakr and Ayatollah Muhsin al-Hakim in 1969 and continuing through guerrilla actions after the end of the Iran-Iraq War. The communiqué called on the Iraqi people to continue their struggle until the "despot Saddam has fallen."[85]

Islamic groups cultivated their relations with other Iraqi opposition groups. In December 1987 the Islamic groups, the major Kurdish parties, Arab nationalist groups, and the New Umma Party met in Tehran.[86] On February 27, 1990, twenty-seven well-known political figures—including Sayyid Muhammad Bahr al-'Ulum, an Islamist; Aziz Muhammad, first secretary of the ICP; and Mas'ud al-Barazani and Jalal al-Talabani, leaders of the two major Kurdish groups—issued a joint statement calling for the overthrow of the Ba'th government.[87] At memorial services for Ayatollah al-Sadr in Damascus in April 1990, one of the speakers was from the Kurdish parties; at the services in Tehran, representatives of the Kurdish parties and the Turkomans were present.[88]

On August 2, 1990, the Iraqi army overran Kuwait, visiting the violence so well known to Iraqis on the Kuwaitis. An international coalition was promptly formed against Iraq, spurring the Iraqi opposition groups to try to form a plan for governing the country in the event of Saddam's ouster. Five Islamic parties met with the Kurdish nationalist parties, the ICP, and dissident Ba'thists in Damascus in September.[89] There they set up the Iraqi National Action Committee, headed by General Hasan Naqib, who had defected from the Iraqi army in 1979. The group called for free elections in Iraq and for Kurdish autonomy. The participants also condemned Zionism and imperialism.

At the end of December, a number of Iraqi opposition groups, including three led by Shi'i clerics, met in Beirut in an attempt to prepare for the hoped-for collapse of the Iraqi government. The conference statement called for a transitional government that would hold elections for an assembly to be charged with writing a new constitution,[90] the scenario Islamists had hoped would come out of the Iran-Iraq War. The groups agreed on a five-man steering committee, consisting of two representatives of the Islamist parties, one Communist, one Kurd, and one Ba'thist, each with the right of veto. The groups agreed on a unity charter outlining steps for a transition to democracy in Iraq, set up a seventeen-man secretariat, and made plans for a forty-eight-person consultative assembly.[91] Signing the unity document were six Shi'i and two Sunni Islamist groups, as well as seven Kurdish groups. The conference statement also promised that a new government formed by the participants would ban the use of weapons of mass destruction.

On January 17, 1991, the U.S.-led international coalition that was formed to free Kuwait from Saddam's control assaulted Iraq in a ruinous, five-week war. The Iraqi opposition groups urgently pursued their efforts to prepare a transitional government. When the war ended with Saddam still in power, the Shi'i population of the south and the Kurdish population of the north rose up against the Ba'th government. Saddam's Revolutionary Guards used napalm and phosphorus to reimpose his control in the south of Iraq and in much of the north. After quelling the uprising, the government conducted mass arrests and mass executions.[92] Among those taken away from Najaf were the *marji'*, 95-year-old Ayatollah Khu'i, and 16 male members of the clerical Bahr al-'Ulum family. (See Appendix 8 for their names and occupations.) The government's fiction that Iraqi Shi'as are Iranians continued to command belief. Western sources reported that 70,000 more "*Iranians*" (emphasis added), "mostly Shiites from Najaf and Karbala," fled Iraq after the Gulf War.[93]

On March 11, 1991, 200 representatives of Iraqi opposition groups, including some eighty Islamists, met again in Beirut.[94] Their hopes for getting recognition and aid from the Arab Gulf states were dashed when their delegation was invited to Saudi Arabia and then left languishing in a Riyadh hotel. For their unproductive pragmatism, the Islamists, who included the Mudarrisi brothers and Hujja Muhammad Baqir al-Hakim, received criticism from non-Iraqi fundamentalists.[95]

Notes

1. Data on Saddam's early years is from Miller and Mylroie, *Saddam Hussein*, pp. 25–33.
2. During my residence in Iraq in the late 1960s and early 1970s, Saddam Hussein was routinely identified by Baghdad's academic community as "the CIA's man in the Ba'th party." When pressed for evidence, cognoscente cited his 1959 attempt to assassinate Abd al-Karim Qasim (whose leftism was regarded as communism by some in the State Department of John Foster Dulles), his zealous killing of Communists, and several instances in his rise that suggested a powerful patron.
3. When the Ba'th government executed people for conspiring with Israel, Iraqi Jews were included, presumably giving the charge credibility. When the government executed people for conspiring with Iran, Iraqi Shi'as were included in the groups, again presumably giving the charges credibility and establishing that Iraqi Shi'as are inclined to disloyalty.
4. Litwak, *Security in the Persian Gulf*, p. 4. Litwak holds that factions in the Ba'th party sought to demonstrate their "Arabness" by taking a hard line toward Iran.
5. *Sawt al-'Iraq al-Tha'ir*, July 1987, p. 10.
6. al-Khatib Ibn al-Najaf, *Al-Harakat*, p. 82. It should be noted that torturing and executing clergymen was without precedent in modern Iraq.
7. Reprinted in *Hayat-e-Hakeem*, pp. 75–77.

8. The government's 1969 suppression of religious activities is frequently recounted in Islamic publications. Cf. *Islamic Revival*, April 1980, p. 1; *Hayat-e-Hakeem*, p. 80; and Siddiqui, *Islamic Movement, 1982–1983*, p. 138.

9. The Twelfth Imam is the savior whose return from occultation is expected by the majority of Shi'as to inaugurate justice in the world.

10. *Al-'Amal al-Islami*, March 5, 1989, p. 2. For biographical data on one of those arrested at this time, see the entry on Muhammad Salih al-Husaini in Table 5.2.

11. al-Khatib Ibn al-Najaf, *Al-Harakat*, p. 96. Al-Khatib Ibn al-Najaf maintains that these three men, and probably others executed at that time, were unequivocally innocent of conspiring to overthrow the government.

12. Khomeini, *Islam and Revolution*, p. 118.

13. As was customary, the bier was transported by vehicle between towns but was carried by men on their shoulders through the towns.

14. For an account of how the Ba'thists promoted Iraqi particularism, see Baram, "Mesopotamian Identity," pp. 426–455.

15. al-Khalil, *Republic of Fear*, p. 136.

16. Lawless, "Iraq: Changing Population Patterns," p. 103.

17. al-Khafaji, "Iraqi Capitalism," pp. 4–9.

18. It is interesting to think back to Carsten Niebuhr's eighteenth-century visit to Iraq and his judgment that Iraqi Shi'as owed the degree of religious freedom they had to the government's need for income brought to Iraq by Shi'i pilgrims. In 1971 the government's ban on Shi'i pilgrims virtually closed that source of revenue. Not long afterwards, in June 1972, the government nationalized a large part of the oil industry, making the state in great measure financially autonomous from societal groups.

19. al-Khatib Ibn al-Najaf, *Al-Harakat*, p. 122; *Al-'Amal al-Islami*, January 15, 1989, p. 5; *Kayhan International*, February 6, 1988, p. 24.

20. Batatu, *Old Social Classes*, pp. 1095–1096.

21. *Al-Jihad*, March 30, 1987, p. 16, contains a report on the arrests of this period.

22. al-Khalil, *Republic of Fear*, p. 12.

23. See Chapter 5 for biographical data on Shaikh al-Basri. The other four activists executed in 1974 were 'Allama (literally, "very learned") Imad al-Din Tabrizi, born in Najaf in 1951; 'Allama Azz al-Din al-Qabanji, born in Najaf in 1951; Ustadh ("professor," a title given to intellectuals generally) Hussein Julukhan, born in Karbala; and Ustadh Nuri Tu'ma, born in Karbala. Cf. Iraqi Islamic Association in America, "Nashra I'lamiya," p. 8.

24. Hanna Batatu has noted that there were economic problems in the Shi'i community because of drought and a reduction in irrigation water caused by Syria's Tabqah Dam. Cf. Batatu, "Shi'i Organizations in Iraq," p. 194. Peasants and landowners, the people directly hurt by problems in the rural economy, have not been numerous in the Islamic movement; but rural economic difficulties necessarily added to economic distress in the holy cities.

25. al-Sadr, "Nida' al-Qa'id." The message was tape-recorded by Ayatollah al-Sadr in 1980 and circulated widely in mimeographed form. An English translation appears in Siddiqui, *Islamic Movement, 1980–1981*, pp. 56–58.

26. Ba'th party, *The 1968 Revolution in Iraq*, p. 113.

27. For data on inflation during this period, see Abdul-Rasool, "Economy of Iraq," pp. 27–40, and al-Khafaji, "The Parasitic Base," p. 79.

28. *Amnesty International 1975–1976*, p. 184.

29. Penrose, "Industrial Policy," pp. 158–159.

30. Economist Intelligence Unit, *Iraq*, p. 55.

31. Safar is the second month of the Islamic year. Details on the *intifada* are from Jawad, "Intifada Safar," p. 4.

32. "Bakr" is Ahmad Hasan al-Bakr, Ba'thist president of Iraq at the time. The organizers of the *intifada* believed fourteen Islamic activists from Najaf had already been executed by the Ba'th government, but a number less than eleven was required to make the refrain rhyme. They therefore used the number four. (1990 telephone interview with the editor of *Sawt al-'Iraq al-Tha'ir*.)

33. The account given here is based on a variety of sources, including conversations with prominent Iraqi Shi'as and details given in Hasan, *Al-Shahid al-Sadr*, p. 58.

34. Bengio, "Shi'is and Politics," p. 3.

35. Mallat, "Iraq," p. 78.

36. Among the leaders outside Iraq by the end of 1977 were Dr. Fadili, Sayyid Murtada al-'Askari, Sayyid Muhammad Hussein Fadlallah, Shaikh Muhammad Mahdi Shams al-Din, Shaikh Muhammad Mahdi al-Asafi, Dr. Dawud al-'Attar, and Hujja Mahdi al-Hakim. Cf. al-Khatib Ibn al-Najaf, *Al-Harakat*, p. 113. Shaikhs Fadlallah and Shams al-Din became leaders of the Islamic movement in their native Lebanon.

37. Farouk-Sluglett and Sluglett, "Iraqi Ba'thism," p. 101.

38. Rajab is the seventh month of the Islamic year. The account of the Rajab *intifada* is from Hussein, "Intifada Rajab," pp. 4–5.

39. *Amnesty International 1980*, p. 332.

40. *Hujja* is the reduced form of *hujjat al-Islam* (proof of Islam), the title of a mujtahid.

41. Adnan Abd al-Jabbar, cited in *At-Tayar al-Jadeed*, September 17, 1984, p. 26.

42. al-Sadr, *Min Fikr al-Da'wa*, p. 37.

43. al-Sadr, "Nida' al-Qa'id."

44. Abu Ali, "An Iraqi Corrects the *New York Times*," p. 12.

45. The quotation is from Ayatollah al-Sadr, as reported in *Sawt al-Da'wa lil-Jamahir*, March 6, 1980, p. 2.

46. *Al-Jihad*, June 1, 1987, p. 6.

47. Dr. Shahristani was presumed dead, but was found alive, his hands and feet crippled from torture, during the March 1991 *intifada*. Released from prison, he escaped to Iran before the Ba'th government was able to reimpose its control. See *Crescent International*, August 1–15, 1991, p. 2.

48. "Reign of Terror," p. 3.

49. I am grateful to Professor Michael Hudson for a mimeographed copy of the *fatwa*, which was issued from Najaf, and was probably written by Hujja Muhammad Baqir al-Hakim, who wrote most of the *fatawin* issued by Jama 'at al-'Ulama'.

50. *Al-Jihad*, September 7, 1987, p. 13.

51. Islamic Task Organization, *Voice of Iraqians* [sic], pp. 4–5; *Kayhan International*, September 26, 1987, p. 8. In the government's version of the incident, the *mujahid* was a Syrian agent and those he killed were Shi'i worshipers, a story intrinsically unbelievable, even in the absence of Islamic movement accounts.

52. Batatu, "Shi'i Organizations in Iraq," p. 196.

53. Matar, *Saddam Hussein*, p. 134.

54. Islamic Task Organization, *Voice of Iraqians* [sic], pp. 5–6.

55. *Islamic Revival*, January–February 1981, p. 6.

56. Iraq, *Al-Niza al-'Iraqi al-Irani*, p. 13.

57. In the belief that Shi'i clerical titles recognized by the Iranian government are the ones likely to prevail, I follow Iranian government publications in titling Shi'i clerics. Because it is sometimes difficult to know what title is appropriate at a given stage in a cleric's life, I ask the reader's indulgence in the matter.

58. Helms, *Iraq*, p. 161. By calling Sayyid Yusuf al-Hakim "Tabataba'i," the government calls attention to the family's Persian origin, *Tabitaba'i* being the Persian name for descendants of the Prophet Muhammad.

59. "Plots Against Saddam Hussein," p. 3.

60. Amnesty International, *Amnesty International Report 1983*, p. 310.

61. *Al-Jihad*, June 1, 1987, p. 6.

62. For accounts of the battle at Dujayl and its aftermath, see the *Economist*, July 31, 1982, pp. 45–46; December 4, 1982, p. 61; and January 29, 1983, p. 30. A detailed account of the attack is given in *Al-Jihad*, June 1, 1987. *Al-Jihad* reports that forty-nine Ba'thists were killed in the fight. If that figure and the *Economist*'s figure of 150 killed overall are correct, Da'wa lost about 100 men in the battle.

The social composition of the settlement at Dujayl is discussed in more detail in the following chapter.

63. See Mallat, "Iraq," p. 81, for a listing of the successive efforts made by Iraqi ulama to replace Ayatollah al-Sadr as leader of the Islamic movement.

64. The Publicity Unit of the High Majlis of the Islamic Revolution in Iraq, *The High Majlis (Supreme Council) of the Islamic Revolution in Iraq*, (Tehran?: 1983), pp. 21–25 and 46, as cited in Batatu, "Shi'i Organizations in Iraq," p. 197.

65. Those killed were Ayatollah Abd al-Sahib, age forty-one; Hujja 'Ala' al-Din, age thirty-nine; Hujja Muhammad Hussein, age thirty-eight; Hujja Kamal, age forty-two; Hujja Abd al-Wahab, age thirty-nine; and Sayyid Ahmad, age thirty-eight. The first three were sons of Ayatollah Muhsin al-Hakim. Kamal and Abd al-Wahab were sons of Yusuf and thus grandsons of Ayatollah Muhsin. Ahmad, the only noncleric, was the son of Muhammad Rida and thereby a grandson of Ayatollah Muhsin. Another of Ayatollah Muhsin's sons, Dr. Abd al-Hadi, age forty-three, was executed somewhat later. Information on those killed, including titles, is from Iraqi Islamic Association in America, *Nashra I'lamiya*, p. 11.

66. Ali Kashif al-Ghita's cooperation with the Ba'th government is in contrast to the nonpolitical or activist stance of most of the Kashif al-Ghita family. Wasim Kashif al-Ghita, Ali's nephew, was arrested and tortured by the government when he reentered Iraq after four years as an engineering student in Switzerland. There were no charges or trial to reveal why he was arrested, but his cellmates believe it was because his brother was in Beirut working with Amal, a politically assertive group of Lebanese Shi'as organized by Imam Musa al-Sadr. Cf. Abu Jameel, "I Was Saddam's Prisoner," p. 3.

67. Particulars about armed forces attached to the Majlis have appeared in several Islamic publications. Among them are *Kayhan International*, October 10, 1987, p. 10, and *Crescent International*, April 1–15, 1988, p. 1.

68. The *mujahida* Um Ma'ad, in an interview reported in *Al-'Amal al-Islami*, November 27, 1988, p. 6.

69. *Al-'Amal al-Islami*, January 29, 1989, p. 4.

70. *Kayhan International*, August 6, 1988, p. 12, reports the execution of Kurdish ulama.

71. As of October 1988, twenty-seven members of the al-Hakim family had been executed by the Iraqi government. The number is reported in the October 1988 edition of *Sawt al-'Iraq al-Tha'ir*, the editor of which is related to the al-Hakims by marriage.

72. Bangash, "Atrocities on Muslims," p. 61.

73. Mallat, "Iraq," pp. 79 and 86n. Mallat's figures come from Abd al-Karim al-Qazwini and Ghalib Hassan, both of whom are well acquainted with Iraq's Islamic activists.

74. *At-Tayar al-Jadeed*, July 1986, p. 2.

75. *Al-Jihad*, June 1, 1987, p. 6.

76. For indications in 1987 and early 1988 that Iraqi groups were being prepared to carry on armed resistance without Iranian participation, see Sick, "A Glimmer of Hope," p. E23; *Middle East International*, September 26, 1987, p. 6; and *Kayhan International*, November 21, 1987, p. 8.

77. See Whittleton et al., "Whither Iraq?" p. 245, for mention of the government's use of chemical weapons in the southern marshes. Western sources in general have not reported this accusation against Saddam's government, but a wide variety of Islamic sources insist upon it. There is nothing incredible about the charge since the Iraqi government had already used chemical weapons against Iranian forces and subsequently used them against Iraqi civilians.

78. Barnes, "Iraq's No-win, No-lose War," p. 38. See also *New York Times*, September 22, 1987, p. A6, and *Kayhan International*, January 9, 1988, p. 11.

79. *Kayhan International*, January 30, 1988, p. 8. Abu Thar died from his wounds in January 1988.

80. *Al-Jihad*, December 21, 1987, p. 7.

81. The account of Majlis's forces is from *Crescent International*, April 1–15, 1988, p. 1; *Kayhan International*, May 7, 1988, p. 1; May 28, 1988, p. 11; and August 13, 1988, p. 16; and *Christian Science Monitor*, August 29, 1988, pp. 1 and 28.

82. *Kayhan International*, September 30, 1988, p. 7; and *Crescent International*, March 1–15, 1988, p. 8, and March 16–31, 1989, p. 8. In comparison to the 4,000 to 5,000 Kurdish *mujahidin*, the United Front of Kurdistan, the alliance of non-Islamic Kurdish parties, had about 26,000 guerrillas. Although not a member of the United Front, KIM has cooperated with the other Kurdish parties. KIM's military wing, Lashkri Qur'an, was reported in 1989 to have some 2,800 *mujahidin*.

83. Jansen, "The Slow Return to Normality," pp. 12–13.

84. *Kayhan International*, April 22, 1989, p. 10.

85. Text of the communiqué is printed in *Al-'Amal al-Islami*, June 24, 1990, p. 2.

86. Whittleton et al., "Whither Iraq?" p. 247. The New Umma party of Iraqi liberals led by Saad Salih Jabr has advocated democracy and Islamic principles, not Islamic government in the fundamentalist sense, but it is very doubtful that the party has any organization inside Iraq.

87. Text of the communiqué with its signatories is printed in *Sawt al-'Iraq al-Tha'ir*, March 1990, p. 1.

88. *Al-'Amal al-Islami*, April 22, 1990, pp. 1 and 2.

89. *Christian Science Monitor*, September 20 and 26, 1990.

90. *New York Times*, December 30, 1990, p. 4.

91. Rodenbeck, "Saddam's Opponents Unite," p. 11.

92. Amnesty International, "Iraq: Human Rights Violations Since the Uprising," pp. 2–14.

93. *New York Times*, June 16, 1991, p. E3.

94. Fandy, "Iraq's Splintered Opposition."

95. *Crescent International*, January 16–31, 1991, p. 1 and February 1–15, 1991, p. 6.

5

Social Bases of
the Islamic Movement

The historical account given in Chapters 3 and 4 reveals that members of the clergy, educated young people, and urban crowds were active in Iraq's Islamic movement. In this chapter I present biographical data on individual leaders and members of the movement, derived largely from eulogies contained in Islamic movement publications. I supplement this data with published research illuminating the social circumstances of groups to which the activists belong.

Clergy

Of the social bases of the Iraqi Islamic movement, the clerical base is foremost. Throughout its existence, the movement has had clerical leadership. In the late 1950s, the ulama organized study groups to politicize believers. When the Ba'th government responded to clerical protests against government actions by torturing prominent clerics and interfering with religious education, the ulama organized nonviolent public protests. When the movement adopted militant tactics in 1979, the ulama were well represented among those who paid with their lives.

Clerical leadership contrasts with the lay leadership of Islamic movements in other Arab countries. In Egypt and Syria, for example, individual Sunni clerics have participated in the Islamic opposition, as indeed have some in Iraq, but the Sunni clerical establishment has been essentially absent. Being a political opposition movement, the Islamic movement has little appeal to groups dependent on the government or beneficially associated with the political establishment, as the Sunni clergy has traditionally been in Arab countries. In contrast, the relationship between the Shi'i clerical establishment and the Iraqi government has usually been one of mutual sufferance. Shi'i clerics are relatively independent of the government because their financial support and their means of rising to prominence rest with their followers, not with the government. Just the opposite tends to be true of the Sunni ulama.

The ulama's motivation for activism was provided by political changes within Iraqi society, particularly secularization. In human societies, religious elites have historically been regarded as the earthly representatives of a supernatural power; thus clerics have been respected as powerful individuals and accorded high social position. In a society undergoing secularization, however, there is a transposition of divinely attributed knowledge and institutional arrangements to human creation and responsibility. Clerics lose educational, judicial, and welfare functions—and their status declines.

Secularization and modernization have been found to present clerics with a threefold problem: their numbers shrink, they lose status (manifested by a drop in income), and they experience role uncertainty as the laity acquires more theological knowledge of its own.[1] Those within the clerical cohort become progressively older as a decreasing number of young men opt for religious careers. By the late 1950s, when Iraq's Islamic movement took form, Shi'i clerics had experienced all of these problems.

Table 5.1 demonstrates the Iraqi clergy's precipitous decline in numbers. From 12,000 in the early 1900s, the number of religious scholars in Najaf had dropped to 1,954 by December 1957. Of these, only 326 were Iraqi, a number insufficient to fill clerical positions in the main cities of Iraq at a time when the rural areas were already very short of clerics.[2] Particularly ominous for Iraq's clerical establishment was that the Iraqi students were primarily among the older scholars. On an immediate level, recruitment of new students was adversely affected by economics. Shi'i seminarians typically receive stipends from funds managed by the mujtahids, whose financial resources had declined substantially beginning with their loss of control over *awqaf* in the 1920s.[3] The deterioration in material situation and prestige affected the whole clerical estate but was acute for the lower ranks of the clergy.

The number of lay students in Islamic schools was also down precipitously. In order to prepare their sons for the world of technology, even pious Iraqi families were selecting government or foreign-operated schools. Traditional religious training, with its emphasis on rote learning and scriptural languages, was of little applicability if the student had any career other than religion in mind, and its irrelevance was becoming apparent. As lamented by Shaikh Riza al-Shabibi, minister of education three times during the 1920s and 1930s, young people were beginning to say that the religious sciences were obsolete.[4]

With increasing urbanization and education, Iraqis from peasants to tribal shaikhs had contact with new groups and new ideas. Non-religious institutions were available to provide meaning for life; thus by the late 1950s, the clergy had lost its monopolistic control over molding the

Table 5.1 Religious Scholars of Najaf

Time Period	Number
Before the British[a]	12,000 scholars[b]
1918	6,000 students[c]
December 1957	1,954 students in twenty-four colleges[d]
1977	600 scholars and students[e]

[a]The British occupied Najaf near the end of 1917.
[b]Muhsin al-Amin, as cited in Ajami, *The Vanished Imam*, p. 40. The term *scholars* presumably includes both teachers and students. In the theological colleges, it was standard practice for the more advanced students to study with a mujtahid while teaching the less advanced.
[c]Batatu, "Shi'i Organizations in Iraq," p. 189.
[d]Jamali, "The Theological Colleges of Najaf," p. 15. The students consisted of 896 Iranians, 665 from the Indian subcontinent, 326 Iraqis, and 67 Arabs from Lebanon, Syria, and the Gulf.
[e]Arjomand, *The Turban for the Crown*, pp. 86 and 234.

worldview of Shi'as. As long as political rulers preserved religious law, religious elites could compromise with new doctrines and secularization; but when not allowed to opt for collaboration, religious elites became declassed and potentially dangerous to the existing order.

A government that eschews collaboration with the clergy, as did the Ba'th government in 1969, runs the risk that religion may provide the necessary social cohesion for a full-fledged political opposition. As Max Weber wrote,

> Two qualities of the hierocracy recommend an alliance to the political authorities. First of all, as a legitimating power hierocracy is almost indispensable even (and especially) to the caesaropapist ruler, but also to the personally charismatic (for example, the plebiscitarian ruler) and all those strata whose privileges depend on the "legitimacy" of the political system. Furthermore, hierocracy is the incomparable means of domesticating the subjects in things great and little.[5]

Not only did the Ba'th government arrest, torture, and even kill prominent ulama, but it added insult to injury with activities such as a nine-day "Mesopotamian" festival that culminated in celebrations at an ancient pagan temple in Hatra.

Despite the clerical decline of the preceding fifty years, Shi'i clerics were consequential opponents when they chose to lead a system-challenging movement. As the interpreters of God's law, the Shi'i ulama had retained religious power, in the sense of influence over the beliefs of the Shi'i community. Using that religious authority, Iraqi ulama moved from their efforts to rectify society through individual reform and enjoined believers to oppose the Ba'th government.

Ayatollah al-Sadr

Of the clerics who initiated and led Iraq's Islamic movement, Ayatollah al-Sadr[6] was preeminent. His innovative use of educated laymen as proselytizers among Iraq's Muslims brought the contemporary Islamic movement into existence. His prestige as a member of the al-Sadr family and as a learned and pious alim gave weight to his reformist ideas and inspiration to Iraqi activists. The presence in Iraq of the activist Islamic circles formed by his followers made possible the resort to violence in 1979.

Ayatollah Muhammad Baqir al-Sadr was born in 1931 in the holy city of Kazymiya. His ancestor, Sadr al-Din, came to Iraq from Lebanon in the eighteenth century. The Arabic word *sadr* means "person holding the highest position in a given area." A *sadr al-din* is, therefore, the chief person in matters of religion (*din* meaning "religion"). The al-Sadr family maintained its position of religious authority within Iraq. Sayyid Hasan al-Sadr was the chief religious figure in Kazymiya when the British arrived there in 1917. As Gertrude Bell, British political officer in Baghdad, wrote in 1920, "Chief among the worthies in Kazymiya is the Sadr family, possibly more distinguished for religious learning than any other family in the whole Shi'ah world."[7] Sayyid Hasan's son Muhammad, likewise a cleric, became a leader of the 1920 Iraqi rebellion against British rule.

Sayyid Haidar al-Sadr, Muhammad Baqir's father, was a mujtahid and was himself the son of a mujtahid, Isma'il al-Sadr. Sayyid Haidar died when Muhammad Baqir was four years old, leaving him to be raised by his very religious mother and by his older brother, Isma'il, also a mujtahid. Muhammad Baqir's maternal grandfather was another Iraqi cleric, Shaikh Abd al-Hussein al-Yasin.[8] His maternal uncles included the clerics Shaikh Murtada al-Yasin, Shaikh Razi al-Yasin, and Shaikh Muhammad Riza al-Yasin.

Muhammad Baqir began his formal schooling at the Imam al-Jawad School, a religious primary school in Baghdad. There he gained a reputation as a precocious student. He then went to study in Najaf, where his teachers included his uncles, his brother, and Ayatollah Muhsin al-Hakim. He distinguished himself in Najaf and was able to begin teaching *fiqh* at an early age. Sayyid al-Sadr married his cousin Fatima, sister of Imam Musa al-Sadr, who organized and politicized Lebanon's Shi'as in the 1960s and 1970s.

Sayyid Muhammad Baqir al-Sadr published twenty-two books and became the only Arab among the eight living Shi'i *maraji'*. Until his death, he lived in a small house in a poor area of Najaf. When hanged on April 8, 1980, he left a son, Ja'far, age 11, three daughters, his wife, and his mother. Ayatollah al-Sadr has been given the title Shahid al-Rabi' (the Fourth Martyr).[9]

Hujja Mahdi al-Hakim

Hujja Mahdi al-Hakim[10] was born in Najaf in 1935. He was the second son of Ayatollah Muhsin al-Hakim, the most widely followed Shi'i authority of the 1960s. The first al-Hakim to settle in Iraq is said to have been Sayyid Ali al-Hakim, court physician to Shah Abbas Safavi (1571–1629), hence the name "al-Hakim," meaning "the physician" in Arabic. Under the Ottomans, members of the al-Hakim family at one time held the high religious office of *al-naqib*. Sayyid Mahdi's mother was the daughter of Hasan al-Bazzi of Lebanon, where the al-Hakim family has a branch.

Sayyid Mahdi became a mujtahid and one of the founders of Jama'at al-'Ulama', the society of activist ulama. He was also a founder of the innovative College of Religious Principles (*kulliya usul al-din*) in Baghdad, where he taught the courses in Islamic economics. Sayyid Mahdi acted as his father's assistant, his duties including the communication of clerical views to the Baghdad government and to the Shi'i community of Iraq. These responsibilities led to his arrest and torture in 1969. He and Ayatollah al-Hakim's assistant for political affairs, Dr. Muhammad Bahr al-'Ulum, fled Iraq later in 1969. Sayyid Mahdi went to Pakistan, where the family has another branch.

In 1971 Ayatollah al-Sadr assigned Sayyid Mahdi to be spiritual guide for the Shi'i community in Dubai, one of the Arab Gulf states. Sayyid Mahdi remained in Dubai until 1980, when he was reassigned to London. There, with the help of Jama'at al-'Ulama', he established Ahl al-Bayt, a charitable organization and Shi'i conference center, which he then directed in its work with Iraqi refugees. Sayyid Mahdi was not involved in the formation of the Majlis, but he "blessed" its creation and avoided any projects outside its auspices.

On January 17, 1988, while attending an Islamic conference in Khartoum, Sudan, Sayyid Mahdi was assassinated by men in an Iraqi embassy car. At funeral services in Beirut, speakers were Shaikh Muhammad Mahdi Shams al-Din, vice-chairman of the Supreme Assembly of Lebanese Shi'i Muslims,[11] and Ali al-Husseini of the Amal[12] movement. At funeral services in Qumm, Iran, Ayatollah Muhammad Riza Gulpaygani spoke. Like Sayyid Mahdi, the speakers have been identified with the moderate line of political thinking among Shi'as, that is, with rejecting clerical rule in favor of a system in which the clerical role is confined to ruling on the acceptability of proposed government actions.

Sayyid Mahdi had two sons, Sayyid Sahib and Sayyid Ali, both of whom live in Iran, and two daughters.

Ayatollah Hasan Shirazi

Ayatollah Hasan Shirazi[13] was born in the holy city of Najaf in about 1933. The name Shirazi indicates that the family was originally from the city of Shiraz in Iran. While Sayyid Hasan was very young, his family moved to Karbala, where he was educated in both contemporary sciences and religious studies. His father, Ayatollah Mahdi Shirazi, was his teacher, as was his older brother, Sayyid Muhammad Shirazi, also a clergyman. In addition, he was taught by Ayatollah Muhammad Hadi al-Milani[14] and Ayatollah Muhammad Riza al-Isfahani. Sayyid Hasan became a poet and an authority on Arabic literature, as well as a mujtahid.

Because he spoke out publicly against the actions of the Ba'th regime in 1969, Sayyid Hasan was arrested, tortured, and forced to spend nine months in prison. Four hospitalizations followed, during which he was treated for both physical and mental problems. Exiled in 1970, he continued to promote Islamic political activism outside Iraq. He established and taught in three centers of religious education, the Hawza al-Zaynabia in Syria, the Hawza al-Imam al-Mahdi in Lebanon, and the Hawza Hashimiya in Sierra Leone. Sayyid Hasan wrote numerous books on Islamic ethics and religion. He was assassinated in Beirut on May 2, 1980.

Ayatollah Muhammad Shirazi, Sayyid Hasan's older brother, resides in Qumm. Two other brothers, also ulama, work elsewhere in Iran.

Hujja Muhammad Baqir al-Hakim

Hujja Muhammad Baqir al-Hakim[15] was born in Najaf around 1944. He is the sixth of Ayatollah Muhsin al-Hakim's ten sons. Like most of his brothers, Muhammad Baqir received a clerical education in Najaf. One of the early members of the Islamic movement, he wrote books and articles for the call to Islam and helped to organize the Safar *intifada* of February 1977. Sayyid Muhammad Baqir was imprisoned by the Ba'th government in 1972, 1977, and 1979. When released in 1980, he fled to Iran.

Sayyid Muhammad Baqir became the leader of Jama'at al-'Ulama' al-Mujahidin and has been chairman of the Majlis since its establishment in 1982. During the Iran-Iraq War, his duties included regular tours of the fifteen Iraqi refugee camps in Iran and inspections of Majlis military forces. Sayyid Muhammad Baqir has reflected the Iranian government's position in his contacts with Iraqi opposition groups in Damascus and elsewhere. He has cooperated with Sunni Arab and Kurdish groups and has supported the election of a consultative assembly to write a new constitution for Iraq.

Ayatollah Muhsin al-Hakim, most
widely followed *marji ‘* of the1960s

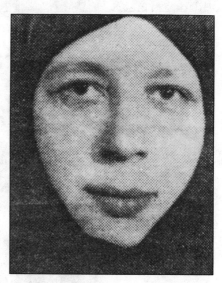

Ayatollah Muhammad Baqir al-Sadr,
Shahid al-Rabi‘ (the Fourth Martyr),
ideologist of the Islamic Movement of
Iraqi Shi‘as

‘Alima Amina al-Sadr (Bint al-Huda), activist
Islamic scholar, sister of Ayatullah al-Sadr

Ayatollah Hasan Shirazi, a
leader of the Islamic
Movement, first in Karbala,
Iraq, and then in Lebanon

Hujja Muhammad Baqir al-Hakim, chairman of al-Majlis al-
A'la lil Thawra al-Islamiya fi al-Iraq (Assembly)

Hujjat al-Islam Mahdi
al-Hakim

These two clerics fled Iraq in 1969 after the Ba'th government sentenced Sayyid al-Hakim to death. In 1988, Sayyid al-Hakim was assassinated in exile, but Dr. Bahr al-'Ulum continues to lead the moderate Islamic opposition. He participated in a conference of Iraqi opposition groups in Washington, D.C. at the beginning of August 1991.

Dr. Muhammad Bahr al-'Ulum

'Alima Bint al-Huda

'Alima Amina al-Sadr, known as Bint al-Huda,[16] was the sister of Ayatollah al-Sadr. (See the section above on Ayatollah al-Sadr for family background.) Bint al-Huda was born in Kazymiya and educated by members of her clerical family in *fiqh*, *usul*, hadith (sayings of the Prophet and Imams), and other theological subjects. She was instrumental in establishing the Madrasa Zahra', a religious school for girls in Baghdad, and the Special Religious School for Girls in Najaf. She supervised both schools, in addition to teaching Islamic awareness and theology to Muslim women in Najaf. Bint al-Huda authored eight books, the first of which, *Kalima wa Da'wa* (An Announcement and a Summons) appeared in the early 1960s. She organized demonstrations against the arrest of her brother in 1979 and was hanged with him on April 8, 1980. Da'wa's largest guerrilla operation against Saddam's person, the 1982 attack at Dujayl, was named for Bint al-Huda.

Shaikh Arif al-Basri

'Allama Shaikh Arif al-Basri[17] was born in the city of Basra in 1937. After completing secondary school in Basra, he entered a college of religious law in Najaf. While in Najaf, he became one of the original organizers of Hizb al-Da'wa. When his studies in Najaf were completed, he was assigned by Ayatollah al-Hakim to teach *usul* in Baghdad at the Imam Jawad School and the College of Religious Principles. In Baghdad he was responsible for many Islamic activities, including the disbursement of charitable funds and broadcasting religious programs over radio and television. Shaikh al-Basri was arrested on July 18, 1974. Sentencing was deferred because of daily demonstrations in front of the court, but he was tortured and, in December, hanged. A unit of the Iraqi *mujahidin* fighting against the Iraqi government in the Iran-Iraq War was named for Shaikh al-Basri.

Other Clerics and Clerical Families in the Movement

The willingness of the *marji'* Ayatollah Muhsin al-Hakim to put the resources of the religious establishment at the service of the reform effort made possible the organization of Jama'at al-'Ulama', the society of activist ulama. The series of recruitment meetings held in 1962 and 1963 was organized by the clerical establishment. It was Ayatollah al-Hakim who dispatched Imam Musa al-Sadr to Lebanon, where Imam al-Sadr organized the Lebanese Shi'as and led them in their political assertiveness of the 1970s.

Ayatollah Abu al-Qasim Khu'i, although not known as a political activist, provided sponsorship and funding for Bint al-Huda's Special Religious School for Girls in Najaf,[18] and his representative in Lebanon,

Sayyid Muhammad Hussein Fadlallah, is a member of Jama'at al-'Ulama' and an acknowledged leader of Lebanon's Shi'i Islamists.

Shaikh Fadlallah, born in Najaf to a Lebanese mujtahid, began his activist writings in Najaf (see Appendix 2) and continued them in Lebanon. In 1976, the second year of Lebanon's civil war, he published *Al-Islam wa Mantaq al-Quwa* (Islam and the Logic of Force), urging Shi'as to abandon their passivity and work for a just and pious Islamic society. He interpreted the withdrawal from politics that the Imams counseled in earlier centuries as a temporary expedient and averred that the time had come to take a stand against oppression. Shaikh Fadlallah defended the use of force in self-defense as not only legitimate but as required for Shi'as. He has not insisted on an Islamic state in Lebanon, with its large Christian minority, but he has insisted that the Shi'as participate in the governance of Lebanon.[19]

Clerics have authored innumerable publications in their efforts to reinterpret religious requirements for Shi'as and to mobilize Shi'as politically. They have made decisions for the Islamic groups and have recruited laypeople to the groups. During the Iran-Iraq War, Shaikh Abu Maythum al-Khafaji, a cleric, was responsible for Iraqi *basij* forces.[20] The president of the general assembly of the Majlis, Sayyid Ali al-Ha'iri, is from a prominent Iraqi clerical family.[21] Each activist group has a clerical guide, the latest for Hizb al-Da'wa being Shaikh Utayfi.

Leaders of the Islamic Task Organization are Hujjat al-Islam Muhsin al-Husseini and Ayatollah Hasan Shirazi's nephews, Muhammad Taqi al-Mudarrisi and Muhammad Hadi al-Mudarrisi. Although neither of the al-Mudarrisi brothers is a mujtahid, both are religionaries, and Muhammad Taqi, the older brother, is considered very knowledgeable in Islam. The younger brother, Muhammad Hadi, is better known for his political efforts on behalf of Islam, among them representing the Majlis at public meetings.[22]

The members of the central committee of the Majlis are ulama. Before the sixth meeting of the general assembly and central committee of the Majlis in Tehran, January 5–6, 1988, all the clerical members of the central committee, which meets with some regularity and performs the organization's coordinating function, met in Qumm.[23] At the meeting of the whole assembly, most of the speakers were clergymen. (Appendix 7 identifies the speakers and other leaders in attendance.)

Virtually all of Iraq's Shi'i clerics have been educated in Iraq's seminaries. They have been brought up in a highly patriarchal environment, studying with their fathers and older brothers, learning to defer to those above them in rank and to expect deference themselves, both for the respect owed their scholarly families and for their own learning. They view obedience to those in authority as a religious duty.

In the formation of Iraq's Islamic movement, three of the country's most prominent clerical families took the lead: the al-Sadr family of Kazymiya, the al-Hakim family of Najaf, and the Shirazi family of Karbala. Clerical leaders in smaller cities formed and maintained their own city-based groups. For example, residents of Karbala are far more likely to join the Islamic Task Organization, headed by the al-Mudarrisi brothers of Karbala, than they are to join Hizb al-Da'wa, which originated in Najaf. Whereas most groups remain city-based, Hizb al-Da'wa and the Islamic Task Organization were able to recruit members outside their cities of origin— Hizb al-Da'wa in Iraq's universities and the Islamic Task Organization in the Arab Gulf states. The Islamic Task Organization was sufficiently involved in Bahrain's August 1979 demonstrations in favor of Islamic government to warrant a Bahraini death sentence for its leader, Shaikh Hadi al-Mudarrisi.

The various Iraqi Islamic groups work together, although a certain amount of rivalry is reflected in their publications. On one level, the competition centers on who has done and is doing the most for the cause of Islam in Iraq. The Shi'i tradition of making clerical advancement depend in large part on public following ensures clerical rivalry and concern with public relations. Thus *Al-Jihad*, a Da'wa publication, has claimed, "The Islamic Da'wa Party is the pivot [*mihwar*] on which activities in Iraq hinge."[24] *Al-'Amal al-Islami*, the weekly newspaper of the Islamic Task Organization, has answered with statements such as, "No group should claim that it alone is responsible for overthrowing the regime of the Ba'th party. The victory promised is divine."[25]

On another level, the competition among Iraq's Islamic groups is ideological. Majlis leaders support Imam Khomeini's prescription of clerical rule as the way to just government; whereas most Iraqi Islamic groups have taken the position that clerical government would be impossible to effect in Iraq, with its large Sunni minority. Revealing a lack of compliance that did not sit well with Imam Khomeini, Hizb al-Da'wa made the issue optional for its members.

Iraq's clerical families intermarry, and both male and female members are highly imbued with traditional values and goals. At least up until the Ba'th purges of the 1970s and 1980s, Iraqi clerical families constituted a tight-knit community devoted to maintaining Najaf in particular and Iraq in general as centers for Shi'i scholarship. Retaining an Arab *marji'* has been sufficiently important to Iraqi clerics to rally them behind one Arab cleric in any given period. Independence of Iran is one of the criteria figuring in the competition among Iraqi clerics; thus members of the Islamic Task Organization, with its support in the Arab Gulf states, aver that it is more independent of Iran than is Hizb al-Da'wa. If the Iraqi clergy is absorbed into the Persian clergy as a result of the large number of Iraqi clerics killed and exiled to Iran and the government control exercised over those remaining, the independence Arab

Shi'i clerics have maintained with difficulty for centuries would be at an end.

Youthful Intelligentsia

Religious leaders can generate a social movement only if there are social groups to whom their message is relevant. In Iraq, pious young Muslims, both the educated and the uneducated, responded to the clergy's message. Like the secular young intelligentsia who opposed the shah's government in Iran, Iraq's young believers began with pacific opposition to Iraqi governments and then took up arms when the government used arms against them. In both Iran and Iraq, young intellectuals were morally indignant at the poverty in their oil-producing countries and the favoritism and autocracy of their governments.[26]

Adding to the indignation of young Iraqis was the economic pressure the Ba'th government put on them. Education was greatly expanded in Iraq in the 1960s and 1970s, making it possible for the Ba'th government to do without the services of those who were unwilling to join the Ba'th Party. With most economic activity under government control by the mid-1960s, virtually the only careers for educated young people were in government; thus they faced great difficulty getting jobs if they were unwilling to join the Ba'th Party: "All jobs are in the hands of the military government. So that one can secure himself or herself a job in Iraq, he or she has to have a recognized qualification plus, most significantly, the recommendation of one of the family members who is very highly respected by the ruling party, hence forcing all families to be members of the party in order to secure their survival."[27] College graduates who did not join the party frequently endured long periods of unemployment that forced young men to postpone marriage and generated resentment. When non-Ba'thists did find employment, the jobs were unlikely to be commensurate with the individuals' qualifications and aspirations.

Table 5.2 gives biographical information on some of the educated young Muslims who followed the clergy into opposition to the Iraqi government. Table 5.3 summarizes the data on educated lay Islamists from Table 5.2. Geographically, they came from all but the northernmost part of Iraq. Nearly all of them were recruited as students, uncertain of gainful employment after graduation. Six of the fifteen were born in one of the Shi'i holy cities. While these fifteen are not necessarily representative of Iraq's educated Islamists, neither are they necessarily atypical. The names and deeds of hundreds of activists are given in Islamic movement publications, but social data is given on relatively few. All the underground activists on whom I have social data are included in the tables.

Table 5.2   Educated Nonclerical Islamists

Abu Du'a was born in 1960 in al-Thawra, the poorest residential area of Baghdad. While a student at Baghdad's College of Administration and Economics, he joined Hizb al-Da'wa and the Mujahidin. Abu Du'a was eventually obliged to flee to Iran, where he joined the military forces of the Iraqi refugees. With his unit, he returned to Iraq and died there fighting the government.
(*Source*: *Al-Jihad*, June 22, 1987, p. 16.)

Samir Nur Ali (called Samir Ghulam by the Lebanese journalist Fuad Matar) was a twenty-year-old student at Mustansariya University in Baghdad when he threw a hand grenade at Deputy Prime Minister Tariq Aziz on April 1, 1980. Samir was a member of the Islamic Task Organization and the *mujahidin*. He was the oldest of eight children, all of whom were executed by the government after the assassination attempt.
(*Sources*: *Islamic Revival*, January–February 1981, p. 2; Islamic Task Organization, *Voice of Iraqians* [sic], pp. 4–5; Matar, *Saddam Husain*, p. 131.)

Abu Mustafa al-Amjadi was born in Karbala in 1955. He joined Hizb al-Da'wa in 1975 while earning a B.A. in economics and business. In 1982 Abu Mustafa fled to Iran, where he joined the Shahid (Martyr) al-Sadr military unit of Iraqi expatriates. Abu Mustafa died near Basra during the Karbala 5 operation (code name of one of Iran's offensives in the Iran-Iraq War).
(*Source*: *Al-Jihad*, February 23, 1987, p. 16.)

Sayyida Salwa al-Bahrani was born about 1937 into a respected Shi'i family of Baghdad. Her father was a government minister during the monarchy. Her brother is, or was, a physician in Baghdad; and both she and her younger sister married physicians. Sayyida al-Bahrani (an Iraqi woman does not assume her husband's surname) became a teacher at the University of Baghdad. She studied theology with Bint al-Huda and established her own circle for the dissemination of religious awareness. In 1980 she was taken hostage by the government in an attempt to make her son Sa'ad Taj al-Din, suspected of being a Da'wa member, surrender. When he had not done so within a month, government authorities poisoned her with thallium and released her. She died two days later at Yarmuk Hospital in Baghdad.
(*Sources*: Cobbett, "Women in Iraq," p. 128; *Islamic Revival*, January–February 1981, p. 2; personal communications.)

Dr. Abu Ali is the nom de guerre of a young Kazmawi (native of Kazymiya) who graduated from the University of Baghdad's College of Medicine. After being arrested three times by the Ba'th government, he fled Iraq. In 1980 and 1982 he served as editor of the bimonthly *Islamic Revival*, published in Washington, D.C., in the name of the Islamic Mujahidin of Iraq. In 1986 Dr. Abu Ali was working as a physician in London and was the London organizer for Hizb al-Da'wa. When he spoke to the sixth meeting of the Majlis in January 1988, he was identified as the Da'wa representative in London.
(*Sources*: *Islamic Revival*, 1980–1981; *Kayhan al-'Arabi*, January 9, 1988, p. 4; personal interview, August 7, 1986.)

(continues)

Table 5.2 (*continued*)

Na'im Fadil was born in Basra in 1957. He graduated from the University of Basra as a civil engineer. A member of Hizb al-Da'wa, he was arrested on November 29, 1979, and died in prison May 31, 1980.
(*Source: Al-Jihad*, May 25, 1987, p. 16.)

Fa'iz Sa'dun al-Hajami was born in 1949 in the district of Suq al-Shayukh in southern Iraq. While in the fourth class of a government secondary school, he joined Hizb al-Da'wa. Fa'iz graduated from the College of Religious Principles in Baghdad and was employed by the City of Baghdad. Fa'iz taught Ayatullah al-Sadr's ideas to the peasants of southern Iraq, meeting with them regularly in village guesthouses. He was arrested on February 25, 1979, and executed on January 29, 1980.
(*Source: Al-Jihad*, April 28, 1986, p. 16).

Sayyid Muhammad Salih al-Husaini[a] was born in Najaf into a poor clerical family. As a student, he became active in al-Shabab al-Muslim (Young Muslim Men). Near the end of 1969, he was arrested by the Ba'th government, imprisoned, and tortured. When released from prison, he moved to Lebanon, where he devoted himself to the Islamic movement "without concern for nationality, popularity, or geography." He was assassinated by Iraqi government agents in Beirut in 1981.
(*Sources: Al-'Amal al-Islami*, March 5, 1989, p. 2, and March 12, 1989, p. 3.)

Abd al-Amir Hamid al-Mansuri was a teacher in Basra. Called a leader of Da'wa by the government, he allegedly divulged the occurrence of a meeting in Qumm at which Da'wa and Iranian government officials made plans to overthrow Iraq's Ba'thist regime. Abd al-Amir's body was returned to his family from the Administration of General Security in Baghdad on February 15, 1980.
(*Sources: Iraq, Al-Niza al-'Iraqi al-Irani*, p. 13; *Al-Mujahidun*, April 1, 1980, p. 11; *Islamic Revival*, June–July 1980, p. 6.)

Abd al-Amir Mashkur was born into a clerical family in Najaf. Joining Hizb al-Da'wa in secondary school, he organized a group to study the Quran. Attending his group were about twenty young men who subsequently carried the Islamic message to the universities of Basra, Mosul, and Baghdad. In 1970, when Abd al-Amir expanded his politicizing efforts to the masses, the government arrested him. In 1971 he entered Baghdad University, majoring in science. Abd al-Amir was obliged to serve in the Iraqi army during its 1974–1975 campaign against the Kurds. Unwilling to kill Muslim Kurds, he contrived to have the artillery crew under his command fail in its assignments. For this he was demoted to the rank of common soldier. In 1979 Abd al-Amir was again arrested. This time, he died in prison.
(*Sources: SawtAl-Da'wa lil-Jamahir*, March 6, 1980, pp. 2–3; Islamic Task Organization, *Voice of Iraqians* [sic], p. 3.)

Sayyid Mustafa Muhammadi was the son of a cleric, Sayyid Azz al-Din Muhammadi al-Shirazi.[b] Sayyid Mustafa was born in Karbala in 1965. He attended the Imam al-Sadiq and Hindiya religious schools. Sayyid Mustafa became a member of the Islamic Task Organization and was arrested in 1983 at the age of eighteen. When he was released after more than two years of prison and torture, he fled to Iran, where he entered the Imam al-Sadiq School in Mashad. There he died of a heart attack at the age of twenty-three.
(*Source: Al-'Amal al-Islami*, April 26, 1989, p. 2.)

(*continues*)

Table 5.2 (*continued*)

Abu Aziz al-Musawi was born in 1960 to a family of peasant farmers in the district of
    Mosul. In 1979, while a student specializing in irrigation at the University of Mosul,
    College of Engineering, Abu Aziz joined Hizb al-Da'wa. In June 1979 he participated
    in the Rajab[c] *intifada* that followed the arrest of Ayatullah al-Sadr. Abu Aziz carried
    a revolver in his missions as a *mujahid*. He was arrested on August 25, 1982, and died
    in prison on August 23, 1983, never having divulged information about other activists.
    Abu Aziz was buried in Najaf.[d]
(*Source*: *Al-Jihad*, June 15, 1987, p. 16.)
Abd al-Husain Qattan was born to a family of landowning date farmers in southern Iraq
    about 1945. He became a veterinarian, joined the Ba'th Party, and was allowed to go
    to England, where he earned a Ph.D. in physiology. Qattan returned to Iraq during the
    Iran-Iraq War and was assigned to teach physiology in the Military College. There, he
    became stricter in his observance of Islam. He was arrested in April 1988 and was
    executed in prison on January 15, 1989.
(*Source*: Personal communications.)
Abu Mujtaba Turkomani, whose name indicates that he was a Turkoman, not an Arab, was
    born in Kirkuk in 1962.[e] Two of his brothers were members of Hizb al-Da'wa. One
    died in prison; the fate of the other is unknown. In 1982 Abu Mujtaba was conscripted
    into the Iraqi army. When able, he deserted to Iran, where he volunteered to mobilize
    forces in the Iraqi refugee camps. Abu Mujtaba fought in the Karbala 2 and Karbala
    5 operations, dying in the latter.
(*Source*: *Al-Jihad*, April 27, 1987, p. 16.)
Um Zaynab (mother of Zaynab) was born in Najaf in 1951 into the well-known clerical
    family of al-Muzaffar. She was educated at a government college for teachers. For
    over three years, Um Zaynab was the student and companion of Bint al-Huda,
    becoming very knowledgeable in several of the theological subjects taught in the
    hawza. Um Zaynab was killed in Mecca during the hajj of 1987.
(*Source*: *Al-Jihad*, August 31, 1987, p. 16.)

[a]At Tehran ceremonies on the eighth anniversary of Sayyid Husaini's death, the speakers were
Sayyid Ali Akbar al-Muhtashami, Interior Minister of the Islamic Republic of Iran, and Sayyid Sadr
al-Din al-Qabanji, member of a well-known family of Bagdad. Attending the ceremony were
delegations from Hizb al-Da'wa, the Palestinian and Libyan embassies, the Majlis, the Islamic Task
Organization, the Islamic Liberation Front of Algeria, and Shaikh Muhammad Mahdi al-Khalisi,
formerly of Kazymiya. A large military unit from Badr was also present.
[b]The use of family names was banned by the government in 1976; thus Mustafa could not use the
name "Shirazi."
[c]Rajab is the seventh month of the Islamic year. The demonstrations of June 1979, protesting the
arrest of Ayatullah al-Sadr, resulted in the execution of tens of Islamic activists, according to *Al-
Jihad*, March 30, 1987, p. 16; and *Al-'Amal al-Islami*, January 29, 1989, p. 1.
[d]That Abu Aziz was born in rural Mosul, where Shi'as are not known to live, and that he was buried
in Najaf, which Sunnis do not choose, are evidence, though not proof, that he was a Shabak. The point
about his bravery under torture may be meant to assure other Muslims that Shabaks are bona fide
Muslims. Islamic movement publications do not refer to Shabaks as a separate religious group.
[e]Although Abu Mujtaba's educational level is not known, he is placed with the educated young
because two of his brothers were Da'wa members and he himself was delegated to mobilize refugees,
suggesting he was of an educated family.

Table 5.3   Profile of Educated Nonclerical Islamists

	Sex	Place of Birth	Father's Occupation	Age (At Time of Affiliation with Movement)	Occupation
1.	M	al-Thawra	?	c. 20	Student
2.	M	?	?	20 or less	Student
3.	M	Karbala	?	20	Student
4.	F	Baghdad	Professional	?	Student/ Professor
5.	M	Kazymiya	?	c. 20	Student
6.	M	Basra	?	22 or less	Student
7.	M	Suq al-Shayukh	?	c. 16	Student
8.	M	Najaf	Cleric	?	Student
9.	M	?	?	?	Student/ Teacher
10.	M	Najaf	Cleric	16 or less	Student
11.	M	Karbala	Cleric	18 or less	Student
12.	M	Rural Mosul	Farmer	19	Student
13.	M	Rural South	Farmer	c. 40	Professor
14.	M	Kirkuk	?	c. 20	Soldier
15.	F	Najaf	Cleric	?	Student

Note: Activists appear in the same order as in Table 5.2.

Urban Poor

The second nonclerical group numerically significant in the Islamic movement is the urban poor. Ba'thist officials have talked convincingly about their many programs for the poor, but the poor's support for a politicized Islam was apparent when the residents of Madinat al-Thawra poured into the streets to celebrate the Islamic revolution in Iran. Large protests also occurred in Madinat al-Thawra after the arrest of Ayatollah al-

Sadr in early June 1979[28] and were presumably the reason for the execution of Hujja Qasim al-Mubarqi', imam of the main mosque in al-Thawra, later that month.[29] In a statement to the United Nations Security Council on October 15, 1980, Sa'doun Hammadi, Iraq's foreign minister at the time, charged that acts of sabotage had been committed in al-Thawra, as well as in Kazymiya, Karbala, Najaf, Amara, Basra, and Nasriya,[30] all of which are Shi'i cities.

In Iraq the urban poor are the progeny of the rural poor, who bring to the city little other than family loyalty and faith in Islam. The Islam they bring is not a separate category of thought; rather, it penetrates every aspect of everyday life. In studying Baghdad's rural migrants, Doris Phillips found that visits to Shi'i shrines were their second favorite recreation, surpassed only by sitting and talking.[31]

Iraq's urban poor have ample grievances against government. With permanent housing for about .25 million people, Madinat al-Thawra harbored well over 1 million people by the late 1970s. Containing one-fourth of the population of Baghdad, al-Thawra existed without city drinking water, sewers, or paved streets. It was not until 1980, in response to Islamist successes in al-Thawra, that the Ba'th government moved to bring essential city services there. This was forty-five years after oil revenues began coming to Iraq and seventeen years after the Ba'thists, with their socialist slogans, came to power. It was twenty years after Qasim's government built al-Thawra's permanent housing.

Although Iraqi governments expanded education and the middle class, they directed relatively little of Iraq's oil wealth to the poorest sectors of the population, either through salaries or through government housing and welfare programs. The Ba'thists kept wages low through the importation of foreign labor. By 1980 there were some 500,000 expatriate workers in Iraq, in an expatriate population of about 1 million.[32] Up to 1976, the average annual rise in prices in Ba'thist Iraq was around 10 percent, while the average growth in wages was about 3.2 percent, indicating an actual drop in real wages, a drop attributable in large part to government policies.[33] Not until the late 1970s did wages increase faster than inflation, and then only in certain sectors.

As actual members of Islamic groups, the urban poor have probably never outnumbered the young intelligentsia; but as sympathizers they showed themselves to be numerous in the demonstrations of the 1970s. Members of the urban poor have also played important individual roles in the movement, as exemplified by the eight activists on whom biographical data is given in Table 5.4. Their occupations would indicate that none of them had more than an elementary school education, although all except perhaps the youngest al-Kufi brother had job skills. They were part of the urban poor and (with the possible exception of Abu Muhannad, whose birthplace is not known) were

Table 5.4 Islamists from the Urban Poor

Hamza Abd al-Kazim was born in Hilla and raised by his father, an elderly woodcutter. Hamza graduated from elementary school and, after helping his father for a few years, joined the army. Becoming a member of Hizb al-Da'wa, Hamza brought weapons from northern Iraq to Islamic activists in central Iraq, transporting them through difficult inspection points. He was the most prominent member of his cell, the Martyr Muhammad Jawad al-Jibouri group. Hamza was arrested on February 18, 1980, and died in Abu Ghraib Prison April 14, 1980.
(*Source*: Al-Jihad, April 21, 1986, p. 16.)

Abu Karar was born in Kazymiya in 1966. He finished intermediate school (ninth grade) at Abi Dhar al-Ghaffari School (a religious school). He then pursued a variety of businesses to support his family. During the battle of Ahwaz, he joined the Shahid al-Sadr force. Abu Karar died on July 11, 1987.
(*Source*: Al-Jihad, September 7, 1987, p. 16.)

Sayyid Abu Baida' al-Husaini was born in 1958 in the small city of Hashimiya. The son of a religious and observing family, he finished primary school, then left to earn a living. He joined the Iraqi army and became a member of al-Ansar al-Da'wa al-Islamiya (Helpers of the Call to Islam). When the Ba'th regime intensified its repression of Islamic political activities, Abu Baida' deserted the army. After Iraq's 1980 attack on Iran, he joined Da'wa's Shahid al-Sadr force and fought in both northern and southern Iraq. He died while returning from an assignment, his group having encountered government forces on the highway leading to the city of Dahuk.
(*Source*: Al-Jihad, December 14, 1987, p. 16.)

Abu Ibrahim al-Kufi was born in Kufa in 1953. He belonged to al-Ansar al-Da'wa al-Islamiya and was a career soldier in the Iraqi army. When Iraq attacked Iran in 1980, he deserted and joined the Islamic forces of Iran, later becoming a member of the Badr brigade.

Abu Ali al-Kufi was born in Kufa in 1958. He became a medical assistant[a] and a member of al-Ansar al-Da'wa. When Iraq invaded Iran, he fled Iraq to join the mujahidin in Iran. Abu Ali died in Iran's Karbala 5 offensive.

A younger *al-Kufi brother* took part in the Safar *intifada* of 1977 and was sent to prison at that time. The remainder of the family, except for two who have disappeared, are in prison.
(*Source*: Al-Jihad, January 25, 1988, p. 16).

Abu Muhannad Salahy was born in Iraq in 1962 and completed four years of schooling. He earned his living as a tailor while working against the Ba'th regime. Abu Muhannad took part in the 1978 antigovernment demonstrations in Kazymiya. In 1980, because of the increasing number of arrests of Islamic activists, Abu Muhannad fled with his family to Iran. In Iran he joined the Islamic Revolutionary Guards and was one of the soldiers who died in the Karbala 5 operation.
(*Source*: Al-Jihad, April 27, 1987, p. 6).

(continues)

Table 5.4 (*continued*)

Abu Muhannad al-Yazdi was born in Madinat al-Thawra in 1965. He was in the seventh
grade when he and his family were expelled to Iran. In the city of Yazd, Iran, he became
a member of al-Ansar al-Da'wa and of Ruwwad al-Markaz al-Thaqafi al-Islami
(Pioneers of the Islamic Educational Center). In 1980 he joined the military. Besides
fighting in the Karbala 2 and Karbala 5 campaigns, he was based for ten months in the
marshes of southern Iraq and for two months elsewhere inside Iraq.
(*Source*: Al-Jihad, March 30, 1987, p. 9.)

[a]In Iraq a "medical assistant" typically has an elementary school education plus a short period of
training in a medical institute.

not rural migrants to the city.[34] The social data on the activists in Table 5.4
is summarized in Table 5.5.

Like their better-educated counterparts, these activists tend to be young,
and half of them are from one of the Shi'i holy cities, Kufa being essentially
a district of Najaf. Unlike the more affluent activists, these young men were
most likely recruited in *husainiyat* and mosques as opposed to the
universities. Da'wa spokesmen told me in 1986 that one regret leaders of the
Islamic movement have is that they did not make earlier and greater efforts to
organize the poor and uneducated.[35] No doubt the role the urban poor played
in Iran's successful revolution in 1978 and 1979 was as instructive for Da'wa
leaders as it was for many other people.

The number of Iraqis in the lower classes make them important, if not
necessary, to any political opposition movement that does not rely on
military force for coming to power. Like the urban poor in Iran, the urban
poor in Iraq were, and probably still are, a fertile field for an opposition
movement. Iraq's poor, despite their preponderance in the society, have
always lacked organization and representation in the government. To the
extent that the poor in particular, and Shi'as in general, have remained
unorganized, they have been unable to compel the state to respect their rights
and interests. As shown by the vigor of Hizbullah in Lebanon and by the
organization of Iraq's urban poor in al-Ansar and other Islamic groups, the
Arab poor, like the Iranian poor, respond to a call to Islam when that call
includes an emphasis on social justice.

Other Societal Groups

The ulama, the urban poor, and young intellectuals who are virtually obliged
to work for the government at its salaries and its choice of place lack any

Table 5.5 Profile of Islamists from the Urban Poor

	Sex	Place of Birth	Father's Occupation	Age (At Time of Affiliation with Movement)	Occupation
1.	M	Hilla	Woodcutter	?	Soldier
2.	M	Kazymiya	?	Teens	Vendor
3.	M	Hashimiya	?	?	Soldier
4.	M	Kufa	?	?	Soldier
5.	M	Kufa	?	?	Medical assistant
6.	M	Kufa	?	20 or less	?
7.	M	?	?	16 or less	Tailor
8.	M	Madinat al-Thawra	?	Teens	Student

Note: Activists appear in the same order as in Table 5.4.

special interest in Iraq's social order as constituted. They are understandably the groups most receptive to an Islamic movement. They are not, however, the only societal groups represented in the Islamic movement. There have been merchants and military officers among Islamic activists, in spite of governmental co-optation of military officers and the economic opportunities available to merchants. Farmers, too, are known to have affiliated with the movement, although the peasantry in general has not been mobilized.

The Farmers of Dujayl

However unreliable and inadequate their income in the city, rural migrants in Iraq have regarded themselves as financially better off in the city than they were as sharecroppers. A survey done in 1974 and 1975 found that rural factors "pushed" migrants to the city, as opposed to urban factors "pulling" them there.[36] Rural migrants cited hunger and landlord oppression as their reasons for moving. Floods, soil salinity, and weather fluctuations interfered with farm productivity, reducing farmers' income. Between 1968 and 1978 agriculture had the lowest growth rate of any sector in the Iraqi economy, despite starting from a very low base.[37] As a 1980 report by the Economist

Intelligence Unit notes, seriously lagging rural incomes pushed Iraqis out of what was already a thinly populated countryside.[38]

Most of Iraq's farmers are Shi'i, unorganized, and unrepresented in the government. The Ba'th government has "organized" farmers into a General Federation of Peasants' Unions and the Higher Agriculture Council, but the groups have offered farmers little, if anything. The first has been essentially a labor contractor, supplying peasant workers to government authorities, and the latter has been devoted to ensuring Ba'th party control.[39]

The immobility, dependence, and geographic dispersal of peasant farmers have always made them a difficult group for counterelites to organize. In Iraq, rural dwellers typically live in small villages of forty or so households, a form of settlement easily supervised by the landowner and his agents. Not surprisingly, there has been little evidence of revolutionary activity among farmers—with the exception of those at Dujayl, a planned agricultural settlement northeast of Baghdad.

In July 1982 two cells of Da'wa *mujahidin* in Dujayl launched a major armed attack against Saddam Hussein and his bodyguards. Approximately 150 men were killed in the gun battle. In the absence of definitive data on the individual activist farmers, the social composition of the original settlement and the control Dujayl farmers had over their own resources offer a plausible explanation for their militance.

Dujayl was settled by a mixed Sunni and Shi'i population between 1946 and 1950, during the period of the Iraqi monarchy. Each of 1,058 families was given 100 donums (62.5 acres) of newly irrigated land on the condition that the family cultivate it for ten years. Because the only criterion for applicants was that they be from the Dujayl area, many of the men given land at Dujayl were not experienced farmers. Land went to retired army and police officers, civil servants, and unemployed *graduates of religious institutions*.[40]

As a group, the Dujayl farmers were not impoverished, uneducated peasants, lacking organizational links to one another. Their educational level, relative independence resulting from land ownership, and organizational links attendant upon Dujayl's being a planned settlement distinguish them from other farmers. Although salinization due to inadequate drainage eventually reduced production, the farmers of Dujayl were much better off than fellahin on private estates. The rebellion at Dujayl lends support to Eric Wolf's theory that the "middle peasantry," not impotent landless laborers and not rich peasants, is the rural stratum most likely to revolt.[41]

The Missing Merchants

Unlike farmers, traditional merchants are a group one might expect to find involved in the Islamic movement. Merchants of the bazaar were part of the coalition that carried out the Islamic revolution in Iran, and merchants have supported the Islamic movement in Syria.[42] Tradesmen, as part of the traditional middle class, seem likely members of a tradition-oriented political opposition. The Shi'i merchants of al-Shurja in Baghdad were known to be major financial contributors to the *maraji'*, which presumably accounts for their hasty deportation by the Ba'th government in 1980.

Even so, references to merchants are infrequent in Iraqi Islamic movement publications, and the references there are do not indicate significant merchant involvement. In a detailed account of the 1977 *intifada*,[43] Sami Jawad describes how one young man was delegated by the organizers to undertake the dangerous task of going to a cloth merchant in Najaf to buy the large amount of fabric needed to make the pilgrims' banners. When the merchant asked the young man, Muhammad Sa'id Jawad al-Balaghi, why he wanted such a large quantity of cloth, al-Balaghi responded that it was for a sports team, a dissimulation that should not have been necessary had Islamic movement leaders had a cloth-merchant ally. The evidence of minimal merchant involvement is corroborated by a statement of Muhammad Baqir al-Hakim. Asked in a 1982 interview who supported the Islamic movement, he said that all sectors of Iraqi society are involved in the movement and then listed laborers, farmers, students, professionals, and ulama—but not merchants.[44]

This is not to say that there have been *no* merchants in Iraq's Islamic movement, merely that merchants cannot be considered one of the social bases of the movement. The wealthy trading family of Riza Alwan, of the Karada district of Baghdad, disappeared into prison in mid-1983, presumably because of the family's friendship with the al-Hakim family, which had been arrested in May 1983.[45] There are also merchants among the *muhajirin*, not surprising because Shi'as are heavily represented among small tradesmen. It is not possible, however, to say what the reasons for their deportations and arrests were, or what the evidence was, since trials, if they occurred, were neither public nor publicized.

Government policies toward merchants may explain their relative absence from Iraq's Islamic movement. The governments of Abd al-Karim Qasim (1958–1963), the Arif brothers (1963–1968), and the early Ba'thists did not pursue policies antagonistic to the traditional middle class to the extent that the shah of Iran did, nor did they nationalize small businesses. Iraqi traders who had import licenses could do much better economically than better-educated people who worked for the government. The crucial element was the import license, the sine qua non of commerce in a country with petrodollars but deficient in industrial and agricultural production. Import licenses have been distributed or withheld by the state at its discretion, obliging merchants to avoid the slightest appearance of disaffection toward the regime.

Government tax policies have also favored merchants. In the late 1970s, none of Iraq's income tax receipts arose from business profits, as compared to 92.7 percent of Iran's income tax receipts in 1977/1978 and 84.7 percent of Syria's in 1976.[46] In the early 1970s, the Ba'th government adopted policies highly favorable to commercial interests. A strategy of widening the range of privately owned light industries, with financing provided through government banks, was inaugurated. Government-owned farmland was leased to private operators for a fraction of the prevailing market rate.[47] A new group of wealthy people, self-employed as contractors, industrialists, and middlemen, joined Ba'thist politicians to form a small new upper class in the affluent suburbs of Baghdad.

Using data published by the Iraqi Ministry of Planning, Isam al-Khafaji, an Iraqi economist, has offered evidence of the development of a new, affluent, Iraqi bourgeoisie, drawn primarily from the middle and lower ranks of the traditional bourgeoisie. As a consequence of the oil price rises of 1973 and the nationalization of the oil industry, GDP more than doubled, going from 1,512.1 million Iraqi dinars ($3.39 per dinar) in 1973 to 3,331.5 million in 1974.[48] A substantial expansion of privately owned wealth occurred, with previously established industrialists consolidating their positions. Several thousand small entrepreneurs rose, and hundreds of small businessmen climbed to the status of big industrialists. For example, the Kubaisis from the town of Kubaisa in al-Anbar Province, part of the Sunni Arab north, went from traditional textile merchants to owners of the most profitable factories in Iraq. Contractors as a group did exceptionally well.

> Some entrepreneurs did not need to contribute any of their own capital. The Industrial Bank granted loans of up to 80 percent of the total cost of construction industry projects, while loans for other projects ranged as high as 40 percent of the total cost in the three main provinces [Baghdad, Basra, and Mosul] and 60 percent of the total cost in the other provinces. An industrialist only had to inflate the cost of a project to obtain a loan which would cover the entire cost.[49]

To enter the world of big profits, the would-be bourgeois needed only some relationship or connection with a politically influential person and a family record of no opposition to the government. Interestingly, high-level government and Ba'th party officials invested *their* new wealth in the Arab Gulf states and abroad.[50]

Co-opted Army Officers

Military officers are another group co-opted by the government. As early as the Abd al-Salam Arif regime (1963–1966), air-conditioned military barracks contrasted with nearby slums, and officers could buy ordinary products at rates below those paid by civilians. The Ba'th regime carried the co-optation further. The spread in income between the highest-paid military officer and the lowest-paid draftees became 46 to 1, not counting officers' housing and servant allowances or the additional pay accruing to those holding positions of command.[51] The military was well supplied with equipment, oil money making it possible for the Ba'th government to spend $2 billion on Soviet military hardware in the mid-1970s.[52] After his accession to the presidency in 1979, Saddam Hussein raised military salaries and gave members of the armed forces priority in purchasing houses and cars. He bought sophisticated Western weaponry, which won him the approval of the armed forces. In 1983 and 1984 about 100 nightclubs were opened in Baghdad to cater to military personnel.[53] After the Iran-Iraq War ended, the government continued to spend huge sums on its military apparatus.[54]

Although the government has co-opted high-ranking officers (those in favorable positions to stage coups), Islamic groups have recruited successfully among enlisted men and low-ranking officers. Not only is the pay for enlisted men very low, but lower ranks are also far more likely to be Shi'as and thus to have less stake in the political system than do Sunni Arabs. Of the twenty-two activists who appear in Tables 5.3 and 5.5, three were enlisted men in the military, two of them career soldiers. Of the thirty-two activists in Table 4.1, two were commissioned officers, four were warrant officers, and a seventh was listed as "soldier." As noted in Chapter 4, air force officers have made at least two attempts to assassinate Saddam Hussein. While the military as an institutional group cannot be considered one of the social bases of the Islamic movement, it is clear that many individual soldiers have received the call to Islam.

A multitude of believers in Iraq could be mobilized should victory appear possible. The more discredited the Iraqi government, the broader the base of the Islamic movement is likely to become. Most Iraqis have been adversely affected by Ba'thist policies, particularly the government's unsuccessful war making. In the past, thousands of Iraqis were mobilized in the cause of Islam while outsiders were judging organized political opposition in Iraq to be insignificant. Suffering from severe misgovernment and war in this world, Iraqis will likely continue to look beyond this world for help.

Notes

1. Towler, "Changing Status of the Ministry?" pp. 73–78.
2. al-Katib, *Al-Thawra al-Islamiya fi al-'Iraq*, pp. 172–173.
3. The shortage of clerics cannot be facilely attributed to weakness of belief. Egypt, like Iraq, has a shortage of clerics. Government mosques there are without regular preachers because none are available, and private mosques feature pious laymen, not trained clerics. Cf. Gaffney, "Authority and the Mosque in Upper Egypt," p. 209. Yet the Muslim Brotherhood and militant Islamic groups in Egypt have repeatedly reconstituted themselves after government purges and do well in elections when they are allowed to compete.

4. Cleveland, *The Making of an Arab Nationalist*, p. 159.

5. Weber, *Economy and Society*, vol. 3, pp. 1175–1176.

6. Hasan, *Al-Shahid al-Sadr*; *Islamic Revival*, June–July 1980, p. 3, and March–April 1981, pp. 3–6; *Kayhan International*, August 15, 1987, p. 11; introduction to al-Sadr, *Our Philosophy*, pp. xiii–xv; preface to al-Sadr, *Rituals*, pp. 7–10; al-Sadr, *Min Fikr al-Da'wa*; Batatu, "Shi'a Movements," p. 593; and Ajami, *The Vanished Imam*, p. 25.

7. Bell, *The Letters of Gertrude Bell*, vol. 2, p. 484.

8. Another alim of the al-Yasin family, Shaikh Muhammad Hasan al-Yasin (Ya Sin) (d. 1891), was *marji'* for Shi'as in the Kazymiya area.

9. The preceding three titled martyrs were, like Ayatollah al-Sadr, high-ranking clerics executed by their governments for activity on behalf of Shi'ism. Al-Shahid al-Awwal ("the First Martyr") was Ibn Makki al-Amili, who established Jabal Amil in present-day Lebanon as an important center for Shi'i studies. He was executed in Damascus in A.D. 1384 on orders of the Mamluk Sultan. Cf. Momen, *Shi'i Islam*, p. 95.

Al-Shahid al-Thani ("the second martyr") was Zayn al-Din al-Amili (1506–1558), who studied under Sunni ulama and taught at Ba'lbak in Lebanon. He was killed as the result of a summons to Istanbul. Cf. Momen, *Shi'i Islam*, p. 320.

Al-Shahid al-Thalith ("the Third Martyr") was Nurullah Ibn Sharif Shustari (b. 1549). A qadi in Lahore, he was flogged to death by the government for heterodoxy. Cf. Hollister, "Shi'ism in the Indian Subcontinent," p. 243.

10. *Hayat-e-Hakeem*, pp. iii, A-23, and A-39; "Iraq on Simmer," pp. 5–6; personal interview with Sayyid Mahdi al-Hakim at Ahl al-Bayt in London, August 6, 1986; *New York Times*, January 24, 1988, p. 6; "Sayyid Mahdi al-Hakim" (Arabic); *Kayhan International*, January 30, 1988, p. 16; *Sawt al-'Iraq al-Tha'ir*, July 1988.

11. Imam Musa al-Sadr is chairman in absentia of the Supreme Assembly of Lebanese Shi'i Muslims. Since Imam Musa disappeared in 1978 (while on a trip to Libya), Shaikh Shams al-Din has been acting chairman, a position that makes him the senior Shi'i cleric in Lebanon. Shaikh Shams al-Din has joined with Sunni and Druze Lebanese leaders in committing to a democratic, parliamentary republic that would preserve differential personal status laws for the various religious groups in Lebanon. Cf. Norton, *Amal and the Shi'a*, p. 93.

12. The word *amal* means hope. The movement is also referred to as AMAL, the acronym for Afwaj al-Muqawama al-Lubnaniya (Lebanese Resistance Battalions).

13. *Hayat-e-Hakeem*, p. A-11; *Islamic Revival*, August–September 1980, pp. 1 and 4; *Kayhan International*, August 15, 1987, p. 11; *Al-'Amal al-Islami*, January 15, 1989, p. 8; personal interview with two Islamic Task Organization members in Hemet, California, November 27, 1987.

14. Ayatollah al-Milani was subsequently *marji'* of Mashhad, Iran.

15. *Hayat-e-Hakeem*, pp. iii and A-23; *Islamic Revival*, January–February 1981, p. 3; Bengio, "Saddam Husayn's Quest for Power," pp. 323–341; *Kayhan International*, June 20, 1987, p. 8; October 27, 1987, p. 10; April 8, 1989, p. 1.

16. *Islamic Revival*, January–February 1981, p. 3; al-Khatib Ibn al-Najaf, *Al-Harakat*, pp. 50–54; *Al-Jihad*, June 1, 1987, p. 6; *Kayhan International*, August 15, 1987, p. 11.

17. *Sawt al-Da'wa lil-Jamahir*, February 28, 1980, pp. 2–3; Hizb al-Da'wa al-Islamiya, *Jara'im Saddam*, p. 219; Iraqi Islamic Association in America, "Nashra I'lamiya," p. 8.

18. al-Khatib Ibn al-Najaf, *Al-Harakat*, p. 54.

19. Information on Shaikh Fadlallah's career in Lebanon is from Norton, *Amal and the Shi'a*, pp. 102–104.

20. *Kayhan al-'Arabi*, January 9, 1988, p. 4.

21. The Ha'iri family takes its name from the *ha'ir*, the sacred enclosure of the shrine of Hussein in Karbala.

22. *Kayhan International*, January 21, 1989, p. 1. The first name "Muhammad" is frequently omitted from Sayyid Hadi's name.

23. *Kayhan International*, December 26, 1987, p. 8. The Majlis does not have regularly scheduled meetings; thus its six meetings have all been "extraordinary."

24. *Al-Jihad*, November 24, 1986, p. 4.

25. *Al-'Amal al-Islami*, November 1, 1987, p. 9.

26. See Abrahamian, "The Guerrilla Movement," pp. 149–152, for the import of moral indignation in young secularists who opposed the shah's government.

27. *Islamic Revival*, May 1980, p. 5.

28. Mujahidin strength in al-Thawra has been noted by various sources, including Batatu, "Shi'a Movements," pp. 580–581, and Farouk-Sluglett et al., "Not Quite Armageddon," p. 29n.

29. Hizb al-Da'wa, *Jara'im Saddam*, p. 220.

30. Statement reprinted in Ismael, *Iran and Iraq*, p. 206.

31. Phillips, "Rural-to-urban Migration in Iraq," p. 417.

32. Sherbiny, "Expatriate Labor Flows," p. 660.

33. al-Khafaji, "The Parasitic Base," p. 84.

34. Studies have shown that urban-born poor are more active politically than are poor rural-to-urban migrants. Cf. Nelson, *Access to Power*, p. 112.

35. August 7, 1986, interview in London with Dr. Abu Ali, Hizb al-Da'wa spokesman, and Brother Ali.

36. al-Jomard, "Internal Migration in Iraq," pp. 116–117.

37. See Abdul-Rasool, "Economy of Iraq," p. 28, for sectoral growth rates.

38. Economist Intelligence Unit, *Iraq*, p. 6.

39. Springborg, "Baathism in Practice," p. 203.

40. Penrose and Penrose, *Iraq*, p. 152.

41. Eric Wolf has written extensively about the revolutionary potential of peasants. A succinct statement of his formulations is contained in Wolf, "Peasant Rebellion and Revolution," pp. 48–67.

42. For the part merchants played in the Islamic revolution in Iran, see Arjomand, "Revolution in Iran," p. 301. For merchant involvement in the Syrian Islamic movement, see Hinnebusch, "The Islamic Movement in Syria," p. 155.

43. Jawad, "Intifada Safar," p. 4.

44. Siddiqui, *Islamic Movement, 1982–1983*, pp. 141–142.

45. *At-Tayar al-Jadeed*, December 17, 1984, p. 8.

46. Askari et al., *Taxation in the Middle East*, p. 218.

47. Springborg, "Iraq's Agrarian Infitah," p. 17.

48. al-Khafaji, *Al-Tatawwur al-Rasmali fi al-'Iraq*, p. 26.

49. al-Khafaji, "Iraqi Capitalism," p. 8.

50. Economist Intelligence Unit, *Iraq*, p. 16.

51. Batatu, "Iraqi Society," p. 387.

52. *Middle East Economic Digest*, December 22, 1977, p. 18.

53. *At-Tayar al-Jadeed*, December 17, 1984, p. 8.

54. Kaslow, "Oil Pays Iraq's Way," p. 1.

6

Epigenesis

While the Islamic political movement of Iraq is part of an assertion of Islam throughout the Muslim world, the assertiveness of Arab Shi'as has another dimension as well. Arab Shi'as have been disadvantaged in their own countries, excluded from political power and the social and economic advantages that accrue to politically dominant groups. Although Iraqi Shi'as are a disadvantaged majority rather than a disadvantaged minority, the emergence of their political activism can be viewed through the political process model of social-movement development advanced by Doug McAdam in connection with the twentieth-century black insurgency in the United States.[1] As outlined in Figure 6.1, social-movement emergence is a process engendered by broad socioeconomic changes, influenced by the state of political opportunities within a society, and formed by the indigenous organizational strength of disadvantaged groups. The determinants of the process serve to effect cognitive changes in traditionally resigned groups, and these changes ultimately cause movements to form.

Broad Socioeconomic Processes

Social changes contributing to the genesis of political activism on the part of Iraqi Shi'as can be traced to the latter years of the Ottoman Empire, when the Turks began efforts to modernize their empire by building schools, improving transportation, and strengthening the government's capacity to govern. Change quickened with the advent of British control in Iraq and the consequent emergence of a new political elite. The expansion of education begun by the Ottomans was accelerated by the British and widened further by all of Iraq's independent governments. Expanded education, abetted by the social-leveling policies of the Qasim government, created a new middle class in Iraq, a social change with far-reaching effects. Literacy made world culture, with its conceptions of economic rights and political freedoms, available to

101

Figure 6.1 Political Process Model of Movement Emergence

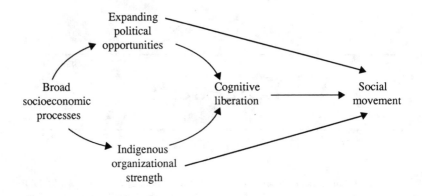

Source: Doug McAdam, *Political Process and the Development of Black Insurgency,
1930–1970*. Chicago: University of Chicago Press, 1982, p. 51. Reprinted with permission.

this class. Schooled in both Arabic and English, members of Iraq's new middle class were able to make choices in their world-view. Literacy affected the way individuals thought about their social and spiritual universe, creating within many of the educated young a need to integrate their new knowledge with the Islamic beliefs they had learned at home. In particular, young Muslims needed to understand how the Quran was compatible with scientific knowledge.

Large numbers of young women were among the Iraqis acquiring education, delaying the age at which women married. As Fatima Mernissi has pointed out in her studies of male-female dynamics in modern Muslim society, "an adolescent unmarried woman is a completely new idea in the Muslim world."[2] In past centuries, Muslim societies largely prevented premarital sex by segregating the sexes and institutionalizing the early marriage of women. In twentieth-century Iraq, both of these societal defenses were breached by female education. The entrance of formerly secluded young women into classrooms and offices and other public places constituted a momentous change in the traditional system. Not only did Iraqi women acquire education and entrance to public places, but they gained powers they had not previously had, both the power of knowledge itself and, arising from that, the possibility of earned income, another source of power.

New social practices such as the education and employment of women were initially embraced by the political and economic elites and then spread down the social scale, displacing customary forms. First the high-status Sunnis, then the Shi'as accepted nontraditional social practices. New sexual, political, economic, and cultural boundaries had to be negotiated between men and women. Reputable women, who had formerly appeared only rarely in public and were invisible under their veils when they did, began working at jobs where a veil was totally impractical, meaning that not only did women appear in public places, but they did so without the traditional veil.

The adoption of new technologies altered the concrete circumstances of lives in multiple other ways, necessitating adjustments in people's understanding of the moral and cognitive map provided by religion. Secularization, with its assignment to human responsibility of an expanded range of societal functions, reduced the domain of religion. The state, not religion, was becoming the prime determinant of societal discourse, forcing all societal groups to respond to the state. Technological and scientific advances in the twentieth century made possible a great expansion of government functions and power. The Iraqi government took control of education and the courts, took possession of major industries (including the oil industry), and engaged in economic planning. The ulama and other Iraqis understandably sought to influence the policies of the government in its performance of these important new functions and in its expenditure of Iraq's oil income.

Government policies that neglected agriculture, the source of livelihood for most Iraqis, spurred the movement of large numbers of fellahin to the cities, where they existed without secure employment and in close proximity to mosques and an array of people for the first time. Urbanization occurred rapidly in Iraq and affected not only the poor but a multitude of young Iraqis. In the process of getting their educations or in employment afterwards, young people were often geographically separated from their families and likely to live in poorly managed environments where housing and recreation were problematic. Changes in traditional patterns of living contributed to normative change by decreasing patriarchal control. A study of kinship ties in Iraq showed that the percentage of families living in extended-family households dropped from 82 percent in the 1940s to 34 percent in 1975.[3]

The ulama perceived foreign cultural influences and the normative changes accompanying modernization to be threats to Islam and initially resisted the transformations. When the ulama clung to tradition, not only the new political elite but many believers came to regard them as "obscurantist," a block to progress. With traditional religious practices and power relationships no longer supported by experience, dissatisfaction with traditional religion and religionaries increased. Eventually, the ulama were impelled to act in defense of religion. The call to Islam was both a defense of religion and traditional values and an adaptation of Islam to new possibilities. Ayatollah al-Sadr sought to bring Islamic practices into congruence with change and to bring Islamic clerics into the management of change in Iraq, in other words, into the governance of Iraq.

Status Incongruity

Fundamental social transformation involves changes in power relationships and in social status, in the sense that status is an effective claim to social esteem in terms of positive or negative privileges.[4] Groups are accorded status positions within the structure of a society according to their economic power, their political power, and their status honor, with status honor being determined in large part by perceived value to society. Similarly, the status of the individual is determined by kinship ties, education, and occupation. The political and economic power of both individuals and groups ordinarily correspond to their cultural prestige; that is, each individual and social group is generally accorded a comparable ranking on all three components of power. In conditions of rapid social change, the economic, political, and honor rankings of individuals and groups are liable to get out of synchrony. When the various statuses of an individual or group are of unequal ranking, status incongruity exists.

In Arab society, social status has traditionally depended in large part on inherited qualities, with moral and physical qualities presumed to be inherited.[5] Iraq's older social forms attach value to noble lineage, knowledge of religion, and possession of sanctity or fighting prowess.[6] Genealogical pretensions have justified social prominence, with notable families from Iraq to Morocco displaying family trees tracing their descent to the Prophet Muhammad. As late as the 1970s, both well-to-do descendants of the Prophet and their former peasant clients in Iraq "legitimated their unequal socioeconomic status in terms of their unequal religious prestige."[7] The historical tendency of Iraqi Shi'as to accord community leadership to religious leaders, the family of the Prophet in particular, has probably intensified Shi'i respect for the qualities associated with religious leaders, namely, religious knowledge, piety, and noble lineage.

In the eyes of the Shi'i community, status inconsistency has characterized Iraqi political leaders from the time the government came under military control in 1958. Probably because the government has always been in Sunni hands and usually under foreign control, Iraqi Shi'as have lamented, not honored, military service on behalf of their government. To Shi'as, the military college has been a last resort for young men unable to get into more estimable schools. Yet since the end of the Hashimite monarchy in 1958, Iraq's governments have been essentially military governments. They have come to power by military means and have been sustained by force. Political leaders have been men with little religious and little social prestige.

The status system was literally turned upside down by the Ba'th political elite that took power in the 1960s. Not only did the new political and economic elite lack noble lineage, but the Ba'th Party itself was regarded as antireligious. President al-Bakr was reputed to be a practicing Muslim, but many Ba'thists, Saddam Hussein in particular, had a reputation for irreligion.[8] Some members of the RCC reportedly "lost their positions because they were praying in party locations and seeking to introduce religion as a measure of being a good party member," practices publicly condemned by Saddam Hussein.[9] Religious rituals, mechanisms for enforcing social solidarity, were in many cases interdicted by the government. Safety, a basic value allocated in any status system, could no longer be effectively claimed by any social group. Even the clergy, long a high-status group, was subject to torture and execution.

In the 1970s, the status deficiency of the political elite was exacerbated as the Ba'th government placed its semirural supporters in positions of political and economic power. Sometimes an official's only qualification for his job appeared to be his origin in Tikrit, the home village of President Ahmad Hasan al-Bakr and the regime's strongman, Saddam Hussein: "The ruling Tikriti clan . . . (many of whom did not even finish high school) were brought from the depth of the country-side to be given significant jobs such as general directors of industrial corporations which require a great deal of technical expertise and managerial capabilities."[10] *At-Tayar al-Jadeed*, the London-based newspaper of Iraqi liberals, has published a list of eleven Iraqi ambassadors and their occupations prior to their appointment as ambassadors. Five were laborers of one sort or another; four were elementary or secondary school teachers; one was a member of the security police; one was a clerk.[11]

In contrast to the Tikritis and the Ba'thist ambassadors, Islamic activists present records of educational achievement. Table 4.1, the list of Islamic activists who died in custody between December 1979 and mid-February 1980, conveys this background. The ten men from Madinat al-Thawra included two clerics, two warrant officers, one college student, one *ustadh* (professor, probably a writer), one college instructor, and one government employee. In Madinat al-Thawra, fellahin built their own *sara'if* from mud when they migrated to the city in the 1940s, 1950s, and 1960s. As rural migrants, they were uneducated and without material assets; yet the executed Islamists from Madinat al-Thawra, most likely their sons and grandsons, had attained education and middle-class positions.[12] Many of the nonclerical Islamists presented in Table 5.2 are graduates of engineering and science colleges. Good marks on the annual national exam are required for admission to these colleges in Iraq; thus non-Ba'thist[13] students who enter them are necessarily high achievers. The Shi'i scientists arrested and accused of "reactionary religious activities" in 1979 were obviously highly educated. Iraq's Islamic activists are unmistakably similar to the Egyptian Islamic militants, whom Saad Ibrahim found to be young, upwardly mobile, and accomplished.[14]

The Ba'th government was able to obscure the humble origins and undistinguished record of its Tikritis somewhat. In 1976 a law was passed decreeing that Iraqis could no longer use names indicating family origin. Thus Saddam, son of Hussein of the village of Tikrit, became Saddam Hussein instead of Saddam Tikriti. The law was widely regarded as meant to cloak the fact that so many people in the government were from the village of Tikrit. It did, but it also had a social-leveling effect of benefit to the semirural Ba'thist elite. Only Iraqi families of some prestige had established family names. Peasants and other people with no pretensions to distinguished lineage had always been known simply by their given names and their fathers' first names. If necessary for identification, the name of the village or tribe was added, as in the case of the Tikritis. By requiring people with family names to drop them, members of the Ba'th elite brought everyone down to their status level in terms of names.

Saddam Hussein probably recognized his problem of insufficient religious status and political legitimacy, for once he had concentrated power in his own hands and become president, he published a family tree that "revealed" that he was descended from Ali, the cousin and son-in-law of the Prophet Muhammad. Copies of his "family tree" were widely distributed.[15] As a member of the Prophet's family, a direct descendant of Imam Ali, he could be regarded as a legitimate Islamic ruler even for Shi'as, making it unnecessary for them to look elsewhere for legitimate government.

Apart from the status of the political elite, there was a broader condition of status incongruity in Iraq. In a modernizing economy, the large, active government bureaucracy and technological advances increase the value to society of groups with technological skills. The social value of groups such as tribal leaders and clerics diminishes. In Iraq the status of tribal leaders and clerics fell in the 1950s and 1960s, as one would expect; but the status of their technologically competent sons encountered barriers in the Ba'thist political and economic systems of the 1970s. Young men from scholarly families were relegated to low-paying bureaucratic jobs or even left without jobs, while the positions they might have taken were dispensed by the government for political reasons. The political system controlled the economy and placed a higher value on political reliability than on technological competence. Opportunities for upward mobility decreased with increased government control of the economy and the establishment of political criteria for hiring and promotion; there was little chance for believing Shi'as to satisfy career ambitions.

Status incongruity is probably not necessary to a social movement, but because it is an indicator that esteem in a social system does not correspond to the contribution groups or individuals are making to society, status incongruity is associated with such movements. Religious social movements enable those whose status is undervalued or negatively valued to nourish their sense of dignity on the belief that a special mission is entrusted to them, their worth guaranteed by an ethical imperative, a task placed before them by God. In the case of Iraq's Islamists, their special mission is a collective effort to establish a new social order.

Islamic activists have a rational interest in a system that would recognize their virtue and achievements and compensate them materially and ideally. On a more immediate level, Islamic groups provide activists a sense of community, strengthen chiliastic hope, and reinforce a sense of virtue resultant from acting in accordance with their internal value system, Islam. Being allied with the virtuous in the cause of Islam assures Islamists they are right.

Movement Emergence

The existence and charisma of Sayyid al-Sadr provided the leadership necessary for organized Islam in Iraq to respond constructively to the broad social changes under way in society. Under Sayyid al-Sadr's leadership, Shi'i clerics engaged in a broad undertaking of study, discussion, and writing aimed at reinterpreting religious law in light of scientific advances, the changing role of women, and government without Islamic legitimacy. Utilizing the greatly increased level of education of Iraqi Muslims, Sayyid al-Sadr and the other clerical activists broadened their support base, offsetting their loss of financial and political backers among the old landowning upper class by means of the young "callers to Islam."

The Islamic movement was built by and through existing Islamic institutions and associations. Ayatollah al-Sadr began his reform effort with ulama resident in the seminaries of Najaf. The conversion of the *marji'* Ayatollah al-Hakim to political activism brought large numbers of ulama and believers, his followers, into the movement. Early lay recruits were young people from the clerical families of Najaf. When the movement expanded beyond Najaf, new groups were organized by the clergy of other cities. Recruitment took place within families, *husainiyat*, mosques, and schools. The network of study groups begun by Ayatollah al-Sadr was expanded as laypeople who had studied in the group of an alim formed their own groups. Sayyida Salwa al-Bahrani, who appears in Table 5.2, is an example of a pious layperson who participated in a group led by an alim, in this case, the *'alima* Bint al-Huda, and then formed her own group. The message of Islamic political activism was carried via the religious establishment to the Arab Gulf states, Lebanon, and elsewhere.

The activist Shi'i ulama were responding to new possibilities. Greatly increased numbers of people in urban areas made mass politics possible.

The congregation of young people in universities constituted an opportunity for political organizers, an opportunity created by modernization. Fifty years earlier, countries like Iraq and Lebanon did not have large numbers of students and even larger numbers of urban poor who could be organized. In college, young people's horizons were broadened and their sense of efficacy strengthened, a cognitive change that facilitated their recruitment to political activism. In the cities, the poor were accessible. The ingenuity of Sayyid al-Sadr and the amenability of the *maraji'* made it possible for Islamists to respond to new opportunities with changes in Islamic educational practices and an innovative approach to the Islamic ministry.

In 1960 a favorable confluence of factors led to the emergence of an open Islamic initiative in Iraq. Within Iraq's political system, the relative political freedom allowed by the Qasim regime (1958–1963) constituted expanded opportunity for organization and activism. Ayatollah Burujirdi's move against land reform in 1960 and then his death in 1961 removed the prohibition on political activity by the Shi'i ulama. The Islamic movement's recruiting drive of 1962 and 1963 occurred near the end of Qasim's rule, a time similar to 1957–1958 in terms of the political weakness of the government and the widely held perception that the regime could not last. Thus a series of social developments and events made possible the founding of a clandestine party, Hizb al-Da'wa, then the fielding of a public political party, the Islamic Party, to be followed by a return to clandestinity when the opportunity for legal political organization was withdrawn. Shi'i Islamists sought and found Sunni allies, as black civil rights activists in the United States sought and found white allies. Had either disadvantaged group sought supremacy as opposed to equality, it would hardly have been successful in its quest for allies in the dominant group.

The recruitment of Iraqi Muslims to political activism in pursuit of an Islamic society necessitated a process of cognitive liberation whereby believers came to see political activism as both legitimate and potentially successful. Ideas of popular participation in governance were familiar, and attractive, to the increasing number of educated Iraqis. Literacy, plus familiarity with the world of ideas, changed people's expectations with regard to political participation and what could reasonably be expected of government.

Formerly quietist Shi'as came to see political opposition as not only legitimate but even required by religion, given the ulama's declarations that the existing government was illegitimate and that believers were responsible for instituting legitimate government. The Ottomans and the Hashimite monarchy, for all their faults, had an Islamic legitimacy that protected them from challenge in the name of Islam. Iraq's subsequent governments, with their secularism and nationalizations, were never accorded the ulama stamp of approval, contributing greatly to Iraq's reputation as "ungovernable." Qasim and the Arif brothers did respond in some degree to ulama admonitions, but they were not descendants of the Prophet, and they furthered secularization, appropriated private property, and otherwise contravened Islamic traditions. The Ba'th government violated tradition even more, responding to ulama advice and requests with repression and violence.

Political legitimacy could have come to Iraqi governments from popular sovereignty rather than from Islam, but Iraqi governments came no closer to a democratic legitimacy than they did to Islamic legitimacy. Narrow-based and unrepresentative, Iraqi governments failed to allow political participation on the part of new groups created by the forces of modernization. Monopolized political power was the rule in Iraq, despite the "elections" and parliament that existed under the monarchy, and the pseudoparticipation decreed by the Ba'th regime.[16]

Political legitimacy could have come to Iraqi governments through economic success, but here also Iraqi governments failed. They did not diversify the economy, nor did they reduce reliance on oil.[17] No development plan was adhered to for long. Despite the creation of a substantial middle class, poverty remained widespread, especially in rural areas. Peasants often existed on bread and dates, without heat in the winter.[18] Young minds imbued with ideas of either Islamic social justice or socialism were aware of the country's oil revenues. They condemned the political situation they judged responsible for the economic injustices. Education and urbanization moved many Iraqis *away* from traditional society, but they did not move *into* a tolerable modern political society.

The political impotence of most Iraqis[19] contrasted with the enormous growth of government. Iraq went from a society in which the government interfered with people's lives only for taxation and conscription to one in which the government, by the 1970s, controlled nearly all jobs, prices, trade, and communication. In democratic political systems, the number of social groups attempting to influence government policies has increased with expanding government control of resources and expanding governmental activities. Not surprisingly, in Iraq, too, citizens sought to influence the increasingly active and wealthy government.

The "callers to Islam" were able to convince many young people that Islamic government is the means to a society characterized by righteousness and justice. The Islamic initiative offered the educated layperson individual religious recognition and an ideologically competitive Islam, the result of modifications Ayatollah al-Sadr made to traditional interpretations. Unable to express themselves in strictly political terms because of monopolized political power, many idealistic young Iraqis responded to the mobilization efforts of Islamists by embracing the Islamic movement as their political language. The goals of any political party are the securing of political power and material advantages for its active members. When religious parties seek political power, they, too, have material as well as ideal goals.

Tactical Adaptations

Figure 6.2, modified from McAdam, outlines the process of tactical adaptations in a social movement once launched. The movement began as a clandestine effort to reform individuals, made use of the 1960 possibility for overt political action, adopted the tactic of mass protests in response to Ba'thist intimidation of the clergy, and finally became revolutionary when government policies interfered with its use of existing religious institutions and decreased the already limited space in Iraq for political organization and dissent. To contend with the Ba'thists, movement leaders broadened their objectives to include reorganization of the government that had come to block their progress.

Figure 6.2 Political Process Model of Movement Adaptation

Source: Modified from McAdam, *Political Process*, p. 51.

Social-Control Responses

During the Abd al-Salam Arif regime (1963–1966), social controls were directed at Islamic activism, but neither concessive nor repressive measures were pursued to an extent unfavorable to the movement. Ostensibly religious activities were unhindered, and political organization by Islamists made gains without serious cost. With environmental factors generally favorable, the Islamic groups were able to expand and develop strength throughout the period from 1957 to 1968, remaining, on the whole, unknown to the government.

With the return to power of the Ba'thists in 1968, the Islamic movement was faced with a social-control strategy uninhibited by any moral values. Using oil revenues, the Ba'thists intensified co-optation of Arab Sunnis and the military. They rigorously repressed Islamic activists and other political opponents of the government. Even nonpolitical Iraqis, guilty of nothing but Iranian origin, were picked up and forced to make the walk to Iran.

Iraq was prosperous in the 1970s, but the economic benefits were far from evenly distributed. Per capita gross national product (GNP) rose from $630 in 1970 to $3,021 in 1978, a result of the oil industry nationalization that began in 1972 and the oil price rises of 1973. Iraq did not honor the 1973 Arab oil embargo against countries supplying Israel, but it reaped enormous economic gains from the embargo as the price of crude oil on the world market increased nearly fourfold. Yet within the same period, there was a drop in real income for many salaried Iraqis. Compensation to employees of large industrial concerns, a group including both administrative personnel and production workers, is reported to have declined in real terms by 20.7 percent.[20]

Because the Iraqi government owned the oil industry, it was in control of the new money coming into Iraq. Prohibitions on political activity by any organization other than the Ba'th Party prevented societal interests from organizing independent labor unions, professional groups, or political parties to try to influence decisions about the use of that money.[21] The percentage of the cost component of GDP accorded employees in Iraq, 20.7 percent, reflects the absence of political input from that large sector of society (see Table 6.1). Only the United Arab Emirates, with its overwhelmingly foreign work force and large capital surplus, accorded a smaller percentage of its GDP to employees.

In the cities, the potential contribution of the increasingly educated populace was underutilized and little rewarded. In comparison with salaries in poor countries such as Egypt, Iraqi salaries would not be considered low, but they were sufficiently low in relation to the cost of living to oblige educated young men to save money for many years before marrying.[22] Inadequate housing in the 1970s, like the inadequate nutrition that prevailed in Iraq well into the 1960s, was a consequence not of poverty as much as of social policies, at least in the view of many young people. In the 1970s, oil revenues were channeled into an expansion of the military, which grew from 100,000 in 1973 to 222,000 in 1978.[23] Needs of nonmilitary Iraqis, including public employees and the urban poor, went unmet, their material

Table 6.1 Cost Components of Gross Domestic Product (in percent)

Country and Year of Measurement	Compensation of Employees	Operating Surplus (Profits, etc.)
Algeria, 1979	37.2	34.7
Egypt, 1980	28.8	66.8
Iraq, 1975	20.7	75.4
Jordan, 1981	38.8	45.9
Libya, 1980	21.7	72.5
Morocco, 1980	33.1	53.0
Saudi Arabia, 1978	24.6	75.7
Sudan, 1977	44.3	35.9
United Arab Emirates, 1981	16.0	78.3
North Yemen, 1981	28.2	53.5

Source: Reprinted from *The Arab World*, Rodney Wilson, 1984, by permission of Westview Press, Boulder, Colorado. Percentages are calculated from data published in the United Nations *Monthly Bulletin of Statistics* 37, 7 (July 1983): xli–xlvi.
Note: Indirect taxes net of subsidies and consumption of fixed capital, included in the source, are omitted here; thus the percentages do not total 100.

well-being eroded by relatively high inflation and government control of the economy.

While economic life for favored Iraqis was improving in the 1970s, political life was worsening for virtually everyone. The private newspapers and political parties of the monarchy and Qasim's time were gone. Individuals who voiced criticism of the government were liable to be arrested and then found tortured and dead in front of their own homes. By the end of 1973, the government had obtained outside assistance in the form of Soviet help in reorganizing Iraq's internal security forces.[24] From the East Germans and the Soviets, the Ba'th government received organizational recommendations, training, and sophisticated equipment for surveillance and interrogation, with the consequence that it became very difficult for government opponents to "oppose" for long.

Making use of its monopoly of violence, the state arrested thousands of its citizens. To be arrested by the Ba'th government was a frightening prospect. As James Barber, chairman of Amnesty International USA, wrote of Iraq's treatment of arrestees, "Iraq has been torturing routinely for years— dragging hundreds of terrified people into torture chambers where they are burned, beaten, cut, shocked with electricity and stretched on special machines."[25] The appalling methods of killing used by the government suggest a deliberate policy of terror.[26]

Another of the government's social-control responses was an apparent effort to change the religious and ethnic composition of the population. Expulsions of Shi'as and Kurds were half of this strategy. Official Iranian sources say Iran had accepted over 500,000 Iraqi Arab refugees by 1988, in addition to a large number of Iraqi Kurds. Tens of thousands of Iraqi refugees lived in exile in Syria. *At-Tayar Al-Jadeed*, whose subscribers are educated Iraqi exiles in the West, puts the total number of educated Iraqis in exile between 500,000 and 1 million. The International Organization for the Defense of Human Rights in Iraq estimates that there are 650,000 Iraqi self-exiles and 500,000 *muhajirin*.[27] The count appears to be around 8 percent of Iraq's 1980 population of 13 million.

The other half of the government's strategy was replacing Iraqi Shi'as and Kurds with Arab Sunnis from other countries, primarily Egypt. Kurdish lands were given to Arab settlers from Iraq, Egypt, and North Yemen. The settlers received government help in the form of services, monetary grants, farm equipment, and guns—assistance not extended to the land's previous farmers. On January 31, 1990, the RCC accorded Arab nationals in Iraq all the working rights and privileges of Iraqis.[28] While the Iraqi government's announcement of a policy does not guarantee that the policy is implemented, this announcement does indicate a continued desire on the part of the government to attract immigrants.

Other measures implemented by the Ba'th government had the effect of depriving the Shi'i religious establishment of its independence. In March 1980 the government took control of the collection, allocation, and distribution of Shi'i religious funds and assumed supervision of Shi'i shrines. Dependent upon the government for both the money and permission to act, the remaining ulama were to be made into government agents ready to cooperate with government action or intent.

After becoming aware of the success Islamists were having with poor Shi'as, the government talked about a massive welfare program for Shi'as; but evidence that large expenditures actually occurred has not been provided. The government did expend funds to pave the streets and bring piped water to Madinat al-Thawra but the government's claim to have spent up to $.25 billion renovating the Shi'i shrines of Najaf and Karbala[29] is hardly believable. In the early 1970s, I observed the shrines to be resplendent with gold and Persian carpets and seemingly well maintained. Although the execution of the shrines' clerical guardians and the confiscation of religious funds later in the 1970s would understandably reduce the clergy's ability to maintain the shrines, why major renovation would be needed is hard to fathom. In any case, government concern for Shi'as remains suspect. As wryly noted in the *Economist* in 1984, the government did not try to stop the shelling of Basra, a city that is about 80 percent Shi'i, even though the offending artillery was just beyond the Iraqi border and could have been knocked out by Iraqi aircraft.[30]

International assistance to the Iraqi government helped the Ba'thists maintain social control. During the Iran-Iraq War, billions of dollars were made available to the Ba'th government by the Arab Gulf states. An estimate of $40 billion in Arab aid is termed "somewhat conservative but well reasoned."[31] Western powers and the Soviet Union also gave Iraq an infusion of resources that bolstered the position of the Ba'th government relative to its opponents. In mid-1982, the Soviet Union resumed arms shipments to Iraq.[32] In December 1982, a U.S. helicopter manufacturer sold helicopters and training in their use to the Iraqi government. By 1984 the United States was supplying the Iraqi government with military intelligence derived from U.S. satellites and AWACS reconnaissance planes and was extending commodity credits to Iraq. During 1984 the Soviet Union concluded major economic and technical agreements with the Iraqi government and extended Iraq loans of $2 billion on easy terms.[33] As of 1987, the United States had granted Iraq over $800 million in agricultural credits,[34] with the Commodity Credit Corporation of the U.S. Department of Agriculture (USDA) guaranteeing the loans. U.S. business and investment interests in Iraq increased steadily, as did investments by citizens of Arab Gulf states. The Soviet Union allowed Iraq to purchase its advanced MiG-29 fighter. Although payments had not been made on the wartime loans, in November 1989 the USDA approved another $.5 billion in export credit guarantees to Baghdad. The large-scale outside assistance extended to the Iraqi government helped Saddam Hussein thwart his political opposition, whether that was the purpose of the assistance or not.

After successfully using mustard gas and nerve gas against Iranian troops, the Iraqi government almost certainly used them against Iraqi guerrillas in the southern marshes and against guerrillas and Kurdish civilians in the mountains of northern Iraq. In the latter months of 1988, after the cease-fire with Iran, the Iraqi government carried out another major purge of its political opponents and potential opponents. Several hundred army officers and a number of civilians, most of them from central and southern Iraq and therefore Shi'i, were executed by firing squad.[35] In a mock judicial appeal, the wives of some of those to be executed were allowed to go before Saddam Hussein to plead for their husbands' lives, even though they did not know what the charges against them were.[36]

In January 1990, government forces moved against thirty Shi'i towns and villages in southeastern Iraq, evicting their populations and killing or wounding many villagers.[37] Little was reported about the attack or what may have preceeded it, but the villagers were reputedly sympathetic to the Islamic movement.

The political and military powers of the Ba'th government and its international supporters are external forces that have imposed themselves on Islamic movement actors. Ba'th policies and modern coercive capabilities have decreased the limited political opportunities that previously existed within Iraq. The government's social controls have promoted the dissolution of Islamic movement membership through execution and exile, the latter both government imposed and voluntary.

The Move to Revolutionary Da'wa

In any society, a variety of individual interests, plus tradition and belief in the legality of the social system, determine individual submission to government.[38] Failure to submit is a portentous decision, likely to involve economic and status losses and perhaps the loss of life itself. Given the losses and dangers incurred by active dissidents, the message protest leaders articulate must be relevant to social groups before it can become a basis of action. People do not rebel against a government accorded a general legitimacy, whether that legitimacy is based in tradition or is due to the government's successes in furthering societal interests in areas like economic development and territorial defense. Only when a government and its policies are regarded as illegitimate, because of its route to power, the estrangement of religious leaders, failure to allow political participation, economic favoritism, or general ineffectiveness, is the public likely to be responsive to rebellion.

The Ba'th government pursued a variety of policies that obliged people to breach Islamic principles or be identified as disloyal. Uninhibited by the Islamic values that have been the essence of social solidarity and the foundation of the social order in Iraq, Saddam Hussein, even before his takeover of full power in 1979, instituted a personality cult that included flooding the country with immense pictures of himself, an aggrandizement of a human being anathema to Islam. *Not* to have a picture of Saddam in one's home and office was to be suspected of being an observant Muslim and a political opponent of the government. Saddam's self-aggrandizement was also apparently functional in elevating him above other Ba'thists, while tying them to him as the one person necessary to maintain the government edifice and their positions of privilege.

The Ba'thists raised pan-Arab hopes, but there is little evidence in the history of the Iraqi Ba'th Party to indicate that the party's expressed ideals of "unity, freedom, socialism" have guided party decisionmakers. Ba'th publications have never indicated how Arab unity might be achieved,[39] and freedom greatly decreased in Iraq under the Ba'th. Rather than becoming socialist, the economy went through various changes in course, ultimately featuring state capitalism and a courting of foreign investors. In the 1970s, Baghdadis rephrased the Ba'th slogan to, "La wahda, la hurriya, la ishtirakiya" (There is no unity, no freedom, no socialism).

The Ba'th government projected an image of efficiency and incorruptibility, but "there is a world of difference between the efficient, high technology computerized tendering system that the Iraqis claim to operate, and the ad hoc manner in which some of the state organizations actually work."[40] Like preceding Iraqi governments, the Ba'th government had some economic successes, thanks to oil revenues, but Ba'thist economic successes were dwarfed by the enormous debts and physical damage resulting from Saddam's 1980 invasion of Iran and the enormous loss of life and infrastructure resulting from his 1990 invasion of Kuwait.

With the possibility for legal political organization nonexistent and illegal organizing extremely dangerous after the Ba'th government received Soviet assistance in training and equipping its secret police, the Islamic movement could no longer expect eventual success through its reform strategy or through its political protest tactic. When the success of the Iranian Revolution confirmed that Muslims would choose Islamic government and generated potential recruits for the movement, Islamist leaders responded to the need and the opportunity for changed tactics. The Iranian revolution promoted cognitive attribution of movement effectiveness, indicating to many people that essentially unarmed masses can overthrow even a repressive government in possession of modern military technology and superpower support.

With the arrest of Ayatollah al-Sadr in June 1979 and the forced retirement of President al-Bakr in July 1979, the Iraqi government's façade of respect for Islam was removed. Although Muslims are forbidden to fight other Muslims and Islamists are highly motivated to do only what is permissible in Islam, violence against the Ba'th government was determined to be justified by the kafir (unbelieving) nature of the regime and by the government's use of violence against its nonviolent opponents. Ayatollah al-Sadr authorized the change to a revolutionary *da'wa*. As Max Weber wrote in the last century, groups from households to political parties resort to physical violence when threatened, *if* they are *able*. Probably obtaining logistic support from the new Islamic government of Iran, Iraqi militants answered government violence with violence of their own. After the Iraqi government's 1980 attack on Iran, its war-induced reliance on outside military and financial support and its forfeiture of moral authority through war making against Muslims supported the Islamist argument that independent and just government requires Islamic government.

Notes

1. McAdam, *Political Process.*
2. Mernissi, *Beyond the Veil*, p. xxiv.

3. Study published by Ihsan al-Hassan in 1981, as cited in Barakat, "The Arab Family," p. 37.

4. The definition of *status* is from Weber, *Economy and Society*, vol. 1, p. 305.

5. Tamadonfar, *Islamic Polity*, p. 66.

6. Batatu, "Iraqi Society," p. 380.

7. Rassam, "Power in Northern Iraq," p. 162.

8. During the war with Iran, top Ba'th leaders increasingly adopted religious practices such as attendance at mosque prayers. Iraqi radio and television devoted more time to religious programming. How convincing the Ba'th "conversion" was to the people of Iraq remains an open question.

9. Helms, *Iraq*, pp. 90–91.

10. *Islamic Revival*, March–April 1981, p. 7. Tikritis are natives of the Arab Sunni town of Tikrit in north central Iraq. It is the home of Saddam Hussein and his kinsman, Ahmad Hasan al-Bakr.

11. *At-Tayar al-Jadeed*, December 10, 1984, p. 1.

12. The two clerics may have come to al-Thawra from elsewhere, but it is highly unlikely that any other educated people would leave their family neighborhoods to move to Madinat al-Thawra.

13. Ba'thist students may get into and graduate from desirable schools by means of political influence. The favorable treatment professors were obliged to accord Ba'thist students was a source of dismay within the university faculty during my residence in Baghdad in the early 1970s.

14. Cf. Saad Eddin Ibrahim, "Egypt's Militant Islamic Groups," pp. 423–453.

15. *Middle East International*, September 28, 1990, p. 28.

16. In the 1970s, the Ba'th government entered into coalitions with both the Kurds and the ICP, but in neither case was the coalition partner allowed real power. In the 1980s, with great fanfare, the government established a parliament, but the parliament's mandate was to approve laws proposed by the RCC. Its approval was not necessary for "decrees" by the RCC.

17. Economist Intelligence Unit, *Iraq*, p. 1 and passim. Although the report was published in 1980, its findings remain valid. No diversification, other than increased weapons manufacture, occurred in the 1980s during the war against Iran.

18. I visited a rural government school in the winter of 1972. The teacher and his Ba'thist overseer wore coats in the unheated room, but the students, all boys, were blue with cold. They lacked coats, socks, and even shoes.

19. The "active" members of the Ba'th Party, people who had voting rights within the party and could hold responsible positions, were no more than 5,000 in 1968, according to the party's own estimate. Cf. Marr, *History of Iraq*, p. 213. In the early 1980s, after more than a decade of Ba'th rule, the number was still only 25,000, or less than .2 percent of the population, according to Helms, *Iraq*, p. 87. A Ba'th recruit had to pass through an initiation period of at least five years, performing a variety of disagreeable tasks, before becoming a full party member; thus the number of people who could legally be politically active was very small.

20. Income figures for employees of large industrial concerns are derived from the Iraqi government's *Annual Abstract of Statistics 1978*. See Batatu, *The Egyptian, Syrian, and Iraqi Revolutions*, p. 17. Per capita GNP figures for the period are from U.S. Department of State, *Country Reports on Human Rights Practices for 1985*, p. 1254.

21. Political activities by the ICP and some Kurdish parties were at times legal for civilian Iraqis.

22. In 1971 the government salary for a beginning teacher with a master's degree was 50 Iraqi dinars per month, the equivalent then of $140. A two-bedroom house in Baghdad rented for about the entire monthly salary of such a teacher; an apartment was not an option, for there were virtually no apartments in Iraq at that time. It should be noted that most teachers did not have master's degrees and therefore began their careers at less than the 50 dinars.

23. Devlin, "Iraqi Military Policy," p. 132.

24. al-Khalil, *Republic of Fear*, p. 12.

25. *New York Times*, June 9, 1986, p. A22.

26. *Al-'Amal al-Islami* on January 15, 1989, published the names of some twenty individuals, with the dates, places, and means by which the government killed them. The methods ranged from the severing of heads to food and water deprivation. As sources for the information, the newspaper cited the families of victims, ex-prisoners, and security personnel who had fled Iraq.

27. The source for the figure on educated Shi'as is *At-Tayar Al-Jadeed*, December 10, 1984, p. 3. The figure for total exiles is from *Kayhan International*, January 2, 1988, p. 10. Obviously, all these figures are estimates. No one really knows how many Iraqis are in voluntary and involuntary exile. In addition to Shi'as and Kurds, a number of Sunni Arabs have also left Iraq, at least in some cases because they lost government jobs when they declined to join the Ba'th Party. Arab Sunnis have generally gone to the West and to the Arab oil states, as indeed have many educated Shi'as.

28. "Chronology," *Middle East Journal 44*, 3 (1990): p. 48.

29. Axelgard, *A New Iraq?* p. 25.

30. *Economist*, March 24, 1984, pp. 31–32.

31. Axelgard, *A New Iraq?* p. 74.

32. The Soviet Union withheld arms shipments after Iraq's September 1980 invasion of Iran.

33. Ross, "Soviet Views Toward the Gulf War," p. 441.

34. For information on U.S. assistance to the Iraqi government, see Cordesman, "The Impact of U.S. and Other Arms Sales on the Iran-Iraq War," p. 29; Keddie, "Iranian Imbroglios: Who's Irrational?" pp. 29–54; and Robert Neumann in foreword to Axelgard, *Iraq in Transition*, p. x.

35. *Al-'Amal al-Islami*, January 29, 1989, p. 1. The bodies of the slain officers were not returned to their families, complicating the task of counting the dead. *Al-'Amal al-Islami* bases its estimate of 900 killed on the number whose properties were confiscated and on information given by informants inside the government.

Amnesty International reported 360 officers killed in November and December 1988. *At-Tayar al-Jadeed* quotes British diplomats to the effect that the Iraqi government was killing any person with an appearance of danger to the ruling elite. Cf. *At-Tayar al-Jadeed*, January 1989, p. 1.

36. Personal communication from one of the wives who went unsuccessfully through the "appeals process."

37. *Middle East International*, February 2, 1990, p. 14.

38. Weber, *Economy and Society*, vol. 1, p. 37.

39. Farouk-Sluglett and Sluglett, "Iraqi Ba'thism," p. 102.

40. Economist Intelligence Unit, *Iraq*, p. 77.

7

The Political Ideology

The core idea of the Islamic movement is a spiritual interpretation of life. According to Ayatollah al-Sadr, "The goal that Islam set up for human beings in their lives is the divine satisfaction."[1] Muslim fundamentalists, whether Sunni or Shi'i, aim for a nomocracy, a state founded on revealed principles, as enacted in Islamic law, the shari'a. Rulers as well as the ruled are to be governed by the shari'a.

Like other monotheists, Muslims believe God sent a series of prophets to guide humans in their behavior toward one another, as well as in their spiritual relationships. First the prophets of the Old Testament, then Jesus, and then Muhammad are believed by Muslims to have brought divine messages and laws to humankind. Had they not done so, Muslims believe, humans would not know divine requirements and would be unable to meet them, a condition that would be a violation of the justness of God and therefore impossible.

Ideal government for Muslims is government according to divine requirements, as revealed by the prophets. In the absence of ideal government, both Sunni and Shi'i ulama have historically counseled acceptance of the existing Muslim governments. Even when the ruler has been impious and despotic, the risk of splitting and weakening the *umma* by revolt has been deemed a greater evil than bad government; but if subjected to government that is not Muslim at all, believers may be obliged to strive for the ideal, which is what Islamists are doing. Islamists stress the need for *tawhid* (unity) in its various senses. In theology, *tawhid* means the unity (oneness) of God, but it also means conformity to God's will. Fundamentalists such as Maulana Mawdudi write of *tawhid* in the sense of integrating human society into the unity of the universe, subjecting all human acts to God's will and making all life God-centered.[2] Reversing secularization and instituting Islamic government are to be the means of helping individual Muslims achieve *tawhid* in its sense of making all life God-centered. In Ayatollah al-Sadr's words: "Any spiritual understanding of life and any moral sense of life

119

that do not result in a complete system of life in which every part of society is taken into consideration . . . does not do anything beyond rendering the atmosphere amiable and reducing the [weight of] calamities."[3]

There are many models of the Islamic state, just as there are many understandings of Islam. Divergent interpretations of revealed principles and "a multitude of approaches to political authority" exist within both Sunnism and Shi'ism, as well as between them,[4] but the base of Islamic government is a legal system consisting of the shari'a and such other laws as are necessary and in conformity with Islamic principles. The shari'a itself outlines a way of life that includes directives on personal hygiene, etiquette, and ethics, as well as laws commonly associated with government. An Islamic state gives legal force to Islamic norms of behavior by requiring that Muslims practice an Islamic way of life. *Hudud* (the prescribed punishments of Islamic law) are to be brought to bear on Muslims, as are all other prescriptions of the Quran and the hadiths. Judges must be trained in religion.

Traditional Shi'i Political Ideology

Shi'as believe that after the death of the Prophet Muhammad, a series of Imams from *ahl al-bayt* continued to guide humans with the help of divine inspiration that passed to them through Ali's line. The Imams should have exercised political power but were wrongfully prevented from doing so. Only during the imamate of Ali (656–661) was political and religious authority actually vested in the infallible Imam, as Shi'as believe should have obtained at all times. In the early decades of Islam, Shi'as looked for and occasionally revolted in the cause of, a descendant of the Prophet who would establish himself as caliph, that is, as political and religious ruler of Muslims; but in the eighth century A.D., on the recommendation of the Sixth Imam, Ja'far al-Sadiq (d. 765), Shi'as largely abandoned rebellion. The majority Shi'i group (the Ithna 'Asharis) expediently adopted a quiescent attitude toward government, so as not to provoke the wrath of the established Sunni state.

The imamate (series of divinely guided Imams) is believed to have ended in A.D. 873 when the Eleventh Imam died without leaving a visible son to be the Twelfth Imam. At least fourteen factions of Shi'as developed, each with a solution to the problem of the absent Imam. Ithna 'Ashari Shi'as eventually adopted the belief that the Twelfth Imam was born in the holy city of Samarra about A.D. 870. His mother was a slave girl named Narjis. Because the political authorities would have put him to death, the boy went into occultation and appeared only to select believers. In occultation, the Twelfth Imam is alive and ever present in the world but is not seen. Expected to return as the savior who will establish justice in the world, he is variously known as the Hidden Imam, the Vanished Imam, and the Mahdi.[5]

In the period from A.D. 873 to 941, called the Era of the Lesser Occultation, the Vanished Imam continued to provide leadership to the community through contact with various believers. At the beginning of the *ghayba* (occultation), a number of *wukala* (agents) who professed to be in contact with the Vanished Imam, came forward to assume leadership of the Shi'i community and to collect the *khums*[6] for the Imam. Direct contact with the Imam ended and the Greater Occultation began when Ali al-Samarri (d. 940/1), the *wakil* (agent) in Baghdad, advised his followers that he was the last designated agent.

With the Greater Occultation, religious authority and leadership of the Shi'i community passed to the ulama. As Islamic jurists, the ulama interpreted religious and personal-status laws. They carried out the lapsed welfare and educational functions of the Hidden Imam, including the collection of the *khums*, but they made no claim to the political authority of the Imam. Political authority was conceded to the existing Sunni rulers. The ulama maintained Shi'i distance from politics, devaluing the political sphere to the point of disinterest but not to the point of disobedience. No agreement was achieved on the nature of the political authority that should obtain in the absence of the Imam. Hope for just government centered on the return of the Imam, although there was also an awareness that it remained incumbent on Muslims to establish a society in which it would be safe for the Twelfth Imam to appear.

Over the centuries, the ulama extended and specified quranic and traditional laws by means of *ijma'* (consensus) and *'aql* (reason), an extension necessary because the Quran decrees few specific laws. In the seventeenth century, the Akhbari movement within Shi'ism rejected *ijma'* and *'aql* as sources of authority. Akhbaris recognize the Quran and *akhbar* (traditions) only and take the position that believers can interpret the *akhbar* themselves.[7] In the eighteenth century, Aqa Muhammad Baqir Bahbahani (1705–1791) popularized the Usuli school of jurisprudence, which takes its name from *usul*, meaning "fundamental principles." Usulis accept all four sources of authority (*ijma'*, *'aql*, *akhbar*, and the Quran) and hold that mujtahids are competent to discern religious laws through the application of reason. Believers are obliged to emulate living mujtahids since only mujtahids are sufficiently learned in the details of religious observances and laws to be able to adhere to them without error.

The eighteenth-century Usuli triumph over the Akhbaris made it possible for Shi'as to adjust to changing needs. By affirming the *ijtihad* of living mujtahids, Usulis foster *'aql* as a source for Islamic jurisprudence and allow for the individual's active participation in shaping human society. Through *ijtihad*, legitimated by ulama consensus, an expanded system of jurisprudence has built up. Mujtahids, the *maraji'* in particular, act as the interpreters of God's laws and the ultimate religious authorities on earth. In matters of religion, the ulama consider themselves, collectively, to be infallible.[8] The Usuli doctrine of taqlid (literally, "imitation") obliges each Shi'a to follow a mujtahid and thereby subjects Shi'as to clerical authority. The number of followers a mujtahid has determines his rank; one with a large following is recognized as a *marji'* and addressed as "ayatollah." Clerics, like other Shi'as, follow a *marji'*, and local clerics are judged by their peers in terms of how faithful they are to the rulings of the *marji'*.

In the middle of the nineteenth century, Marji' al-Taqlid Murtada Ansari (1800–1864) categorized "the duty to emulate the most learned jurisprudent as an absolute duty,"[9] thus introducing the concept of centralized leadership into the community of Shi'i clerics. Shi'ism has no institutionalized clerical hierarchy, but the *maraji'* are at the top of an informal hierarchy, which has at times been capped by a *marji' al-taqlid al-mutlaq*, that is, a *marji'* whom the other *maraji'* recognize as the most learned. There is no prescribed method for determining who, if anyone, is the most learned, and *maraji'* have vied for the position, with group leadership obtaining for long periods (see Table 7.1). Abbas Amanat has argued persuasively that a sole authority emerges only when the laity, by directing religious taxes and deference to a particular *marji'*, obliges the other *maraji'* to defer to the one the public has singled out.[10]

The *maraji'* are charged with deciding what is permitted in religion. When there is a *marji' al-taqlid al-mutlaq*, his religious pronouncements are not to be contradicted by other ulama. Some *maraji'* have interpreted their clerical responsibility narrowly to exclude action; others have interpreted it broadly to include action. Ayatollah Kazim al-Yazdi and Ayatollah Burujirdi interpreted their responsibility narrowly. In the words of Ayatollah Arbab Isfahani, also of the quietist school, "Our duty is to advise, not to fight."[11] The broad or activist interpretation is represented by Ayatollah Muhammad Taqi Shirazi, a principal actor in the 1920 Iraqi revolt against the British, and by Imam Ruhullah Khomeini. The latter authorities interpreted their responsibility to include action to bring about what they regarded as right. When there is a *marji' al-taqlid al-mutlaq*, his view necessarily influences the posture adopted by the ulama of his time.

Clearly, Islamic scholars have claimed a right and a responsibility to advise governments, but does the laity have any such right? Two quranic verses appear to require *shura* (consultation) with the people, a directive that may be interpreted to require the people's participation in their own governance. One verse promises everlasting life with God for "those who . . . conduct their affairs by mutual consultation" (Sura 42, verse 38). The above verse is part of a long enumeration of the characteristics of virtuous

Table 7.1   Maraji' al-Taqlid al-Mutlaq (Sole Supreme Authorities)

	Years[a]	Residence
Shaikh Murtada Ansari	Late 1850s–1864	Najaf
Group leadership	1864–1882	
Mirza Hasan Shirazi	1882–1896	Samarra
Group leadership	1896–1911	
Muhammad Kazim Yazdi	1911–1919	Najaf
Muhammad Taqi Shirazi	1919–1920	Karbala
Shaikh Fatu'llah		
Isfahani (al-Shari'a)	1920–1920	Najaf
Group leadership	1920–1942	
Abu al-Hasan Isfahani	1942–1946	Najaf
Aqa Husain Qummi	1946–1947	Karbala
Ayatullah Muhammad		
Husain Burujirdi	1947–1961	Qumm
Group leadership	1961–1978	
Ruhullah Khomeini[b]	1978–1989	Tehran

Sources: Compiled from Momen, Shi'i Islam, pp. 247–249 and 303; Hairi, Shi'ism, p. 64; and Amanat, "The Designation of Clerical Leadership," pp. 98–132.
[a]Apart from the date of a rival's death, there is no precise date when a marji' becomes the marji' al-taqlid al-mutlaq.
[b]Imam Khomeini's political triumphs in Iran provided him a following far beyond that of the other maraji'. In 1982, he was even able to effect the demotion of his principal clerical opponent, Ayatullah Shari'at-Madari.

individuals and hence is not necessarily applicable to government. The other verse gives direction from God to the Prophet Muhammad and is more obviously pertinent to the relationship between ruler and ruled. It seems to direct Muhammad to "consult" but to make the ultimate decisions himself:

> It is part of the mercy
> Of God that thou [Muhammad] dost deal
> Gently with them.
> Wert thou severe
> Or harsh-hearted,
> They would have broken away
> From about thee: so pass over
> [Their faults], and ask
> For [God's] forgiveness

> For them; and consult
> Them in affairs [of moment],
> Then, when thou hast
> Taken a decision,
> Put thy trust in God.
> For God loves those
> Who put their trust [in Him].
>
> (Sura 3, verse 159)

The Quran's directives relative to *shura* have generally been interpreted to mean that government should consult with notable citizens, not everyone, and is not obliged to take the advice given. In practice, governments in Muslim countries have often abjured even consultation.

In applying the shari'a, there is some support among both Sunnis and Shi'as for a collective *ijtihad*, that is, for arriving at consensus on the intent of the shari'a by means of a group or council of high-ranking clerics;[12] but individual Shi'i mujtahids continue to make individual rulings. Probably because Shi'as are a minority within Islam and because the Quran does not command binding consultation, Ithna 'Ashari ulama have refused to admit that majority opinion is necessarily true or right.[13] Within Shi'ism, however, the clerical ranks and notable families have figured large in determining religious leadership. Practicing Shi'as choose the clerical guides whom they follow and to whom they pay their religious taxes. Thus clerical leaders depend for their positions on voluntary support within the Shi'i community, especially from other clerics and that part of the observant community with large assets and large incomes.[14] In the case of an organization like Hizb al-Da'wa, members choose a clerical guide, who then serves as a group leader. The process ensures that clerics are initially responsive to opinion among their followers and potential followers, but there is no ready means of "impeaching" a clerical leader once he has a position of authority.

In the area of personal-status law, the shari'a, as historically interpreted, accords men greater rights than it does women. As in pre-Islamic Arab society, marriage in Islamic society has involved the passing of a woman from one man to another, ordinarily from the bride's father to the future husband. A Muslim man may marry outside the Muslim community, but a Muslim woman may not. A man may have more than one wife,[15] but a woman may not have more than one husband. A husband may divorce his wife without her consent and without any justification or review by society, but a wife may divorce her husband without his consent only in exceptional cases in which a judge has the final decision. Custody of children above a certain age is automatically given to the father.

In the time of the Prophet, the sexes were not segregated, nor were

Muslim women veiled, a symbolic form of sexual segregation. Subsequently, Sura 24, verse 31 of the Quran was interpreted to require segregation and *hijab* (covering all of a woman except the hands and part or all of the face):

> And say to the believing women
> That they should lower
> Their gaze and guard
> Their modesty; that they
> Should not display their
> Beauty and ornaments except
> What [must ordinarily] appear
> Thereof; that they should
> Draw their veils over
> Their bosoms and not display
> Their beauty except
> To their husbands, their fathers,
> Their husbands' fathers, their sons . . .

The Quran also directs men to "lower their gaze and guard their modesty" (Sura 24, verse 30), but Islamic societies have traditionally enforced female modesty while allowing males considerable latitude in making their own choices.

With regard to Shi'i ideas toward Sunni Muslims, accommodation has been a persistent feature of contemporary Shi'i thinking. As early as 1950, Ayatollah Muhammad Hussein Al Kashif al-Ghita (1876–1954), who was *marji'* for many Iraqi Shi'as, strongly advocated efforts to achieve solidarity with Sunni Muslims.[16] He even ruled that belief in the imamate, the most significant theological difference between Sunnis and Shi'as, was not compulsory. Ayatollah Burujirdi (1875–1961), *marji' al-taqlid* throughout the 1950s, worked with the shaikh of al-Azhar in Cairo, Mahmud Shaltut, to promote rapprochement between Shi'ism and the four Sunni schools of thought.[17]

Ayatollah al-Sadr's Interpretations

Ayatollah al-Sadr's response to the Iraqi ulama's problem of how to obtain legitimate government, given the continued absence of the Imam and the demise of Iraq's Hashimite monarchy, was to work for the establishment of an Islamic polity and thereby enlist government in the service of God's directive obliging believers to "enjoin the good and forbid the evil." He considered human beings inherently good but weak, and he desired society to protect Muslims from their frailties, making submission to God's will more likely. He expected a Muslim social order to help people adhere to their religious obligations by making time for obligatory prayers during the workday, by adjusting work schedules during the month of fasting, and by otherwise facilitating the observance of religious injunctions. Transgressors were to be exhorted to abide by the law, and orthopraxy to be bolstered in every way possible.

As *marji'* for most Iraqi Shi'as, Ayatollah al-Sadr considered the ulama responsible for exercising leadership in the struggle for Islamic government:

> As [the] imamate was a continuation of prophethood, similarly after the major occultation imamate ended in *marja'iyat* [*marji'iya*] (religious authority of the eminent divines) . . . the Shi'ah divines, with the help of the virtuous and downtrodden Muslims . . . continued to strive for a government of the prophets and imams, which was the only true and just government and for which all the good people of every age and the lovers of humanity have always struggled and fought.[18]

When Muhammad died, prophethood was replaced by the imamate, and the imamate was replaced by the *marji'iya* when the Twelfth Imam went into occultation. Decisionmaking by Muhammad was replaced with decisionmaking by the Imams and then with decisionmaking by the *maraji'*.

God's directive to Muhammad to consult with the people continued to apply, but with the means of consultation still not specified. Although in the past it was believed that consultation with influential persons was sufficient, Ayatollah al-Sadr held that "changed circumstances" and the juristic supervision in an Islamic government made it both necessary and possible to form "an assembly whose members are the real representatives of the people."[19] In the preface to *Iqtisaduna*, Ayatollah al-Sadr emphasized that man is *khalifat Allah* (vice-regent of God) in the world and that this concept implies delegation of power and responsibility.[20]

In 1979 Ayatollah al-Sadr listed four principles of an Islamic republic:

1. Absolute sovereignty belongs to God.
2. Islamic injunctions are the basis of legislation. The legislative authority may enact any law not repugnant to Islam.
3. The people, as vice-regents of Allah, are entrusted with legislative and executive powers.
4. The jurist holding religious authority represents Islam. By confirming legislative and executive actions, he gives them legality.[21]

Ayatollah al-Sadr did not charge the ulama with the responsibility to govern. Rather, he envisioned the Islamic community governing itself within the parameters of Islamic law, with the power of the state restricted by Islamic law and the clergy serving as interpreters and judges of that law, as has been traditional in Islamic society. He held that people do not require a full clerical education to understand and interpret the word of God, as long as Islamic jurists are in a position to see that popular interpretations do not go awry. Political authority he delineated as diagrammed in Figure 7.1. He specified three branches of government, with the executive and legislative branches elected by the people. He did not indicate how the judiciary was to be chosen, nor did he deal with the relationship between the legislature and the executive. The legal principles for governance he found revealed in the Quran and the hadiths, but details of implementation he left to be worked out by political leaders.

Figure 7.1 Political Authority as Formulated by Ayatullah al-Sadr

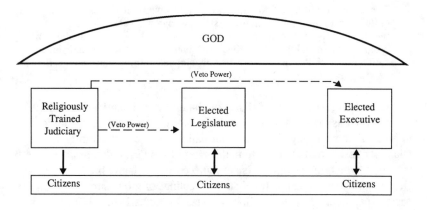

Ayatollah al-Sadr is said to have been the first *marji'* to adopt the principle of *shura* for choosing the executive authority for an Islamic government.[22] Even so, his vision of Islamic government is not majority rule. A state whose judiciary is charged with upholding God's laws, without a popular right to change those laws, is not democratic in essence. Ayatollah al-Sadr rejected majority rule as entailing human submission to humans.[23] In the common Shi'i view, only God is believed to have the right to arrange human life-style.

Ayatollah al-Sadr's strategy for achieving Islamic government required reversing the depoliticization effected by the Sixth Imam, Ja'far al-Sadiq. Ayatollah al-Sadr blamed Shi'i aloofness from politics for allowing society to develop in unacceptable ways. Being detached from politics, the ulama had applied *ijtihad* only to laws affecting individuals, ignoring laws applicable to society. Ayatollah al-Sadr blamed the resultant deficiency in societal laws for the problematic state of Muslim society.[24] His remedy was (1) to raise the Islamic consciousness of the people so they would want Islamic government and would strive for it and (2) to reinterpret certain Islamic laws, eliminating inappropriate interpretations from the past and thereby increasing the appeal of Islam as a modern ideology. The means to the second objective was to be the mujtahids, who, through their ability to interpret the law, would give consideration to the background and social circumstances of the various texts rather than to tradition alone.[25]

The means to the first objective, Islamic government, was the people:

> The basic condition of the success of any operation to set up a new culture or to make an extensive struggle against backwardness is to move the masses, for it is their movement which is the sign of their progress, the development of their will, and the liberation of their inner capabilities. If the masses are not developed, nothing can change the existing position.[26]

Reflecting the universalism of Islam, the Islamic movement is international as opposed to national in ideology. The focus of citizen loyalty in an Islamic state is to be Islam, not nationalism, either Arab or Kurdish. Islamists assert that Arab nationalism is the modern counterpart of Arab tribalism, which the advent of Islam replaced with Islamic brotherhood. The Quran expressly condemns tribalism and feelings of group superiority on any basis other than piety. Ayatollah Murtaza Mutahhari (d. 1979), who was highly esteemed by Iraqi Islamists, quotes 'Allama Tabataba'i to the effect that "Islam has annulled the role of tribal and national distinctions, and denied them any effective role in the evolution of [the structure of] human society."[27]

Economic Principles

Ayatollah al-Sadr held that Islam has all the principles for organizing economic life because Islam is a comprehensive system that provides guidance for all facets of life. From the given laws and laws deduced from the given laws, Ayatollah al-Sadr expected an Islamic economic system to evolve for contemporary Muslim society—when Muslims had attained self-government and were in a position to make their own economic decisions.

In *Iqtisaduna*, Ayatollah al-Sadr outlined the basic principles of an Islamic economy.

1. Multi-faceted ownership, that is, both private and public ownership.
2. Economic freedom, limited by revealed law, in the fields of production, exchange, and consumption.
3. Social justice, whose foundation is mutual responsibility and balance.[28]

In *Falsafatuna*, written in 1959, Ayatollah al-Sadr charged the Islamic state with two functions: educating mankind in Islam and bringing people back to principles if they deviate.[29] In his 1979 treatise on Islamic government, written when Islamic government was actually being implemented in Iran, Ayatollah al-Sadr enumerated three responsibilities of the Islamic state: disseminating knowledge of Islam, enforcing Islamic law, and ensuring social justice.[30] The principle of social justice has always existed in Islam, but by assigning to government the responsibility for achieving social justice, at a time when he could influence the actualization of Islamic government, Ayatollah al-Sadr emphasized the principle.

The Quran contains laws on zakat and *khums*,[31] the two taxlike charitable obligations of Muslims, and on inheritance, all of which bear on economic justice within families and within the larger society. Pious Shi'as have traditionally paid the *khums* to the ulama for disbursement, but Ayatollah al-Sadr assigned Islamic government the obligation to provide the means of living to all who are unable to participate in production. This would imply government collection of the *khums*, but when the Islamic government of Iran tried to make the ulama hand over part of the *khums* to finance the national budget, it failed.[32] In order to collect the *khums* successfully, a government would probably have to assess the tax directly on all the people, a course of action that would likely be unpopular with those unaccustomed to paying the tax, and possibly with those accustomed to directing the *khums* to their own clerical guides.

In *The General Bases of Banking in the Muslim Society*, Ayatollah al-Sadr sought to resolve popular doubts about the possibility of operating a modern economy in accordance with Islamic principles. He rejected the contention that Islamic economic thought has to explain scientific questions such as the relationship of price to demand and the means to economic development and maintained that the only legitimate demand upon Islam in the area of economics is that it organize economic life based on the Islamic concept of justice: "Justice in distribution lies in ensuring a certain standard of living to all members of society and giving them the freedom to earn more."[33]

Interest on the use of money is believed disallowed by Islam, but an owner may charge for the use of his nonmonetary property. Owning land without using it is considered unjust, and from this law it is deduced that hoarding is forbidden. The religious prohibition on hoarding is expected to encourage Muslims in an Islamic society to loan money even without interest. In an Islamic banking system, people with capital can allow societal use of their capital in two ways: (1) By placing funds with a government bank for loan without interest, the owner of the capital is guaranteed his capital will be returned at full value, without depreciation due to inflation, *and* he will be excused from paying zakat on the money so lent. (2) By using the bank to invest capital in economic projects, the owner of the capital receives profit and bears loss according to the outcome of the economic project. The capital so lent is exempt from zakat.[34]

Economic modernization is a goal supported by Ayatollah al-Sadr in his preface to *Iqtisaduna*: "The holy Quran says: 'And provide for them whatever force you can.' The provision of force includes economic force which is measured by the yardstick of production, and is of utmost importance for the preservation of [the] entity and sovereignty of the Muslim *Ummah*."[35]

In *Falsafatuna*, Ayatollah al-Sadr endorsed scientific knowledge and its pursuit: "In fact, the theological notion of the world does not mean dispensing with natural causes or rebelling against any one of the sound scientific truths. Rather, it is the notion that considers God as a cause beyond [nature]."[36] The young laypeople attracted to the movement have accepted modernization as a desideratum, studying medicine, engineering, economics, and administration in an effort to obtain the modern knowledge judged to be needed in their sought-after Islamic society. Following Ayatollah al-Sadr, Iraq's Islamists work to blend revelation with technological modernity in a "reconstruction" of society.

Ayatollah al-Sadr criticized both capitalism and communism, proposing a middle way that would protect private property but would be tempered with such constraints as are necessary to avoid genuine deprivation for anyone. He proposed to devote one-fifth of Iraq's oil income to social security and housing and to provide free education and health services to all.[37] At the international level, Ayatollah al-Sadr viewed materialistic systems as transgressing against peaceful countries, utilizing the wealth of those countries.[38] He rejected the Marxist idea that the social order is determined by the method of production, but he recognized that the social order does have material significance in that the distribution, or sharing out, of nature's bounty depends on the social order. Because he viewed the social order as the outcome of human choices, he viewed it as amenable to change.[39] With regard to the country's oil resources, Ayatollah al-Sadr interpreted Islam to reject private ownership since natural resources are not the products of any individual's labor. In Iraq, state ownership of the oil industry already exists so no change would be required in that area.

Social Principles

In Ayatollah al-Sadr's world-view, both society and individuals have objective existence and are accorded equal importance.[40] Because humans are intrinsically needful of others, they always live in groups. Individuals are responsible not only for their own actions but also for the actions of their society, as indicated by the quranic verse that says, "Every *umma* shall be summoned to its record" (Sura 45, verse 28), a verse that buttresses the ayatollah's interpretation of the people's right and responsibility to participate in their own governance.

Ayatollah al-Sadr included women within the masses to be developed and accorded social justice. He sought to educate women and to better their position, rejecting the validity of some traditional practices relative to women. The responsibilities he accorded his sister, Bint al-Huda, are evidence of a degree of nontraditionalism in his view of women. Without losing respectability, Bint al-Huda lived in a household headed by her mother, not by a man, as would have been traditional. Reputable families sent their daughters to Bint al-Huda's schools, where the girls were taught by teachers like the wife of Shaikh Muhammad Mahdi al-Asafi and her sister.[41] On Da'wa's thirtieth anniversary, Shaikh Muhammad Mahdi al-Asafi, speaking for Da'wa, listed one of its achievements as "introducing Islamic awareness (*wa'y*) to the female population *for the first time*" (emphasis added).[42]

Non-Muslims in an Islamic state would be free to observe their religious rites and to take part in political activities, both of which are rights guaranteed to them by quranic injunctions. Non-Muslims would pay the *jizya*, a tax in lieu of the zakat and military service required of Muslims. In return, they would be afforded the protection and services received by Muslims.[43] Non-Muslims would be expected to comport themselves in accordance with Islamic social sensibilities, as has traditionally been the case in Islamic society.

Ayatollah al-Sadr believed that the source of error in Western social systems is making individual interest the top priority. He criticized the way in which people in individualistic systems feel responsibility only for themselves and considered that personal interests do not always bring forth society's interests. He held freedom in Islam to be liberation from slavery to the false gods of material possessions and passions,[44] and freedom from domination by humans, for, according to the Quran, "No one of us shall take others from among ourselves as lords other than Allah" (Sura 3, verse 64).

Iraqi Islamic activists, following Ayatollah al-Sadr, have undertaken to reconstruct society themselves, as opposed to the traditional Shi'i stance of waiting for God to send the Mahdi to accomplish the task for them. Decisions about what is modern and desirable, as opposed to merely foreign and corrupting, are to be made by religious authorities. With his ideas for solving the problems of the Muslim community, his personal piety, and his family's prestige, Ayatollah al-Sadr met the leadership requirements of Iraqi Shi'as, and his understanding of Islam remains highly valued.

System Effected by Imam Khomeini

It was not Ayatollah al-Sadr but Imam Khomeini who actually implemented Islamic government. Imam Khomeini's ideas about Islamic government were not the same as those of Ayatollah al-Sadr; but neither were they completely rigid. In *Kashf al-Asrar* (Uncovering the Secrets), published in 1943, he espoused the traditional Shi'i opinion that the ulama should support even bad Muslim governments. He also maintained an equally established position that the governments of Islamic countries should govern by Islamic law, as interpreted by the ulama: "We do not say that government must be in the hands of the faqih (Muslim jurisprudent); rather we say that the government must be run in accordance with God's law, for the welfare of the country and the people demands this, and it is not feasible except with the supervision of the religious leaders."[45]

After the Iraqi government's 1969 attacks on Shi'as, many ulama despaired of getting existing governments to function within the boundaries of Islamic law. Early in 1970, in a series of lectures delivered in Najaf, Ayatollah Khomeini advanced the radical political concept of hierocratic government, calling on the ulama to exercise the political authority of the Vanished Imam. To support his position, Khomeini cited the "established principle" that the faqih has authority over the ruler, and he cited traditions that refer to the ulama as heirs of the prophets.[46]

Khomeini's 1970 lectures called for *wilayat al-faqih* (guardianship of the jurist),[47] in effect extending the ulama's authority from the religious domain to the political domain. Khomeini did not indicate at that time that an Islamic government should be headed by *one* supreme Islamic scholar who designates his own successor. He said that the jurist selected as faqih had to surpass all others in knowledge of the law and in justice,[48] but he also said, "The *fuqaha* [faqihs] do not have absolute authority in the sense of having authority over all other *fuqaha* of their time, being able to appoint or dismiss them. There is no hierarchy ranking one faqih higher than another or endowing one with more authority than another."[49] While thus acknowledging the limited religious authority one *marji'* has over the other *maraji'*, at about the same time Khomeini wrote in his *Kitab al-Bay'* (Book of Sale) that the faqih who serves as political ruler does have political superiority over other faqihs and that they must obey his political rulings.[50]

Like Ayatollah al-Sadr, Ayatollah Khomeini contended that Muslims have an obligation to establish Islamic government, but Ayatollah Khomeini did so in severe and forceful language.[51] He insisted that religious leaders abandon taqiya (concealment of convictions) and act politically on the basis of their religious convictions: "Any person who claims that the formation of an Islamic government is not necessary implicitly denies the necessity for the implementation of divine law, the universality and comprehensiveness of the law, and the eternal validity of the faith itself";[52] "when the Prophet appointed a successor, it was not for the purpose of expounding articles of faith and law, it was for the implementation of law and the execution of God's ordinances."[53]

Khomeini's early political formulations were without liberalizing innovations. In the 1960s he protested the shah's election law allowing women to vote, and in his 1970 conceptualization of Islamic government, he pronounced a legislative assembly unnecessary.[54] He initially rejected any need for community consent regarding the choice of a faqih. Later, under pressure from reformist clerics and the Iranian public, he acceded to consultation with the people. Presumably, similar pressures led him in March 1979 to acknowledge that "Islam grants women a say in all affairs just as it grants men a say."[55] Women as well as men are allowed to vote for legislative candidates approved by the clergy in the Islamic Republic of Iran, and one woman was included in the Assembly of Experts set up to produce a constitution for the Islamic Republic.[56] Even one woman in the group of about seventy people is evidence of an erosion in the tradition attributed to the Sixth Imam, Ja'far al-Sadiq, which describes it as "moral degradation" to have "women occupying places in the assemblies just as men do."[57]

Like other prominent Shi'i clerics in the twentieth century, Imam Khomeini sought accommodation with Sunni Muslims. In his first hajj message, delivered in 1970, he stressed the unity of all Muslims and urged the rejection of publications and individuals seeking to sow discord between Sunnis and Shi'as.[58] After the Islamic revolution in Iran, Imam Khomeini introduced the systematic teaching of the four Sunni madhabs into the curriculum of the hawza in Qumm "to further awareness among Shi'i Muslims of the potentialities of the Sunni traditions and to draw, if it appears appropriate and necessary, on those potentialities for the solution of particular problems in Iran."[59] In 1980 Imam Khomeini ruled that Shi'i Muslims may pray behind a Sunni imam. He advised his followers to offer their five daily prayers separately, as the Sunnis do, instead of combining them into three prayer times as Shi'as have traditionally done.[60] He also wrote, "In Islam there is no distinction between the rich and the poor, between black and white, between Shi'i and Sunni."[61]

Other Iranian clerics have also sought accommodation with Sunnis. Called upon to lead prayers at the 1983 Islamic conference in Colombo, Sri Lanka, Ayatollah Zanjani, the senior Shi'i cleric present, ended the prayers in the Sunni manner. In Shi'i Abadan, a few weeks later, the muezzin (announcer of the hour of prayer) for a group of visiting Sunnis, gave the *adhan* (call to prayer) as in the days of the Prophet, rather than in the traditional Shi'i manner.

Imam Khomeini's differences with Ayatollah al-Sadr center primarily on the degree of clerical control of government. Whereas Ayatollah al-Sadr assigned clerics responsibility for judging the legitimacy of laws enacted by representatives of the people, Imam Khomeini imposed a system in which one cleric, the faqih, has the final word on who peoples the government as well as on the laws government passes. In the Islamic Republic of Iran, the concept of *shura* is subordinated to *wilayat al-faqih*. Candidates for the legislature and actions taken by the legislature are subject to veto by the faqih, as are actions by the judiciary and the executive. The faqih appoints a council of divines whose powers derive from his. The council helps the faqih determine the acceptability of actions by the government and the suitability of candidates for government positions. The hierarchy of political authority established by Imam Khomeini is diagrammed in Figure 7.2. As God's representative, the faqih oversees the government and has the power to declare its acts null and void. Imam Khomeini became the first supreme faqih by public acclamation, but he established the principle that future supreme faqihs should be selected by their predecessors, as the Twelve Imams were designated by their predecessors.

Imam Khomeini endorsed "unhampered scholarly debate" for arriving at specific courses of action, but the word *scholarly* excludes most nonclerics, and opponents of Islamic government have not been eligible to participate even if they are clerics[62] (witness the house arrest inflicted on Ayatollah Shariat-Madari in his late years). When Ayatollah Montezeri had differences with Imam Khomeini, he called for opening the media to opposition views. "Our society must be an open society in which all people can voice their views through the press, the radio, the television, and other mass communications media."[63] Shortly thereafter, he was obliged to resign his position as designated successor to Imam Khomeini. Secularists who were elected to the legislature in 1980 were not allowed to take their seats, revealing how severely circumscribed "scholarly debate" is.

As Islamic government has been implemented in Iran, Imam Khomeini and the other leaders have departed from their original formulations in some areas. In January 1988 Imam Khomeini asserted that, as faqih, he had the authority to supercede Islamic regulations, a claim that appears to conflict with the raison d'être for Islamic government, namely, the implementation of God's laws. Another change occurred in 1989, when constitutional requirements in the area of the faqih's qualifications were altered. In 1970 Khomeini had stipulated that the faqih had to surpass all other *maraji'* in knowledge of the law and justice. When he was ready to choose the faqih ultimately to be his successor, none of the living *maraji'* were judged to have

Figure 7.2 Lines of Political Authority as Actualized in Iran

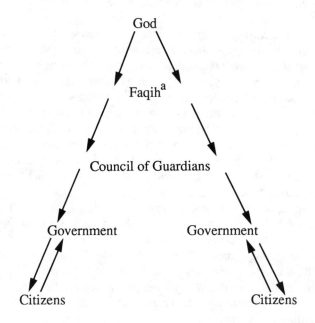

God

Faqih[a]

Council of Guardians

Government   Government

Citizens   Citizens

[a]Believers are not obliged to follow the faqih in nonpolitical matters.

the political ability necessary to the position (indeed, none of them were strong advocates of the concept of *wilayat al-faqih*). A council revised the constitution, reducing the qualifications for faqih so that any mujtahid would be eligible.[64] As revised, the constitution makes it possible for the government to continue to pursue "the line of the Imam [Khomeini]."

In the area of economic policy, a degree of pluralism has been allowed. Iranian legislative candidates accepted by the Council of Guardians and elected legislators have represented differing economic points of view, notably in the area of rural social justice. Because the Islamic requirement of social justice necessitates improving the economic situation of the rural masses, land reform has been on the political agenda. Many clerics support the idea of allowing farmers ownership of the land they farm, but such a remedy runs into the problem that Islamic law also protects the private property of the landowners. In order to take some action on rural poverty, Iran's governing clergy, despite division within clerical ranks, has resorted to the doctrine of *zarurat* (temporary waiving of Islamic law in conditions of overriding necessity), allowing the government to transfer some land from landlords to cultivators.[65]

In manufacturing and commerce, small businesses have been given interest-free loans by the government, although private banks that loaned money for interest were taken over by the government in 1979. In terms of the international economy, self-sufficiency is termed the most important goal of the *umma*. Economic dependence is believed to cause political and social dependence, relegating the dependent society to satellite status; thus it is considered essential that Islamic countries break the chains of economic dependence.[66] The constitution of the Islamic Republic forbids foreign investment in Iran, but shortly after the Iran-Iraq War ended, President Ali Khamenei indicated that Iran's parliament could allow such investment.[67] Need appears to have impinged on ideology.

Restrictions on women are close to traditional practice. The Islamic government at first made wearing the chador (a tentlike veil covering all of a woman except face, hands, and feet) compulsory in government and public offices, prompting women in Tehran to march for five days in March 1979 in opposition to the dress restrictions and for women's rights.[68] The government then redefined *hijab* to mean wearing head scarves, loose clothing, and nontransparent stockings, which is the way Sunni Islamists had been interpreting it for years.

The Islamic government in Iran reimposed sexual segregation in education. Females were stopped from studying "subjects that were not useful for them and society."[69] All women judges lost their positions, and women were barred from the legal profession. Economic and social opportunities for women remain greater than in traditional Islamic society but less than in the more recent secular period. When the Islamic Republic adopted an austerity program, it classified washing machines and vacuum cleaners, labor-saving devices used by women, as "false needs." Electric shavers, cars, and televisions, imports enjoyed by men, were not included in the list of "false needs" citizens could forgo.[70] As for the export of Islamic revolution, Imam Khomeini supported the conversion of all humanity to Islam, but he emphasized that the export of an idea by force is not "export." Rather, the export of Islam is to occur through the Islamic Republic's setting an example of good behavior.[71]

Iran's respect for human rights has been obviously deficient. How much of the abuse is attendant upon revolutionary conditions and the Iran-Iraq War and how much is due to the system of Islamic government is unclear. Executions for crimes like drug abuse are common. "Warring with God" is a charge the government has made against some people. Those so charged, while allowed defense attorneys, are not allowed to plead innocent.[72] Exactly what the offenses are is not clear, but Imam Khomeini has written that "since God Almighty has commanded us to follow the messenger and the *holders of authority*, our obeying them is actually an expression of obedience to God" (emphasis added).[73] By logical extension, questioning decisions of the "holders of authority" would be questioning God. Unavoidably, the very idea that any one or any group knows God's will leads to authoritarianism if that person or group has ultimate political power.

Although Imam Khomeini was not, in the opinion of many observers, a dictator, in his capacity as ultimate governmental authority, he on occasion exercised dictatorial power.[74] Iranian dissidents, and even others, may be harsher in their judgments, particularly given Imam Khomeini's January 7, 1988, letter to President Khamenei advising him that the supreme faqih has authority to override even Islamic injunctions.

Internal Contradictions

Like all ideologies, the ideology of Islamic government contains contradictions. Authorities would have to deal with the problem of perfunctory Muslims who would not willingly submit to any prescribed shari'a. Coercing perfunctory Muslims into apparent submission would create a contradiction in that Islam calls for *submission* to God's will, not coercion to comply with what someone interprets God's will to be. The Quran itself says, "Let there be no compulsion in religion" (Sura 2, verse 256). As Ayatollah al-Sadr explained, "Religion . . . is an ideology and a way of thinking. Hence by its nature, it cannot be forced on anyone."[75] Ayatollah al-Sadr did not envision coercion. Quite the contrary, he expected the Islamic government in Iran to "make a pleasant impact on the whole world,"[76] an expectation belied by the world's actual reaction to the Islamic Republic. After reviewing the difficulties confronting individual Muslims living in systems inconsistent with the teachings of the Quran, Ayatollah al-Sadr wrote of his expectation that "if an Islamic government comes to power . . . man will regain the true unity and total harmony of his personality."[77]

Ayatollah al-Sadr's belief that individuals would be satisfied with Islamic government could prove as idealistic as was his expectation regarding the international reaction to Islamic government. With many Muslims in the habit of slighting obligatory prayers and otherwise failing to comply with Islamic laws, resistance to an enforced shari'a cannot be discounted, especially if interpretation of the law is by jurists who are less reform-minded and less compassionate than was Ayatollah al-Sadr. In the face of dissidence, the Islamic government could take an absolutist attitude, stringently defining and enforcing religious laws, or it could allow considerable latitude in religious observation. The first option would require repressive measures.

The second option would in all probability encounter opposition from hard-liners who would want the government to enforce morality.[78]

Ayatollah al-Sadr combined the idea of Islamic government with the "reconstruction" of society through *ijtihad*. Inappropriate traditions were to be jettisoned and the necessary adaptations made to modernize Islamic society. Seeking societal benefit from achievements in science and education, Ayatollah al-Sadr advanced reformist and progressive programs, but it is questionable that the government he proposed could remain progressive. Divine law is immutable. Religion has historically been an ideological tool of political control. Once society is "reconstructed" and inapt applications of tradition disallowed, Islamic government could be profoundly conservative, with proposed changes resisted as attempts to change God's law.

Islamists seek to promote Islamic orthopraxy, but damage to Islam as a religion could well be an unintended consequence of Islamic government. From the seventh to the twentieth century, from Morocco to Indonesia, Islam has adapted flexibly to existing conditions. In an Islamic nomocracy, there would be one interpretation of Islam and that interpretation would be implemented by state authorities, with the powers of modern government enforcing the definition and implementation. Flexibility would ipso facto be lost. Governmental failures would redound to Islam. There is already some evidence that religiosity has declined in the Islamic Republic of Iran as a result of resentment toward the government. Overt religious observances have been noted to wax and wane in parallel with public support for the Islamic regime.[79]

With *wilayat al-faqih*, the unity of the law interpreter and the law enforcer in the person of one faqih disposes to rigidity and a failure of justice. A government so structured is responsive to the faqih, not to the changing needs and interests of the people. Even the reevaluation of tradition begun by Ayatollah al-Sadr might not be completed because "reconstruction" of society would depend in the first instance on the faqih. Imam Khomeini reinterpreted Shi'i political ideology and supported economic redistribution, but he adhered largely to traditional practices in social relations, for example, in the matter of women's capacity for responsibility. Each new faqih will have his own views.

A system of Islamic government featuring *wilayat al-faqih* lacks safeguards against abuse of power or incompetence on the part of the faqih, an omission likely to become problematic, given the historical proclivity of humans to use power for their own ends as opposed to the ends of any other human being or group. The expectation that any government operated by humans will be perfect is probably delusive.

There is also a potential contradiction between the political elitism of *wilayat al-faqih* and Islamic government's commitment to social justice. As implemented in Iran, Islamic government is theoretically not accountable to anyone on earth. History would indicate that the interests of social groups are respected in the sharing-out of society's resources only when those groups have the means to compel such respect. Given the Islamic government's concentration of political power in the hands of a clerical elite and the absence of specific definitions of social justice, the disinherited have some reason to be skeptical about their prospects for social justice.

None of these contradictions means the ideology cannot be implemented or that Islamist programs cannot be made to work. They do indicate pitfalls for those Iraqis trying to effect self-government within an Islamic framework.

Notes

1. al-Sadr, *Our Philosophy*, p. 27.
2. Mawdudi, *The Islamic Movement*, p. 30.
3. al-Sadr, *Our Philosophy*, p. 31.
4. Tamadonfar, *Islamic Polity*, p. 29.
5. Details on the early occultation are after Sachedina, *Islamic Messianism*, pp. 39–56.
6. *Khums*, meaning one-fifth, is the annual portion of an individual's increase in wealth and net income that the Quran (Sura 8, verse 41) stipulates individuals must assign to God and the needy.
7. Today Akhbarism survives in Iraq only in a band of territory stretching across the southern part of the country, from Suq al-Shayukh to the Iranian border, including part of the city of Basra. Cf. Momen, *Shi'i Islam*, p. 225.
8. Akhavi, *Religion and Politics*, p. 7.
9. Cole, "Role of the Ulama," p. 44.
10. Cf. Amanat, "Clerical Leadership," p. 124.
11. Quoted in Millward, "Modernism in Shi'a Islam," p. 115.
12. Tamadonfar, *Islamic Polity*, pp. 90 and 107.
13. Enayat, *Modern Islamic Political Thought*, p. 19. Historically, there have been Shi'i sects whose governments were quite democratic relative to other governments of their time, but Ithna 'Ashari Shi'as have considered quranic directives on *shura* to be fulfilled by government consultation with the ulama.
14. I once heard this reality expressed by one Iraqi Shi'a of social position to another when he said, "Where would Ayatollah [Muhsin] al-Hakim have been without men like your father and mine?"
15. As is well known, the Quran discourages polygyny by requiring a husband to treat all wives equally, a virtual impossibility, albeit a condition difficult to define legally. My point, though, is that Muslim tradition allows polygyny. Polyandry is not allowed.
16. Akhavi, *Religion and Politics*, p. 223n. The *Al* in *Al Kashif al-Ghita* means "family of." The original Kashif al-Ghita was Shaikh Ja'far al-Najafi (1743–1812) who authored the book *Kashf al-Ghita'* (Uncovering of Error). Shaikh al-Najafi became known as "Kashif al-Ghita" ("Uncoverer of Error"), and his sons, several of whom became high-ranking ulama, were then called "Al Kashif al-Ghita," "the family of Kashif al-Ghita." A descendant, Hasan Al Kashif al-Ghita (d. 1846), was the leader of Iraqi Shi'as in his era. Cf. Momen, *Shi'i Islam*, p. 315.
17. Algar, *The Roots of the Islamic Revolution*, p. 42.

18. al-Sadr, *Islamic Political System*, p. 72.

19. Ibid., p. 82. Ayatollah al-Sadr does not, in this discussion of the Islamic political system, explain what the changed circumstances are, but it is probable that he refers to the greatly increased amount of education and communication in modern societies, changes that have made citizens more able to participate in their own governance and increased their expectation of doing so.

20. al-Sadr, *Islam and Schools of Economics*, p. 29. Ayatollah al-Sadr was not the only Shi'i cleric to contend that legislative and executive authority are entrusted to the people collectively. An Iranian cleric, Asad Allah Mamaqani, published a book in 1956 in which he held that during the absence of the Twelfth Imam, functions of government devolve on "the just believers," not the ulama. Cf. Arjomand, "Ideological Revolution," p. 183.

21. al-Sadr, *Islamic Political System*, pp. 75–80.

22. *Islamic Revival*, March and April 1981, p. 5.

23. al-Sadr, *Contemporary Man and the Social Problem*, pp. 165–172.

24. al-Sadr, *Islamic Political System*, pp. 45–48.

25. Ibid., pp. 51–53.

26. Ibid., pp. 25–26.

27. Mutahhari, *Society and History*, p. 34.

28. al-Sadr, *Iqtisaduna*, pp. 117–123.

29. al-Sadr, *Our Philosophy*, p. 32.

30. The article entitled "Islamic Republic," pp. 70–84, in al-Sadr, *Islamic Political System*, is dated 6 Rabi' al-Awwali, A.H. 1399 (early February 1979), that is, immediately after the triumph of the Islamic revolution in Iran. Ayatollah al-Sadr wrote the article in response to a query from a group of Lebanese clerics about the basis of an Islamic republic.

31. Interestingly, the newspaper *At-Tayar al-Jadeed* has interpreted the quranic specification of *khums* to mean that 20 percent is the maximum tax a legitimate Islamic government can collect from individuals. Cf. *At-Tayar al-Jadeed*, September 10, 1984, p. 31.

32. Afshar, "The Iranian Theocracy," p. 235.

33. al-Sadr, *Islam and Schools of Economics*, pp. 128–129.

34. al-Sadr, *Banking in the Muslim Society*, pp. 17–19.

35. al-Sadr, *Islam and Schools of Economics*, p. 28.

36. al-Sadr, *Our Philosophy*, p. 151.

37. Muhammad Baqir al-Sadr, as cited in Batatu, "Shi'i Organizations in Iraq," p. 182.

38. al-Sadr, *Islam and Schools of Economics*, pp. 59–60.

39. Ibid., p. 34.

40. al-Sadr, *Islamic Political System*, p. 45.

41. al-Khatib Ibn al-Najaf, *Al-Harakat*, pp. 50–54.

42. *Al-Jihad*, November 24, 1986, p. 4.

43. Mutahhari, *Jihad*, p. 65. Ayatollah Mutahhari was one of Ayatollah al-Sadr's students. In the early 1960s, Ayatollah Mutahhari organized a group of modernist Iranian ulama for the purpose of reforming Shi'i thought and organization. Cf. Akhavi, "The Pahlavi Era," p. 225. Although associated with a liberal interpretation of Islamic political principles and not infrequently in opposition to Ayatollah Khomeini on political issues, Ayatollah Mutahhari was the first chairman of the Revolutionary Council set up by Imam Khomeini on his return to Iran in 1979.

Queried about the specifics of the society for which Iraq's Islamic movement strives, Hujja Mahdi al-Hakim gave me several books by Ayatollah Mutahhari.

44. al-Sadr, *Islam and Schools of Economics*, pp. 91–97.

45. Khomeini, *Islam and Revolution*, p. 170.

46. Ibid., pp. 99–100. In the same year, 1970, at least two other prominent Iranian clerics, Hasan Farid Gulpaygani and Shaikh Ali Tihrani, also called for hierocratic government, specifying that the ulama collectively should exercise the governing authority of the Hidden Imam. Cf. Arjomand, "Ideological Revolution in Shi'ism," pp. 190–191.

47. *Wilayat al-faqih* (*vilayat-i faqih* in Persian) is usually translated as "guardianship of the jurist" or "guardianship of the jurisprudent authorized to lead in the absence of the Imam Mahdi," but other translations are possible since the word *wilaya(t)* has a variety of meanings.

48. Khomeini, *Islam and Revolution*, pp. 59–60.

49. Ibid., p. 64.

50. Enayat, "Ayatollah Khumayni," pp. 341–342.

51. A conspicuous difference between the writings of Ayatollah al-Sadr and those of Imam Khomeini is their tone. Whereas Ayatollah al-Sadr is reasoned and charitable in his expressions, Imam Khomeini is often hostile in tone.

52. Khomeini, *Islam and Revolution*, p. 43.

53. Ibid., p. 40.

54. Ibid., pp. 55–56.

55. Ibid., p. 264.

56. Azari, "The Women's Movement in Iran," p. 200. Although the Council of Experts was purported to draft the constitution submitted to the public for ratification, Azari indicates that the constitution had already been written in secret and that the Council of Experts had little more input than did the public.

57. The tradition is cited by Momen, *Shi'i Islam*, p. 167.

58. *Kayhan International*, November 7, 1987, p. 3.

59. Algar, *The Roots of the Islamic Revolution*, p. 59.

60. See Siddiqui, *Islamic Movement, 1982–1983*, pp. 305–306, for Shi'i concessions to Sunni practices. Kalim Siddiqui, the editor of the *Issues in the Islamic Movement* series, is a Sunni Muslim who chronicles the international Islamic movement.

61. Cited in Tamadonfar, *Islamic Polity*, p. 53.

62. Ramazani, "Editorial," pp. 166–167.

63. *Kayhan International*, February 18, 1989, p. 8.

64. Hujja Abbas Ali Zanjani, in an interview reported in *Crescent International*, July 1–15, 1989, p. 5. The other living *maraji'* are Ayatollah Khu'i in Iraq, and Ayatollahs Gulpaygani and Mar'ash-Najafi in Iran. None is closely associated with Khomeini's political interpretations.

65. Cf. Bakhash, "Land, Law, and Social Justice," pp. 186–201.

66. Abbas Mirakhor, a contemporary Muslim expert on Islamic economics, cites Ayatollah al-Sadr regarding the importance of economic self-sufficiency. Cf. Mirakhor, "Economic Dependence a Denial of Islam," pp. 158–159.

67. Haeri, "Opening the Doors," p. 12.

68. Schahgaldian, *The Clerical Establishment*, p. 94.

69. *Kayhan International*, February 6, 1988, p. 9.

70. Afshar, "The Iranian Theocracy," p. 239. The bias in the list may be because there were no women in the group that drew up the list.

71. Ramazani, "Iran's Foreign Policy," p. 55.

72. Akhavi, "Iran: Implementation of an Islamic State," p. 41.

73. Khomeini, *Islam and Revolution*, p. 91.

74. Cf. Cottam, "Khomeini, the Future, and U.S. Options."

75. al-Sadr, *Islamic Political System*, p. 112.

76. Ibid., p. 73.

77. Ibid., p. 30.

78. Obviously, this problem is not unique to Islamic government. Even secular democratic governments come under pressure from people who are convinced the government should prevent immoral acts as *they* perceive immorality.

79. Hegland, "Two Images of Hussein," p. 205.

8

What Will Iraq's Islamists Accept?

In terms of Shi'i political ideology and practice, the significance of the Islamic initiative is the abandonment of traditional Shi'i quietism in favor of political involvement. The Shi'i *maraji'* have reinterpreted clerical functions and obligations in the direction of political assertiveness, leading their clerical followers to mobilize the Shi'i community politically. This mobilization of a large, traditionally disadvantaged group has upset the established distribution of political privilege in Iraq and Lebanon and could threaten the distribution of power in Bahrain and other Gulf states.

The ideology that inspires the Islamic movement is a credible and comprehensive set of beliefs if one accepts the basic premise that a divine being sent a prophet with laws for mankind, including laws concerning the organization of social systems on earth. Following from that first premise, action to effect government that meets revealed requirements is value-rational, the only requisite being a conscious belief in the value of implementing the divine will. The political theory of the Islamic movement is determined by first principles. No arcane reasoning is required.

Ayatollah al-Sadr's proposed Islamic government allows the people a greater measure of self-government than does Imam Khomeini's system of *wilayat al-faqih*. The divergent interpretations of Islamic government make it necessary to ask which vision of Islamic government Iraqi Islamists pursue. The answer is that all except the leadership of the Majlis strive to keep their distance from Iran. Hizb al-Da'wa allows its members to support *wilayat al-faqih* or not, as they see fit, a position the leadership adopted after it took up residence in Iran. Despite Imam Khomeini's displeasure, prominent members of Da'wa, such as Murtada al-'Askari, have never accepted *wilayat al-faqih*.[1] The Islamic Task Organization is on the side of the moderates, committed to real representative rule within the bounds of Islamic requirements.

The leadership of the Majlis accepted *wilayat al-faqih* as a condition for Imam Khomeini's approval and the organization's existence. Iraqi supporters of *wilayat al-faqih* envision an Iraqi government with structures homologous to those of the Islamic Republic of Iran. Iraq would have its own executive and its own constitutional assembly, and the two countries would have the same faqih, representing Islam. Governmental acts would be subject to review by the faqih. Among Iraqi supporters of *wilayat al-faqih*, there is preference for an Iraqi legislature that would have a larger role than does the legislature in the Islamic Republic of Iran.[2]

Whether Ayatollah al-Sadr would have supported the evolution of the Iranian government is not known, but his past deference to clerical rank leads one to believe that he would have avoided opposing it. Many of his followers accepted Imam Khomeini's version of Islamic government by volunteering for the Iranian war effort. Hundreds of Iraqi POWs sought asylum in Iran at the end of the war.[3]

In both visions of Islamic government, governors would themselves be governed by a higher law, as interpreted by religiously trained judges. Neither system would be majority rule in that changing the fundamental law would not be within human province. Interpretation could, of course, respond to societal interests, particularly in Ayatollah al-Sadr's version, with its larger measure of citizen participation.

Whatever Islamists might prefer, political opposition movements operate in the world of the possible. What is possible in Iraq differs from what is possible in Iran. It was not just personality or accident that led Ayatollah Khomeini to advocate a hierocratic system of rule and Ayatollah al-Sadr to advocate an elective system in which the clergy exercises only a judicial function. Ayatollah Khomeini was leader of the political opposition in an overwhelmingly Shi'i country when he advanced the principle of *wilayat al-faqih*, whereas Ayatollah al-Sadr was seeking to solve the problem of illegitimate government in a religiously divided country. Those Iraqi Islamists who adopted *wilayat al-faqih* did so after Ayatollah al-Sadr's death and their own exile to Iran.

A salient characteristic of Iraqi Shi'i ulama is their pragmatism. While they have shown a willingness to die for government that meets the minimum requirements for Islamic legitimacy, they have not survived as an Arab minority within Shi'ism, and as a Shi'i minority within the Arab world, by taking maximalist stands. Given that Iraq is around 56 percent Shi'i and 40 percent Sunni, Islamic brotherhood is a political necessity if Iraqi Islamists hope to reverse secular advances and establish a government that acknowledges Islamic law. That fact has played a central role in the course of Iraq's Islamic movement. In Ayatollah al-Sadr's last message to the Iraqi people, he clearly absolved Sunnism of responsibility for the Ba'thist government:

> The actual [Iraqi] rule today is not a Sunni rule although the ruling gang deceitfully claims to belong to the Sunni branch of Islam. Sunni rule

does not mean the rule of a person who descended from Sunni parents. . . . The tyrant rulers of Iraq today . . . violate Islam, and they abuse Ali and Omar together every day in every step they take.[4]

In most Muslim countries, accommodation between Shi'as and Sunnis is not a critical political issue, but in Iraq there is little prospect of integrating the country on the basis of Islam unless the two sects do harmonize their programs and efforts. The guardianship of a faqih based in Iran or even the guardianship of a Shi'i faqih based in Iraq would be difficult if not impossible to effect in a religiously mixed country. Ayatollah al-Sadr's proposals, though, may fit Iraqi needs, moving the government to legitimacy and the country substantially toward self-government. The Sunnis who have participated in Iraq's Islamic movement appear to believe a mutually acceptable system is possible. The Ba'th government has certainly acted as though Sunni-Shi'i cooperation is an actual threat to the government. Significantly, the first cleric to die at the hands of the Ba'th government was Shaikh al-Badri, a Sunni Islamist working with the Shi'i reformers. Other Sunni clerics have since joined their Shi'i counterparts in being executed by the Ba'th government for their Islamist political activities.

That Iraqi Islamists strive for a partnership between Shi'as and Sunnis, and that they need that partnership, does not make alliance inevitable, but there is ample evidence of cooperation. The political alliances effected between religious Iraqi Sunnis and Shi'as in 1919 and in 1960 were discussed in Chapters 2 and 3. The membership of Sunni groups in the Majlis is a more recent example of Shi'i Islamists' disposition to appeal to other believers. Sunni and Shi'i dissidents are known to have collaborated in various military operations against the Iraqi government, including the bombings of government-controlled television stations and air force headquarters in Baghdad in spring 1983. In 1985, Da'wa links with Sunni clerics in Mosul were reported.[5] Qusay Fahmi, a leader of the Iraqi Ikhwan al-Muslimin, which is of course Sunni, has characterized Iran's revolution as Muslim, not Shi'i, and called on Iraq's Muslims to resist efforts to divide them on a sectarian basis.[6] Sunni Kurdish theologians, members of the Ulama Movement of Iraq's Kurdistan Province, worked with Shi'i Iran in its war effort against the Iraqi government and have called for unity among Muslims.[7] Obviously, some Iraqi Sunnis have responded in kind to Shi'i efforts toward Islamic brotherhood.

Granted a cooperative spirit on the part of observant Iraqi Muslims, could Islamists succeed in free elections? They have repeatedly called for free elections[8] and say they would win them. That does not prove they would, but neither is there convincing evidence that they would not. To assume, as some theorists have done, that Saddam's Islamic opposition would have triumphed during the Iran-Iraq War had it had significant internal support is to overlook the power of the government's repressive apparatus, the government's control of the economy, and the rally to the flag that occurs in wartime. Failure of any people to rebel may well be rational self-preservation—not support for the government.

Iraq's Islamic movement does face a variety of obstacles. One difficulty in the path of Sunni-Shi'i alliance is inherent in fundamentalism itself. By nature, fundamentalists fear heterodoxy and are often religiously scrupulous in the extreme; thus some Sunni fundamentalists may prefer not to risk association with Shi'as. This kind of scrupulosity appears to have been overcome in the past by Iraqi Muslims, and Ayatollah al-Sadr's participatory form of Islamic government allows input from both sects. The Shi'i and Sunni communities could each have a council of high-ranking clerics to adjudge laws, in the manner of Lebanon with its Supreme Shi'i Council and Sunni Grand Mufti (top religious authority) and his council, or Sunni and Shi'i clerics could sit together on one supreme court.

Another serious obstacle to Islamic government is posed by nationalism. Neither Arab nor Kurdish secularists would willingly accept a government featuring *wilayat al-faqih*. Iraqi Islamists benefit from the general discrediting of Arab nationalism, but nationalism retains a strong hold on the leadership of the Kurds. Anti-Arab feeling generated among Kurds by Saddam's atrocities could also militate against future cooperation between the Kurdish and Arab populations. Islamists may or may not be correct in their belief that nationalism is a surmountable obstacle and that even indifferent Muslims would accept Ayatollah al-Sadr's vision of representative institutions limited only by Islamic law.

The obstacle that gets the most attention in Islamic movement literature is that posed by foreigners. The literature is replete with calls for self-government, by which Islamists mean removing foreign political "agents" and influences from Iraq. The present international political era is viewed by Islamists from a North-South perspective. Third World countries are presumed to be indirectly controlled by either the West or the Soviet Union through economic, political, and intellectual means.[9] Iraqis are predisposed to believe, given their past experiences, that the West is a puppeteer, able to pull strings attached to Third World governments. They cite the experience of neighboring Iran, where an elected government was overthrown in 1953 with the help of the United States and Britain, and their own experience with British behind-the-scenes control between 1932 and 1958. Iraq's Ba'th government remained in power during the Iran-Iraq War only by means of foreign support. Until the war waged against Iraq in 1991 by the U.S.-led coalition, Islamists considered Saddam Hussein to be beholden to the United States.[10] Shortly before the 1980 Iraqi attack on Iran, Imam Khomeini referred to Saddam Hussein as a "humble servant of America."[11] Reflecting the same basic view, Muhammad Baqir al-Hakim said in a 1982 interview that the struggle is between Islam and imperialism, with Saddam Hussein representing imperialism. According to this analysis, the West and the Soviet Union aided Saddam Hussein in his war against Iran because an independent Islamic government in Tehran constitutes a fissure in superpower control of the Third World.

Obviously, there are flaws in this political analysis. Neither the West nor the Soviet Union has been able to pull the strings on client governments in the manner of a puppet master pulling the strings on a puppet. If Saddam was ever a "humble servant of America," by 1990 he had clearly lost both humility and servility.

Although Islamists may not assess blame accurately, there is no gainsaying the sincerity of their belief that Iraqis are not in charge of their own country, that dictatorial whim and perceived superpower interests affect Iraqi government policies more than does domestic opinion. Islamic activists consider their struggle to be defensive, an effort to save Iraq and Islam from further decline and foreign exploitation.

Interests to Which Islamic Government Appeals

Groups standing to benefit from Islamic government include the Shi'i clerical stratum and, quite likely, the Sunni clerical stratum. As actualized in Iran, Islamic government has transformed the clergy from a declining social group to a politically powerful group. Under *wilayat al-faqih* the ulama have collectively arrogated to themselves the political prerogatives of the Vanished Imam. Although heterodox in the context of Muslim tradition, clerical assumption of political power solves the problem of how to effect an Islamic social order, and in a way that simultaneously reverses the dispossession of the clergy. Even in the system advanced by Ayatollah al-Sadr, the ulama would be assured high status with real power.

Practicing Iraqi Muslims in general have an interest in the integration of Iraq as a nonracial, nonsectarian community of the faithful. In an Islamic republic, they would be esteemed for their piety and not excluded from political and economic power because they are not Ba'thists or Arabs or Sunnis. Observance of religious injunctions would be easier to effect, and moral example and knowledge of Islam would be socially rewarding. Those Muslims who believe God mandated Islamic government expect religious credit for their support of Islamic government.

Males in an Islamic republic would likely maintain their privileged position vis-à-vis females. Even debate on women's issues could be suppressed, as it has been in the Islamic Republic of Iran. Only high-ranking ulama would have the authority to question the reliability of traditions denying self-determination to women, and the executions of Ayatollah al-Sadr and Bint al-Huda removed the most authoritative voices supporting women's capacity for self-responsibility. Their example and the commitment of Arab Shi'as to the reinterpretation of traditions contributing to women's inferior position do militate in favor of more self-responsibility for Iraqi women than exists for Iranian women. Arab Shi'i women have been participating in the contemporary Islamic political movement for decades, not only in Iraq but elsewhere. In Lebanon, the sister of Imam Musa al-Sadr, Rabab al-Sadr, is a member of the Presidential Council of Amal and director of a large vocational school in south Lebanon.[12]

Even if not particularly enamored of the idea of Islamic government, many exiles who hope to return home and people within Iraq who desire revenge for family members lost to the Ba'thist security apparatus and a halt to the Ba'th government's wars would initially welcome *any* alternative to the existing government. The Ba'th regime in Iraq has established the closest thing to a totalitarian order anywhere in the Arab world. As the Arab Organization for Human Rights reported at its January 1987 meeting:

> The conditions of human rights in Iraq are unique in terms of the rampant flagrant violations of civil and political rights even before the Iran-Iraq War of 1980. The rights of citizens are almost non-existent, even if one is a member of the ruling party. . . . He is always subjected, without probable cause, to questioning, detention, disappearance, abusive treatment and torture. Many times, these violations include deprivation of life without due process and without a public accusation, hearing or trial.[13]

Factors Rejected as Determinants

Several factors sometimes suggested as causative agents should be rejected. One such factor is sectarianism. Although the majority of Iraq's population is Shi'i and the government has historically consisted of urban Sunnis in alliance with foreigners, first the Turks and then the British, Shi'i Islamists view their struggle as Muslims versus an infidel political system, not Shi'as versus Sunnis. In the hundreds of books and papers on the Islamic movement I read for this study, I encountered no derogation of Sunnism. Rather, believing Sunnis are presented as allies or potential allies against the kafir government. The Ba'thist regime is condemned not for Sunnism but for its deeds. In the words of Sayyid Hadi al-Mudarrisi, leader of the Islamic Task Organization, "The issue in Iraq is between the people and the depraved [*fasid*] regime, and with Iraqis [is the obligation to] intensify their struggle until fulfillment of their divine goal."[14] The idea of Shi'as fighting Sunnis for a Shi'i version of Islamic government was abandoned in the eighth century, and Shi'i clerics continue to anathematize bloodshed among Muslims.

The division of Iraqis into disadvantaged Shi'as and Kurds and co-opted Sunni Arabs preceded the Islamic movement and has complicated the movement's effort to organize and unite Iraqis. To maintain its privileged position, the Ba'th government has exploited Iraq's sectarian division.[15] It has co-opted military officers and others from the Sunni Arab triangle of north central Iraq, while expelling and executing Shi'as and Kurds and importing non-Iraqi Arab Sunnis. With the political and economic elites belonging largely to the Arab Sunni minority, the existing system of dominance is protected by the obvious community of interests between the government and the Sunni Arab community, even though many Sunni Arabs abhor Ba'th Party methods and have gone into self-exile for their own safety. Iraqis falling into neither the scapegoated non-Arab groups nor the favored Ba'thist group are the majority. As Arab Shi'as, they have been hindered in asserting their interests by what happens to protesters and by their vulnerability to being designated "Iranian" and expelled. Dependence on state employment has dissuaded Iraqis of all ethnic and religious groups from joining the political opposition to Ba'th rule.

Claims that Iran is the cause of Islamic opposition in Iraq should also be rejected. Iraq had an Islamic movement long before Iran had an Islamic government that might want to export revolution. The example of Iranian revolutionary success in 1979 and the possibility of military assistance did, however, encourage the 1979 adoption of a strategy of armed resistance to the government.

Individual anomie, as Talcott Parsons[16] and others associated with social protest movements, has to be ruled out in this social movement. Although family control has diminished in Iraq, it has not evanesced. Unattached individuals are virtually inconceivable in Iraq. Even rural-to-urban migration has been by family groups, not by individuals.[17] In the city, migrants have tended to join other migrants from their villages and tribes of origin, approximating the familiar rural community. With family ties in Iraq remaining strong, individual anomie is an unlikely eventuality. Indeed, membership in the Islamic movement is often by family group.

Nor is Islamic fundamentalism a causative factor, although Islam as a value system has greatly influenced the choice of goals and the course of action taken by Islamic groups. With its values of social justice and the brotherhood of believers, Islam is well suited to be an ideology of protest against despotic rule and socioeconomic favoritism, but the ideology obviously existed long before individual clerics used it to organize this political opposition movement. The conscious effort by Muslims to get control of the government in Iraq derives from societal changes and governmental failures, not from the ideology that has been the means of its organization and the normative guide for its course.

Extrapolation

A movement that has never been in power cannot be expected to have fully developed political, economic, and social programs, but alternate elites do have to proffer programs of a general nature. The images framed by elites provide evidence not only of their intentions but of what their followers are supporting. Although political forces operating at the time a new political system is being actualized would affect the formation of specific institutions, a projection of their tenor is possible.

On a right-left spectrum, with the left representing diffusion of political power and the right representing concentration of political power, even Imam Khomeini's *wilayat al-faqih* is to the left of Iraq's present government. Ayatollah al-Sadr's delineation of Islamic government specifies a much greater diffusion of political power than Iraq has experienced to date. In his vision of Islamic government, only Islamic principles and the superior position of the ulama in the proposed judiciary constitute brakes on majority rule.

In economic ideology, Iraq's Islamic movement is neither rightist nor leftist. A strong defense of private property was the first issue around which the ulama rallied in opposition to General Qasim in the late 1950s. In the ensuing years, the ulama have continued to cite quranic approval of private property and wealth, at the same time stressing the necessity of social justice and the obligation of Islamic government to prevent the people's genuine need.

In an Islamic polity, the operation of the economy would change to a degree in that the banking system would be modified to eliminate interest on capital, but the banking system outlined by Ayatollah al-Sadr allows capital to be accumulated and lent by public banks. Since commercial banks were nationalized by the government in 1964, the banking changes would not require any expropriation of property. Iraqi owners of economic assets would retain their assets, with the possible exception of owners prominently associated with the Ba'th government.

War-related debts incurred by the Ba'th regime would be at risk. The Majlis has declared numerous times, one of which was at its January 1988 meeting, that an Islamic government of Iraq would have no commitment to honor foreign loans given to the Ba'thist regime for military purposes.[18] Islamist leaders have, however, pledged to assume responsibility for loans made to Iraq for purposes of economic development.

Social freedoms would unmistakably decrease. If social freedoms are viewed on a right-left spectrum, with the left representing individual freedom and the right representing societal domination, the Islamic movement is very rightist, despite the protestations of some Islamists that societal controls actually give individuals more freedom.[19] Political power would serve normative ends in that Islamic values and practices would have the power of government behind them. One can imagine the political participation in the system and the experience educated Islamists have had with other cultures leading to some reinterpretations of inhibiting traditions, but only implementation of the system would reveal whether or not that occurs. There has been reinterpretation of some requirements in Iran, for example the move from the chador to less restrictive *hijab* for women.

Women and perfunctory Muslims would initially be allowed fewer choices, although quranic injunctions afford both groups a level of protection no group has had under the Ba'thists. Religious minorities, as in any state organized on the basis of religion, would be second-class citizens—although they, too, are protected by quranic precepts. One group that would lose more than social freedom is the Ba'thist security forces. Having killed believers, the security forces are in a category specifically condemned by the Quran.

Iraqi experience with modern government has been unpromising. "Democracy" under the British brought Iraqis elections rigged to return governments that met British requirements. "Socialism" under the Ba'thists brought them a "parasitic"[20] economic elite and a would-be totalitarian government. For Iraqis, both communism and democracy are further sullied by the deeds of their international models, not the least of which is the arming of Saddam Hussein. Iraqis who have experienced democracy embrace it, as evidenced by the support for democracy among Iraqis who live, or have lived, in the West;[21] but it is difficult to conceive any scenario in which Western-style democracy could be implemented in Iraq.

A relevant question regarding Islamic government is, What is the minimum that Iraqi Islamists will accept? My opinion is that they are highly unlikely to accept any system of government that does not subject laws or proposed laws to clerical review. The ulama and their followers may retreat from their maximum goal of government by the righteous, but they feel religiously obligated to ensure that governmental laws do not contravene Islam. If allowed their minimum demands, current Iraqi Islamists will likely compromise with secularists to get the most adherence to Islamic law they can in a new system. The clerical leaders of Iraq's Islamic movement are not men of war, nor is there evidence they are grasping for personal power. They will almost certainly opt for a political solution if given an opportunity to do so.

Iraq's Islamic movement is appropriately seen as part of the larger movement toward Islam that has been occurring among Muslim peoples at least since the end of World War II. The activist ulama were inspired by Egyptian Sunni fundamentalists and a perceived need to defend Islam. The move to Islam in Iraq is being carried out through the political mobilization of the majority group, the Shi'as. Shi'as have made concessions to Sunni beliefs, aimed at promoting sectarian cooperation. Devotion to Islamic brotherhood and cooperation with observant Sunnis is an intrinsic feature of the Shi'i movement in Iraq. The movement appeals to observant Muslims generally and to less pious Shi'as who stand to benefit from a fairer distribution of political power in the country.

Shi'as do not seek the breakup of Iraq and would not do so. Arab Shi'as are a minority in the Arab world but a majority in Iraq. In Iraq they can hope to have an influence they could not have in a unified Arab nation or in a unified "Shi'i state" where Iranians would be the majority group. Some outsiders have completely misjudged the political interests of Iraqi Shi'as because they have little knowledge of them. The idea that Iraq needs a strong dictator to hold it together flies in the face of political reality for the Shi'as. Arab Sunni military domination of the 80 percent of Iraqis who are not Arab Sunnis is a formula for vicious and unending repression and resistance. Assuming that the Shi'as will revert to quietism is unrealistic in the twentieth century. The politically relevant population in Iraq has broadened, and efforts to prevent their participation can succeed only in the short term, if at all.

The Shi'as have not sacrificed for political participation qua participation. Each social group in the movement has specific objectives, only one of which deals with the hereafter. The ulama feel morally obligated to effect a system of government that meets Islamic requirements, and they seek to stem the decline in their own status. The young intelligentsia are acting in accordance with their belief system, and they stand to benefit socially and economically from a system in which merit plays more of a role. As for the urban poor, they are obeying their traditional religious leaders and working to place social justice on the political agenda in Iraq. Just as the belief that government was insufficiently pious and economic discontent coalesced with partisanship for Imam Ali in Umayyad Iraq, so moral indignation and economic discontent coalesce with support for Islamic government in contemporary Iraq.

Notes

1. Farhad Ibrahim, "The Iraqi Shi'a," p. 13.
2. August 8, 1986, interview in London with Dr. Abu Ali, Hizb al-Da'wa spokesman, and Brother Ali, Da'wa member.
3. A total of 482 Iraqi prisoners of war were granted political asylum in Iran on December 16, 1988, according to *Kayhan International*, December 19, 1988, p. 8.
4. al-Sadr, "Nida' al-Qa'id." Omar, the second caliph of Islam, is highly esteemed by Sunnis, whereas Ali, the fourth caliph, is the most revered Imam of the Shi'as. The two caliphs are often used, as Ayatollah al-Sadr uses them in this epistle, to symbolize the two sects.
5. Riley, "Letter from ath-Thaghir," p. 20.

6. *Crescent International*, January 1–15, 1988, p. 3.

7. *Kayhan International*, May 30, 1987, p. 2.

8. One such call for elections was reported in the magazine *Arabia*, April 1985, p. 26.

9. Among the innumerable expositions of this view are Hashim, "About the World Political Situation," and *Da'wah Chronicle*, June 1984, p. 3.

10. The oil nationalizations of 1972 cast doubt on the view of Saddam Hussein as the CIA's man, but the belief was reinvigorated by Iraq's 1980 attack on Iran and the subsequent U.S. assistance extended to the Ba'th government.

11. Khomeini, *Islam and Revolution*, pp. 301–302.

12. Norton, *Amal and the Shi'a*, pp. 39 and 89. Rabab al-Sadr is the sister of Ayatollah Muhammad Baqir al-Sadr's wife, Fatima.

13. Aruri, "Human Rights in the Arab World," p. 11.

14. *Al-'Amal al-Islami*, January 22, 1989, p. 2.

15. I do not contend that the Ba'th government is sectarian in belief, only that Iraq's sectarian division has been exploited to the benefit of the ruling minority. It is doubtful that any ideology has motivated the leaders of the Ba'th Party.

Marion Farouk-Sluglett and Peter Sluglett make the argument that personal relationships, not ideology, have been the decisive factor in Ba'th Party affiliation in Iraq. When Fu'ad al-Rakabi founded the Iraqi Ba'th Party, its members were almost entirely his Shi'i relatives and classmates. When Ali Salih al-Sa'adi headed the party, his "supporters were generally petty criminals like himself from the Bab al-Shaikh area of Baghdad, and the Ahmad Hasan al-Bakr/Saddam Hussein group that came to power in 1968 had a following based in the first instance on Sunnis from Takrit." Quotation from Farouk-Sluglett and Sluglett, *Iraq Since 1958*, pp. 108–109.

The newspaper *At-Tayar al-Jadeed* has wryly dubbed Saddam Hussein "democratic" in his choice of victims. "He is from Tikrit, but he has executed a number of Tikritis; he is a Ba'thist, but [as of 1986], he had executed 31 Ba'th Party leaders; he is a Sunni, but he has not hesitated to execute Sunni ulama . . . along with his extensive executions of Shi'as and Kurds." *At-Tayar al-Jadeed*, April 7, 1986, p. 6.

16. See Parsons, *Essays in Sociological Theory*, pp. 126–141.

17. Cf. Phillips, "Rural-to-urban Migration in Iraq," p. 412, and Lawless, "Iraq: Changing Population Patterns," p. 119.

18. *Kayhan International*, January 9, 1988, p. 1.

19. Some Islamic publications contend, for example, that *hijab* enhances freedom by minimizing sexual stimulation and the tyranny of fashion. See, for example, *Crescent International*, December 16–31, 1987, p. 10.

20. The new economic elite is termed "parasitic" in that it depends for its existence on the state and the state's oil revenues.

21. At a two-day conference of Iraqi opposition groups in Washington, D.C., on August 1–2, 1991, representatives of eighteen organized groups headquartered in North America, Europe, and Syria put their organizations on record in favor of democracy, although the Kurdish groups also wanted guarantees regarding Kurdish autonomy. For years, the New Umma Party, headquartered in London, advocated democracy in Iraq. In the late 1960s, when I was teaching in Iraq, many Western-educated individuals, including some Ba'thists, were working for democracy. When some of them began turning up tortured and dead in front of their homes, however, the others became politically inactive.

Appendixes

Appendix 1: Partial List of Members of Jama'at al-'Ulama'

Ayatollah Murtada al-Yasin
Shaikh Hussein al-Hamdani
Shaikh Khadir al-Dujayli
Sayyid Isma'il al-Sadr
Sayyid Muhammad Taqi Bahr al-'Ulum
Sayyid Musa Bahr al-'Ulum
Shaikh Ali Haraj al-Wa'ily
Sayyid Muhammad Jamal al-Hashimi
Shaikh Muhammad Juwwa
Shaikh Radi
Shaikh Muhammad Hasan al-Jawahri
Sayyid Mahdi al-Hakim
Shaikh Muhammad Hussein Fadlallah

Sources: The first eleven members listed are from al-Khatib Ibn al-Najaf, *Tarikh al-Harakat al-Islamiya al-Mu'asira fi al-'Iraq*, pp. 16–17. Hujja Mahdi al-Hakim gave me his own name. The membership of Shaikh Fadlallah (who is Lebanese) is reported in Mallat, "Religious Militancy in Contemporary Iraq," p. 716.

Appendix 2: Islamic Movement Publications

• *Periodicals*

Title: *Al-Adwa' al-Islamiya* (The Islamic lights)
Publisher: Jama'at al-'Ulama' in Najaf
Featured Writers: Sayyid Muhammad Baqir al-Sadr
                    Shaikh Muhammad Amin Zain al-Din
                    Dr. Abd al-Hadi al-Fadili
                    Sayyid Muhammad Hussein Fadlallah

Title: *Al-Najaf*
Publisher: College of Jurisprudence in Najaf
Featured Writers: Shaikh al-Muzaffar
                    Hujja Muhammad Taqi al-Hakim
                    Graduates and students of the college

Title: *Al-Tadamun al-Islami* (Islamic solidarity)
Publisher: Islamic Solidarity Association in Nasriya
Featured Writers: Shaikh Muhammad Baqir al-Nasri and brothers

Title: *Iman* (Faith)
Publisher: The preachers al-Ya'qubi and Sayyid Hadi al-Hakim of Najaf

Content: Poems, recitations, and articles on ethics

Title: *Risala al-Islam* (The Message of Islam)
Publisher: College of Religious Principles in Najaf
Featured Writers: Sayyid Murtada al-'Askari
                    Shaikh Arif al-Basri
                    Dr. Dawud al-'Attar
                    Sayyid Muhammad Baqir al-Hakim
                    Sayyid Muhammad Baqir al-Sadr
                    Shaikh Murtada Al Yasin

Title: *Al-Nashat al-Thaqafi* (Educational Zeal)
Publisher: Organization for Educational Purity in Najaf

Title: *Al-Balagh* (The Report)
Publisher: Society for Islamic Studies in Kazymiya

* *Books (by author)*

Sayyid Muhammad Baqir al-Sadr
    Falsafatuna (Our Philosophy)
    Iqtisaduna (Our Economy)
Shaikh Muhammad Amin Zain al-Din
    Al-Islam: Yanabu'hu, Manahujhu, Ghayatuhu (Islam: Its Sources,
    Its Methods, Its Goals)
    Ila al-Tali'a al-Mu'mina (To the Believing Vanguard)
    Asha''tun min al-Qur'an (Rays from the Quran)
Shaikh Baqir al-Qurashi
    Al-'Amal wa Huquq al-'Amil fi al-Islam (The Task and Duties of a
    Worker for Islam)
    Al-Nizam al-Siyasi fi al-Islam (The Political System in Islam)
Dr. Abd al-Hadi al-Fadili
    Mushkila al-Faqr fi Nazar al-Islam (The Problem of Poverty in the
    View of Islam)
Shaikh al-Asafi
    Al-Nizam al-Mali wa Tadawal al-Tharwa fi Al-Islam (The Monetary
    System and Circulation of Wealth in Islam)
Shaikh Muhammad Mahdi Shams al-Din
    Nizam al-Hukm wa Idara fi al-Islam (The Governmental and
    Administrative System in Islam)
Shaikh Muhammad Baqir al-Nasri
    Qissata ma'a Sadiq Mushakak (My Story for a Doubting Friend)

Shaikh al-Saghir
 Al-Shuyu'iya Mabda' Haddam (Communism Is a Destructive
 Concept)
Dr. Abd al-Razzaq Muhi al-Din
 Sha'b Asil wa Hizb Dakhil (Steadfast People and an Alien Party)
Dr. Muhammad Hadi al-Amini
 Al-Shuyu'iya 'Aduwat al-Shu'ub (Communism is the Enemy of the
 People)

• *Islamic Series* (a sequence of religious instruction booklets)

 • On Islamic Guidance:
  Shaikh Muhammad Mahdi al-Asafi
   Al-Madkhal ila al-Tashri' al-Islami (Introduction to Islamic
   Regulations)
   Al-Imama fi al-Tashri' al-Islami (The Imamate in Islamic
   Legal Relations)
  'Alima Bint al-Huda
   Al-Fadila Tantasar (Virtue Overcomes)
   Al-Marrat ma'a al-Nabity (The Times in Relation to the
   Prophet)
  Sayyid Muhammad Hussein Fadlallah
   Qadayana 'ala Dau' al-Islam (Our Problems Through the
   Light of Islam)
  Sayyid Muhammad Baqir al-Sadr
   Nazarat fi I'lan al-Huquq (Views of Human Rights in
   Revelation)
 • On Selected Subjects (issued by Madrasat al-Khalili al-Kubra, a
  seminary in Najaf):
  Shaikh Muhammad Mahdi al-Asafi
   Min Hadith al-Da'wa wa al-Du'at (Discussion on the Call
   and the Callers)
  Dr. Abd al-Hadi al-Fadili
   Min al-Ba'tha ila al-Daula (From the Mission to the State)
  Shaikh Muhammad Hussein Fadlallah
   Uslub al-Da'wa fi al-Qur'an (The Method of the Call in the
   Quran)
  Sayyid Adnan al-Bika'
   Al-Usra al-Muslima (The Muslim Family)
  Shaikh Muhammad Mahdi Shams al-Din
   Baina al-Jahiliya wa al-Islam (Between Unbelief and Islam)
  Sayyid Abd al-Rasul Al Ali Khan al-Madani
   Tahdid al-Nasl (Birth Control)

Sayyid Abd al-Karim al-Qazwini
Al-Saum: Tarikhhi wa Fawa'iduhu (Fasting: Its History
and its Benefits)
Sayyid Muhammad Taqi al-Hakim
Ahadith Tashayyu' fi Naduwat al-Qahira (Discussions in
Cairo Circles on Becoming a Shi'a)
• Booklets on the Building Phase (issued in Najaf under the direction
of Ustadh Abd al-Hussein al-Bahbahani):
Ustadh al-Bahbahani
"Kaifa wa Nahnu Samituun" (Why We Are Silent)
"Al-Uslub al-Amthal fi Khidmat al-Madhab" (The Ideal
Tactic for the Sake of the Madhab)
Dr. Abd al-Hadi al-Fadili
"Mustalahan Asasiyan" (Established Fundamentals)
Sayyid Muhammad Baqir al-Sadr
"Al-Qanun al-Islami" (Islamic Law)
Shaikh Muhammad Mahdi al-Asafi
"Sa'at al-Faragh" (Idle Hours)

Source: al-Khatib Ibn al-Najaf, *Tarikh Al-Harakat al-Islamiya al-Mu'asira fi al-'Iraq*, pp. 28–36. Translation from Arabic is by the author.

Appendix 3: Clerics Executed by the Ba'th Government

Name	Duty Assignment	Year of Execution
Muhammad Baqir al-Sadr	Najaf	1980
Qasim Shubbar	Nu'maniya	1979
Muhammad Tahir al-Haidari	Baghdad	
Abd al-Sahib Muhsin al-Hakim	Najaf	1983
Bint al-Huda	Najaf	1980
Mahdi al-Samawi	Samawa	1979
Arif al-Basri	Madinat al-Salam [Baghdad]	1974
Hussein Ma'un	Najaf	1980
Qasim al-Mubarqi'	Madinat al-Thawra	1979
Abd al-Jabbar al-Basri	Baghdad	1979
Azz al-Din al-Qabanji	Najaf	1974
Imad al-Din al-Tabataba'i	Najaf	1974
Abd al-Rahim al-Yasri	Jizan [Diyala]	1980
Khaz'al al-Sudani	Baghdad	1979
Kamal Yusuf al-Hakim	Najaf	1983
Abd al-Wahab Yusuf al-Hakim	Najaf	1983

Muhammad Hussein Muhsin al-Hakim	Najaf	1983
'Ala' Muhsin al-Hakim	Najaf	1983
Muhammad Taqi Jalali	Hilla	1981
Abd al-Jalil Malallah	Diyala	1980
Abd al-Aziz al-Badri	Baghdad	1969
Muhammad Ali al-Jabri	Nasriya	1979
Sharif Sakhur al-Jabri	Najaf	1980
Abbas Hussein Tahir al-Shawki	Madinat al-Thawra	1979
Jasim Mahmud Mubaraqi'	Madinat al-Thawra	1979
Abd al-Jabbar al-Musawi	Najaf	1979
Hasuni Abd al-Mun'im al-Fartusi	Najaf	
Abd al-Khaliq Salih al-Awadi	Najaf	1979
Abbas Fadil al-Turkomani	Najaf	1979
Ibrahim Hammudi Qunbar	Najaf	1979
Salih Hadi al-Hasnawi	Najaf	1980
Salih Rifa'i	Najaf	
Qasim Hadi Daif	Baghdad	1980
Abd al-Amir al-Sa'idi	Amara	1980
Mahmud Hasan al-Ka'bi	Madinat al-Thawra	1979
Farhan al-Baghdadi	Kazymiya	1980
Nazim Mizhur al-Jaza'i	Najaf	1980
Sadiq al-Karbala'i	Najaf	
Nijah Habib al-Musawi	Madinat al-Hurriya	1979
Tahir Abu Raghif	Basra	1977
Sadiq Hasan al-Ya'subi	Baghdad	
Salim al-Baghdadi	Madinat al-Hurriya	
Ahmad Farij al-Bahadili	Najaf	
Ziyad al-Musawi	Najaf	
Hussein Mashkur al-Halu	Basra	1980
Muhammad Sijad al-Yusufi	Najaf	1980
Abbas al-Halu	Najaf	1983
Muhammad Hasan al-Hakim		1985
Isam Arif	Sulaimaniya	1985
Rami Tuskharmatu'i	Kirkuk	1985

Sources: Hizb al-Da'wa al-Islamiya, *Jara'im Saddam*, pp. 75–78; and Zafar Bangash, "Ba'thists Continue to Inflict Atrocities on Muslims," p. 61.

Note: Hizb al-Da'wa presents all but the last three names as part of its legal indictment of Saddam Hussein and, as such, the list includes only clerics who indisputably died in government custody, without revealed charges or trials. Iraqi clerics who were assassinated outside Iraq, almost certainly by the Iraqi government, include Sayyid Abd al-Mun'im al-Shawki, killed in Kuwait; Ayatollah Hasan Shirazi, killed in Beirut; and Hujja Mahdi al-Hakim, killed in Khartoum, Sudan.

Appendix 4: Islamic Liberation
Movement Press Release of July 31, 1979

The Islamic revolution in Iran has induced the people to speak out. Popular zeal was soon translated into numerous delegations pouring on [sic] Ayatollah Muhammad Baqir al-Sadr from all over Iraq—expressing allegiance to him and accepting his leadership of the Islamic revolution. Ayatollah al-Sadr, who resides in Najaf, is the leader of the masses in Iraq, one of the major religious leaders in the Muslim world. The Ayatollah welcomed these delegations and publicly denounced the Ba'thist regime on many occasions.

The Ba'thist regime, which was taken by surprise, reacted violently to these events; they soon put the Ayatollah under house arrest and embarked on a wave of mass arrests of all delegations in Najaf to visit the Ayatollah. When Ayatollah al-Sadr protested against these measures, the Ba'thists immediately arrested the Ayatollah and took him to Baghdad for interrogation. This move sparked off widespread demonstrations all over Iraq, protesting against the measures and demanding the immediate release of Ayatollah al-Sadr. The Ba'thists, embarrassed by this popular outburst, could not face the reality of the situation. They, though they released Ayatollah al-Sadr one day later, have indulged in mass arrests of all demonstrators, including all representatives, relatives, and close associates of the Ayatollah. This aggravated the situation further and led the demonstrators to attack and kill key party and "security" officers like: Abd al-Rahman Ubayd Musa, head of the Party unit in al-Thawra; Ali al-Dhalimi, head of Najaf "security" unit; and Muhammad Barham, leader of the "People's Army"[1] in Khalis.[2]

The Ba'thists reacted by putting Ayatollah al-Sadr under house arrest once again and embarked on further and continued mass arrests.

The latest situation is that there are more than 10,000 people detained (400 women)—all facing the inevitable brutality of the Ba'thist "security" apparatus. So far, 36 people have died under torture; about 100 others—mostly mullahs—[are] sentenced to death, and about 600 [are] sentenced to life imprisonment.

The Ba'thist regime is obviously facing the most crucial moments since they came to power in 1968. They are facing a triple enemy: the Kurdish revolution in the north, the Islamic revolution, and the communists.

Nevertheless, the Islamic Liberation Movement shall resort to all means to deprive the Ba'thist regime, and the Saddam Hussein faction particularly, from [sic] their power to dominate and tyrannize the people of Iraq.

The Islamic Liberation Movement in its present form represents a coalition of the main Islamic Parties that have been operating in Iraq for decades. The aims of the Liberation Movement are to:

1. Expose the fallacy of the Ba'thists to the people of Iraq in particular and to world opinion at large;
2. Mobilize the people of Iraq to speak out against the Ba'thist regime;
3. Win the support of other movements in the world and particularly in Iraq;
4. Isolate the Ba'thist regime from their power to control and brainwash the people.

Source: The source for this appendix is the Islamic Liberation Movement, as reported in "Documents File," *Middle East International*, August 3, 1979, p. 14.
Notes
1. The People's Army is a paramilitary adjunct to the Ba'th Party. It was created in 1976 and built up sufficiently to constitute a counterweight to the regular armed forces.
2. Khalis is a city in Diyala province in east central Iraq.

Appendix 5: Islamic Groups Formed
After the 1979 Adoption of Militant Tactics

Name of Organization	Activities
Hizb al-Da'wa al-Islamiya al-Mujahid (Militant Party of the Call to Islam)	Works to get accurate news of Iraq to exiles in Iran
Rabitat al-Mar'at al-Muslima fi al-'Iraq (League of Muslim Women in Iraq)	Performs religious and educational services (composed of female relatives of Hizb al-Da'wa members)
Harakat al-Mujahidin al-'Iraqiyin (Movement of Iraqi Religious Fighters)	Works to get accurate news of Iraq to exiles in Syria
Jama'at al-Shahida Bint al-Huda (Society of the Martyr Bint al-Huda)	Performs religious and educational services (composed of female relatives of members of Harakat al-Mujahidin al-'Iraqiyin)
Haraka Jama'at al-'Ulama' al-Mujahidin fi al-'Iraq (Movement of the Society of Militant Ulama in Iraq)	Coordinates Iraqi Islamic groups (Hujja Muhammad Baqir al-Hakim is the group's Secretary General)

Rabitat al-Mujahidat al-
Muslima fi al-'Iraq (League
of Militant Muslim Women
in Iraq)

Assists in the work of the Islamic
Task Organization

Sources: al-Khatib Ibn al-Najaf, *Tarikh al-Harakat al-Islamiya al-Mu'asira fi al-'Iraq*, pp. 135–139; and Al-'Amal al-Islami, January 29, 1989, p. 2.

Appendix 6: Publications by Exile Groups

Hizb al-Da'wa al-Islamiya al-Mujahid
(Militant Party of the Call to Islam)

   Sada al-'Iraq (Echo of Iraq) - Bimonthly political newspaper
   Al-Qari'a (The Hour of the Last Judgment) - Periodical
   Ansar Allah (God's Followers) - Periodical
   Sawt al-'Iraq (Voice of Iraq) - Periodical (in Europe)
   Al-Kashif (The Examiner) - Reports on the tenth political
                              committee of Hizb al-Da'wa
   Li Hukm al-Islami wa Wilayat al-Faqih (In Favor of Islamic Government
      and Guardianship of the *Faqih*) - Book

League of Muslim Women

Al-Muslima bil-Mawadi' al-Islamiyat al-Ra'ida (The Muslim Woman as an
Islamic Pioneer) - Periodical

Harakat al-Mujahidin al-'Iraqiyin
(Movement of Iraqi Religious Fighters)

   Al-Shabab al-'Arabi (The Young Arab Men) - Pamphlet
   Al-Kifah al-Musallah (The Armed Struggle) - Book
   Al-Qa'id wa al-Umma (The Leader and the Community) - Book

Jama'at al-Shahida Bint al-Huda (Society of the Martyr Bint al-Huda)

   Al-Mujahida (The Woman Freedom Fighter) - Religious Periodical

Islamic Task Organization

   Al-Shahid (The Martyr) - Periodical

Jund al-Imam (Soldiers of the Imam)

   Al-Mustad'afun (The Oppressed) - Periodical

Tawhid al-Quwan al-Islamiya fi al-'Iraq (The Unity of Islamic Forces Inside Iraq) - Book

Source: al-Khatib Ibn al-Najaf, Tarikh al-Harakat al-Islamiya al-Mu'asira fi al-'Iraq, pp. 134–139. Translation from Arabic is by the author. This is by no means a complete list. Iraqi exile groups, highly motivated both to witness for Islam and to reveal the deeds of the Ba'th government, are prolific when it comes to publications.

Appendix 7: Speakers at the Sixth Extraordinary Meeting of Majlis, January 5–6, 1988, Tehran

Sayyid Ali al-Ha'iri	president of the general assembly
Hujja Muhammad Baqir al-Hakim	chairman of the central committee
Hujja Muhammad Ali Rahmani	commander of exile mobilization, Islamic Republic of Iran
Shaikh Muhammad Khalid Barazan	Hizbullah leader of Iraqi Kurds and member of the central committee (a Kurd)
Snaikh Muhammad Mahdi al-Asafi	member of the central committee
Shaikh al-Kurani[a]	member of the general assembly
Sayyid Abd al-Rahim al-Shawki[b]	member of the general assembly
Sayyid Muhsin al-Husaini	Islamic Task Organization delegate
Shaikh Hasan Bashira	Imam Jum'a[c] of Kirkuk (a Turk)
Dr. Abu Ali[d]	Da'wa representative in London

Source: *Kayhan al-'Arabi*, January 9, 1988, p. 4. Translated from the Arabic by the author. Some first names and titles added.
[a]Spoke about the establishment of Hizbullah cells inside Iraq.
[b]Spoke about progress in the establishment of Hizbullah units inside Iraq.
[c]Friday prayer leader, an influential position.
[d]Layman.

Appendix 8: Members of the Bahr al-'Ulum Family Arrested in Najaf in March 1991

'Ala' al-Din, age 58	Religious scholar at the Islamic Religious University of Najaf (IRU-N) and congressional prayer leader at the Holy Shrine of Imam Ali
'Ali, age 27	Seminarian
Mustafa, age 24	Seminarian
Amin, age 22	Engineering student
'Azz al-Din, age 55	Lecturer at IRU-N, leader of

	congressional prayers at the courtyard of the Holy Shrine of Imam Ali, and author
Hasan 'Azz al-Din, age 27	Seminarian
Ja'far, age 53	Delegate for Ayatollah Khu'i
Ahmad, age 35	Civil engineer
Muhammad Jawad, age 27	Seminarian
Hasan, age 48	Lecturer at IRU-N and imam of the Great Mosque of Kufa
Muhammad, age 18	Student
Muhammad Hussein, age 45	Lecturer at IRU-N
Muhsin, age 18	Engineering student
Muhammad Rida, age 38	Lecturer at IRU-N
Muhammad 'Abud, age 29	Civil engineer
'Ammar, age 19	Student

Source: United Activists for a Democratic Iraq, "Appeal to Human Rights Organizations." The arrestees were taken to an unknown location. Another member of the family, Sadiqa Bahr al-'Ulum, age 36, was killed by the secret police near the Holy Shrine of Imam Ali during the March uprising against the government. Sadiqa was the daughter of Dr. Muhammad Bahr al-'Ulum, one of the Iraqi opposition leaders based in London.

Glossary

With the exception of a few words that are familiar to the public, Arabic words that are not found in *Webster's Third New International Dictionary* are transliterated according to the system adopted by the Library of Congress and the Middle East Studies Association. Diacritical marks are included only in the Glossary, not in the text. The words are set in italic and their plurals are formed as in Arabic, e.g., *fatwā, fatāwin*. The 'ayn is represented by the symbol ' and the hamza by '.

Arabic words that are found in a complete English dictionary are included in the Glossary for the reader's convenience. They are set in roman text, and their plurals are formed with s—e.g., mujtahid, mujtahids—unless the Arabic plural is also known in English, e.g., alim, ulama. Proper nouns are set in roman text.

The Arabic prefix *al-* is discounted in the alphabetic order.

abu: father, frequently used as part of a name, for example, Abu Ali, Father of Ali.

A.H.: (Anno Hegirae): year after the A.D. 622 emigration of Muhammad from Mecca to Medina.

ahl al-bayt: lit., "family of the house (of the Prophet Muhammad)," the immediate descendants of the Prophet; a term used to refer to Shi'as collectively; (capitalized) a London-based organization ministering to Iraqi refugees.

akhbar: traditions; information.

Al: family of, in contrast to *al-*, which means "the."

'Allāma: "Very Learned," a title.

alim: religious scholar, cleric.

'alima: female religious scholar.

Allah: lit., "the God."

al-Anṣār al-Ḥizb al-Da'wa al-Islāmīya (Followers of the Call to Islam): an

167

organization of working-class men formed in 1962 to assist in the call to Islam.

'aql: reason.

Ashura: tenth day of the month of Muharram, the anniversary of Imam Hussein's death.

awqaf: pious endowments (plural of waqf).

Ayatollah: lit., "Sign of God," title of a high-ranking Shi'i cleric.

Badr: special Iraqi Islamic military forces.

basij [Persian] forces: volunteer soldiers who receive elementary military training and light weapons but no pay.

Bint al-Huda: "Daughter of the Righteous Path," public name of Amina al-Sadr, Islamic scholar and sister of Ayatollah Muhammad Baqir al-Sadr.

caliphate: political authority accorded the Prophet's successors.

caliphs: successors to the political power of the Prophet Muhammad.

chador [Persian]: tentlike veil covering all of a woman except the face, hands, and feet.

al-da'wa: the call or invitation to believe in and defend Islam.

din: religion.

faqih: Muslim jurisprudent, expert in Islamic law.

fatwa (pl. *fatawin*): authoritative opinion based on religious law; religious injunction.

Fayliya Kurds: the 40,000 to 60,000 Kurds who are Shi'i Muslims.

fellahin: sharecroppers, peasant farmers.

fiqh: Islamic jurisprudence.

hadiths: recorded sayings and deeds of the Prophet Muhammad and the Imams.

Hashimites: the family that served as guardians of the holy cities of Mecca and Medina from the seventh century until the 1920s. The Hashimites are so called because they claim direct descent from the Prophet Muhammad, who was a member of the Banu Hashim clan.

hawza: center of religious education.

hijab: covering or veil.

Hizb al-Da'wa al-Islamiya: Party of the Call to Islam, founded by Muhammad Baqir al-Sadr in 1957.

Hizb al-Fatimi: Fatimid Party, name reportedly invented by Ba'thists for the Islamic movement. *Fatimid* denotes "Shi'i" since *ahl al-bayt* is descended from Fatima, the daughter of the Prophet Muhammad.

Hizb al-Tahrir al-Islami: Islamic Liberation Party, a Sunni fundamentalist party associated with the Muslim Brotherhood. Hizb al-Tahrir became active in Iraq in the mid-1950s.

Hizbullah: Party of God, a militant grouping of underprivileged Shi'i men, active in Lebanon and the Gulf states, including Iraq.

holy cities: Najaf, Karbala, Kazymiya, and Samarra; Iraqi cities in which one or more of the Twelve Imams are buried.

Hujja: title of a mujtahid, reduced form of *Hujjat al-Islam*, proof of Islam.

husainiya (pl. *husainiyat*): religious studies and ceremonial center for male Shi'as.

ICP: Iraqi Communist Party.

ijma': consensus.

ijtihad: making religious judgments and interpretations, deducing laws in cases to which no express religious text is applicable.

al-Ikhwan al-Muslimin: the Muslim Brotherhood, a Sunni fundamentalist group with adherents in a number of countries, including Iraq.

imam: in the root sense, "religious leader"; prayer leader in charge of a mosque; (capitalized) religious leader invested with political authority.

imamate: in Shi'i belief, the series of twelve "rightful rulers," Imams who came after the Prophet Muhammad. They were denied political authority by the Muslim community but are accorded religious authority by Shi'as.

intifada: an unarmed uprising or large public protest.

iqta': a system of tax farming in which the government sold concessionaires the right to collect taxes in given areas.

Islamic Task Organization (Munazzamat al-'Amal al-Islami): Islamic political group formed by ulama in Karbala in 1961. The Islamic Task Organization has been active in the Arab Gulf states as well as in Iraq.

Islamists: advocates of Islamic government.

Ithna 'Ashari Shi'as: the majority group of Shi'as, including those of Iraq. Ithna 'Ashari (Twelver) Shi'as recognize twelve Imams.

Ja'faris: Ithna 'Ashari Shi'as, so called because they follow the legal interpretations of the Sixth Imam, Ja'far al-Sadiq.

Jama'at al-'Ulama': Society of Ulama, formed in Najaf in 1958 to coordinate the activities of reformist ulama.

jihad: lit., "struggle," frequently referring to military efforts on behalf of Islam but also applicable to striving against evil in society and in individual souls.

Jund al-Imam: Soldiers of the [Twelfth] Imam, a militant group of Iraqi Shi'as, originally formed in 1969, then allowed to lapse until 1979.

kafir: infidel, one who does not believe in God.

Kazmawi: native of the city of Kazymiya.

khalifat Allah: deputy or vice-regent of God.

khums: lit., "one-fifth," the annual portion of an individual's increase in wealth that the Quran stipulates must be assigned to God and the needy.

KIM: Kurdish Islamic Movement (al-Harakat al-Rabitat al-Islamiya fi Kurdistan).

madhab: a school of Muslim jurisprudence.

Madinat al-Thawra: lit., "City of the Revolution," the name of the suburb Abd al-Karim Qasim built for Baghdad's poor (renamed Saddam City in 1982).

Mahdi: Savior, the Twelfth Imam.

Majlis: parliament, assembly; popular name for the Supreme Assembly of the Islamic Revolution in Iraq, the organization headquartered in Tehran, which coordinates the activities of the various Iraqi Islamic opposition groups.

marji' (pl. *maraji'*): a religious authority consulted by other mujtahids.

marji' al-taqlid al-mutlaq: sole or absolute supreme authority, source of imitation.

muhajirin: deportees.

Muharram: first month of the Muslim year, the month in which Imam Hussein's death is commemorated with ritualized funeral processions.

mujahid (pl. *mujahidin*): fighter in a holy cause (masc).

mujahida (pl. *mujahidat*): fighter in a holy cause (fem.).

mujtahid: cleric authorized to issue authoritative opinions on Islamic law; doctor of Islamic law.

mulla: Shi'i cleric, often a rural teacher of religion.

Muslim: one who submits to God.

mutasarrif: provincial governor.

Najafi: native of the city of Najaf.

naqib: highest religious official in a given geographical area of the Abbasid and Ottoman empires.

qadi: judge in a religious court.

Rajab: seventh month of the Muslim year.

Ramadan: ninth month of the Muslim year, the month of obligatory fasting.

RCC: Revolutionary Command Council, the supreme executive and legislative body in Ba'thist Iraq.

Safar: second month of the Muslim year.

sara'if: mud huts.

Sawt al-Da'wa: lit., "voice of the call," early publication of Hizb al-Da'wa al-Islamiya.

sayyid (fem. sayyida): descendant of the Prophet Muhammad; the title by which such a descendant is addressed.

shahid: martyr.

Shahid al-Rabi': the Fourth Martyr, the title accorded Muhammad Baqir al-Sadr.

shari'a: Islamic law, covering both private and public life.

Shatt al-Arab: lit., "the Arab shore," the 100-mile confluence of the Tigris and Euphrates rivers.

shaikh: in the root sense, an elderly, venerable gentleman; Muslim cleric; leader of a tribe.

Shi'as: Muslims who regard Imam Ali as the legitimate successor to the Prophet Muhammad.

Shi'i: of or pertaining to Shi'as.

shūrā: consultation, taking counsel.

sunna: authoritative Muslim tradition.

Sunni: of or pertaining to Sunnis.

Sunnis: Muslim followers of the sunna, the path of tradition.

taqlid: lit., "imitation," the doctrine that obliges all Shi'as except mujtahids to follow a living religious authority.

tawhīd: unity of God in theology; unity of religion and politics in the social order; conformity to God's will.

ta'ziya: religious ritual of condolence held forty days after a death or the anniversary of a death. A *ta'ziya* is held annually for Imam Hussein.

Tikritis: people from the village of Tikrit in north central Iraq.

Twelfth Imam: the Savior whose return from occultation is expected by the majority of Shi'as to inaugurate justice in the world.

Twelve Imams: in the belief of the majority of Shi'as, the series of "rightful rulers" after the Prophet Muhammad. The Prophet's cousin and son-in-law, Ali, was the First Imam; the other eleven were his direct descendants.

ulama: religious scholars who teach in seminaries (plural of alim).

umma: the community of believers in Islam.

Ustādh: "Professor," title for any intellectual, but particularly for writers.

uṣūl: fundamental principles by which mujtahids derive religious laws from the sunna.

wilāyat al-faqīh: guardianship or authority of the jurisprudent.

zakat: wealth tax mandated by the Quran.

Bibliography

Abdul-Rasool, Faik. "Growth and Structural Change of Output in the Economy of Iraq: 1958–1978." *OPEC Review* 6 (1982): 27–40.

Abrahamian, Ervand. "The Guerrilla Movement in Iran, 1963–1977." In *Iran: A Revolution in Turmoil,* ed. Haleh Afshar, 149–174. Albany: State University of New York Press, 1985.

Abu Ali, Dr. "An Iraqi Corrects *The New York Times.*" *Islamic Revolution,* October 1981, 11–13.

Abu Jameel. "I Was Saddam's Prisoner." *At-Tayar al-Jadeed,* February 18, 1985, 3.

Abu Malik. "Al-Qadiya al-'Iraqiya—Waqi'ha wa Mustaqbalha" (The Iraqi Situation—Its Present and Future). *Sawt al-'Iraq al-Tha'ir,* September 1987, 4, and November 1987, 8.

al-Adhami, M. M. "The Elections for the Constituent Assembly in Iraq, 1922–1924." In *The Integration of Modern Iraq,* ed. Abbas Kelidar, 13–31. London: Croom Helm, 1979.

al-Adib, Salih. "Al-Hizb al-Fatimi" (The Fatimi Party). *Al-Jihad.* February 8, 1988, 7.

———. "Min Mazahir Taghyir Ijtima'i" (Thoughts on the Phenomena of Social Changes). *Al-Jihad.* February 15, 1988, 12.

Afshar, Haleh. "The Iranian Theocracy." In *Iran: A Revolution in Turmoil,* ed. Haleh Afshar, 220–243. Albany: State University of New York Press, 1985.

Ajami, Fuad. *The Vanished Imam.* Ithaca: Cornell University Press, 1986.

Akhavi, Shahrough. *Religion and Politics in Contemporary Iran.* Albany: State University of New York Press, 1980.

———. "Iran: Implementation of an Islamic State." In *Islam in Asia,* ed. John Esposito, 27–52. New York: Oxford University Press, 1987.

———. "The Pahlavi Era." In *Expectation of the Millennium,* eds. Seyyed Hossein Nasr, Hamid Dabashi, and Seyyed Vali Reza Nasr, 218–229. Albany: State University of New York Press, 1989.

Algar, Hamid. *The Roots of the Islamic Revolution.* Markham, Ont.: Open Press, 1983.

Ali, Abdullah Yousuf, trans. *The Meaning of the Glorious Quran.* 2 vols. 3rd ed. Cairo: Dar al-Kitab al-Masri, 1938.

Amanat, Abbas. "In Between the Madrasa and the Marketplace: The Designation of Clerical Leadership in Modern Shi'ism." In *Authority and Political Culture in Shi'ism,* ed. Said Amir Arjomand, 98–132. Albany: State University of New York, 1988.

Amnesty International. *The Amnesty International Report 1975–1976*. London: Amnesty International, 1976.

———. *The Amnesty International Report 1980*. London: Amnesty International, 1980.

———. *Iraq*. London: Amnesty International, 1981.

———. *Amnesty International Report 1983*. London: Amnesty International, 1983.

———. *Iraq: Human Rights Violations Since the Uprising.* London: Amnesty International, July 1991.

Arjomand, Said Amir. "Shi'ite Islam and the Revolution in Iran." *Government and Opposition* 16, 3 (1981): 293–316.

———. "Ideological Revolution in Shi'ism." In *Authority and Political Culture in Shi'ism*, ed. Said Arjomand, 178–209. Albany: State University of New York Press, 1988.

———. *The Turban for the Crown*. New York: Oxford University Press, 1988.

———, ed. *From Nationalism to Revolutionary Islam*. Albany: State University of New York Press, 1984.

Aruri, Naseer. "Disaster Area: Human Rights in the Arab World." *Middle East Report* 17, 6 (1987): 7–16.

al-Asafi, Muhammad Mahdi. "The Life of al-Shaikh Muhammad Rida al-Muzaffar." In Muhammad Rida al-Muzaffar, *The Faith of Shi'a Islam*, 83–86. Cambridge: Muhammadi Trust, 1982.

Askari, Hossein, John T. Cummings, and Michael Glover. *Taxation and Tax Policies in the Middle East*. London: Butterworth Scientific, 1982.

Axelgard, Fred. *A New Iraq?* New York: Praeger, 1989.

———, ed. *Iraq in Transition*. Boulder: Westview Press, 1986.

Azari, Farah. "The Post-revolutionary Women's Movement in Iran." In *Women of Iran*, ed. Farah Azari, 190–255. London: Ithaca Press, 1983.

Bakhash, Shaul. "The Politics of Land, Law, and Social Justice in Iran." *Middle East Journal* 43, 2 (1989): 186–201.

Bangash, Zafar. "Ba'thists Continue to Inflict Atrocities on Muslims." In *Issues in the Islamic movement, 1985–1986*, eds. Kalim Siddiqui and Muhammad Ghayasuddin, 61–63. London: Open Press, 1987.

Barakat, Halim. "The Arab Family and the Challenge of Social Transformation." In *Women and the Family in the Middle East: New Voices of Change*. ed. E. Fernea, 27–48. Austin: University of Texas Press, 1985.

Baram, Amatzia. "Mesopotamian Identity in Ba'thi Iraq." *Middle Eastern Studies* 19, 4 (1983): 426–455.

Barnes, John. "Iraq's No-win, No-lose War." *U.S. News and World Report*, October 12, 1987, 38–39.

Batatu, Hanna. *The Old Social Classes and the Revolutionary Movements of Iraq*. Princeton: Princeton University Press, 1978.

———. "Iraq's Underground Shi'a Movements: Characteristics, Causes and Prospects." *Middle East Journal* 35, 4 (1981): 578–594.

———. *The Egyptian, Syrian, and Iraqi Revolutions*. Washington, D.C.: Center for Contemporary Arab Studies, 1984.

———. "Class Analysis and Iraqi Society." In *Arab Society*, eds. Nicholas Hopkins and Saad Eddin Ibrahim, 379–392. Cairo: American University in Cairo Press, 1985.

———. "Shi'i Organizations in Iraq: Al-Da'wah al-Islamiyah and al-Mujahidin." In *Shi'ism and Social Protest*, eds. Juan R. I. Cole and Nikki Keddie, 179–200. New Haven: Yale University Press, 1986.

Ba'th party. *The 1968 Revolution in Iraq* (The Political Report of the 8th Congress of the Arab Ba'th Socialist Party in Iraq, January 1974). Trans. Iraq Ministry of Information. London: Ithaca Press, 1979.

Bell, Florence. *The Letters of Gertrude Bell*, vol. 2. London: Ernest Benn, 1927.

Bengio, Ofra. "Saddam Husayn's Quest for Power and Survival." *Asian and African Studies* 15 (1981): 323–341.

———. "Shi'is and Politics in Ba'thi Iraq." *Middle Eastern Studies* 21, 1 (1985): 1–14.

Bill, James A. "Resurgent Islam in the Persian Gulf." *Foreign Affairs* 63, 1 (1984): 108–127.

Burgoyne, Elizabeth. *Gertrude Bell*. London: Ernest Benn, 1961.

Burns, Norman. "The Dujailah Land Settlement." *Middle East Journal* 5, 3 (1951): 362–366.

Chirri, M. Jawad. *The Shiites Under Attack*. Detroit: Islamic Center of America, 1986.

Cleveland, William L. *The Making of an Arab Nationalist*. Princeton: Princeton University Press, 1971.

Cobbett, Deborah. "Women in Iraq." In *Saddam's Iraq*, ed. Committee Against Repression and for Democratic Rights in Iraq, 120–137. London: Zed, 1986.

Cole, Juan R. I. "Imami Jurisprudence and the Role of the Ulama: Mortaza Ansari on Emulating the Supreme Exemplar." In *Religion and Politics in Iran*, ed. Nikki R. Keddie, 33–46. New Haven: Yale University Press, 1983.

Cordesman, Anthony H. "Arms to Iran: The Impact of U.S. and Other Arms Sales on the Iran-Iraq War." *American-Arab Affairs* 20 (1987): 13–29.

Cottam, Richard W. "Khomeini, the Future, and U.S. Options." Policy Paper 38. Muscatine, Iowa: Stanley Foundation, 1987.

Dann, Uriel. *Iraq Under Kassem*. New York: Praeger, 1969.

Devlin, John. "Iraqi Military Policy: From Assertiveness to Defense." In *Gulf Security and the Iran-Iraq War*, ed. Thomas Naff, 129–156. Washington: National Defense University Press, 1985.

Dowson, V.H.W. "Date Cultivation and Date Cultivators of Basra." *Journal of the Royal Central Asian Society* 26, 2 (1939): 247–260.

Economist Intelligence Unit. *Iraq*. Special Report No. 88. London: Economist Intelligence Unit, 1980.

Enayat, Hamid. *Modern Islamic Political Thought*. Austin: University of Texas Press, 1982.

———. "Ayatullah Sayyid Ruhullah Musawi Khumayni." In *Expectation of the Millennium*, eds. Seyyed Hossein Nasr, Hamid Dabashi, and Seyyed Vali Reza Nasr, 334–343. Albany: State University of New York Press, 1989.

Esposito, John L. *Islam: the Straight Path*. New York: Oxford University Press, 1991.

Fandy, Mamoun. "Iraq's Splintered Opposition." *Christian Science Monitor*, April 29, 1991.

Farouk-Sluglett, Marion, and Peter Sluglett. "Iraqi Ba'thism: Nationalism, Socialism and National Socialism." In *Saddam's Iraq*, 2nd ed., ed. Committee Against Repression and for Democratic Rights in Iraq, 89–107. London: Zed, 1989.

———. *Iraq Since 1958*. London: KPI, 1987.

Farouk-Sluglett, Marion, Peter Sluglett, and Joe Stork. "Not Quite Armageddon: Impact of the War on Iraq." *Middle East Report* 125/126 (1984): 23–30.

Fernea, Elizabeth Warnock. *Guests of the Sheikh*. Garden City, N.J.: Doubleday, Inc., 1965.

Floor, Willem. "The Revolutionary Character of the Iranian Ulama: Wishful Thinking or Reality?" *International Journal of Middle East Studies* 12, 4 (1980): 501–524.

Foster, Henry A. *The Making of Modern Iraq*. New York: Russell and Russell, 1935.

Gaffney, Patrick D. "Authority and the Mosque in Upper Egypt: The Islamic Preacher as Image and Actor." In *Islam and the Political Economy of Meaning*, ed. William R. Roff, 199–225. Berkeley: University of California Press, 1987.

Haeri, Safa. "Opening the Doors." *Middle East International*, September 9, 1988, 11–12.

Hairi, Abdul-Hadi. *Shi'ism and Constitutionalism in Iran*. Leiden: E. J. Brill, 1977.

Haldane, Aylmer. *The Insurrection in Mesopotamia, 1920*. London: William Blackwood and Sons, 1922.

Harris, George L., ed. *Iraq*. New Haven: Hraf Press, 1958.

Hasan, Ghalib. *Al-Shahid al-Sadr Ra'id al-Thawra al-Islamiya fi al-'Iraq* (The Martyr Sadr, Leader of the Islamic Revolution in Iraq). Tehran: Ministry of Islamic Guidance, 1980.

Hashim, Hussain. *About the World Political Situation*. Trans. Yasin al-Jibouri. Washington, D.C.: Islamic Revival Movement, 1980/1981.

Hayat-e-Hakeem (Life of Aqae Sayyed Mohsin al-Hakeem). Trans. Sayyed Murtaza Hussein. Karachi: Peermahomed Ebrahim Trust, 1973.

Hegland, Mary. "Two Images of Hussein: Accommodation and Revolution in an Iranian Village." In *Religion and Politics in Iran*, ed. Nikki R. Keddie, 218–235. New Haven: Yale University Press, 1983.

Helms, Christine Moss. *Iraq*. Washington, D.C.: Brookings Institution, 1984.

Hemphill, Paul. "The Formation of the Iraqi Army, 1921–1933." In *The Integration of Modern Iraq*, ed. Abbas Kelidar, 88–110. London: Croom Helm Ltd., 1979.

Hinnebusch, Raymond. "The Islamic Movement in Syria: Sectarian Conflict and Urban Rebellion in an Authoritarian-Populist Regime." In *Islamic Resurgence in the Arab World*, ed. Ali Dessouki, 138–169. New York: Praeger, 1982.

Hizb al-Da'wa al-Islamiya. *Jara'im Saddam* (Crimes of Saddam). Tehran: Islamic Center for Political Studies, 1983.

Hodgson, Marshall. "How Did the Early Shi'a Become Sectarian?" *Journal of the American Oriental Society* 75 (1955): 1–13.

Hollister, John. "Shi'ism in the Indian Subcontinent." In *Expectation of the Millennium*, eds. Seyyed Hossein Nasr, Hamid Dabashi, and Seyyed Vali Reza Nasr, 242–246. Albany: State University of New York Press, 1989.

Hudson, Michael C. "Islam and Political Development." In *Islam and Development*, ed. John Esposito, 1–24. Syracuse: Syracuse University Press, 1980.

Hussein, Ghalib. "Qira'a fi A'maq Intifada Rajab 1399" (Discourse on the Profoundness of the Rajab *Intifada* of 1979). *Al-Ansar*, March 12, 1987, 4–5.

Ibrahim, Farhad. "The Iraqi Shi'a and Their Relations with Iran." Paper delivered in Toronto at the 1989 meeting of the Middle East Studies Association.

Ibrahim, Saad Eddin. "The Anatomy of Egypt's Militant Islamic Groups: Methodological Note and Preliminary Findings." *International Journal of Middle East Studies* 12, 4 (1980): 423–453.

International Bank for Reconstruction and Development. *The Economic Development of Iraq*. Baltimore: Johns Hopkins University Press, 1952.

Iraq, Ministry of Foreign Affairs. *Al-Niza' al-'Iraqi al-Irani fi al-Qanoun al-Dawali* (The Iraqi-Iranian Dispute in Terms of International Law). Baghdad: Freedom Printing House, 1981.

Iraq, Ministry of Planning. *Annual Abstract of Statistics 1968.* Baghdad: al-Zahra Press, 1968.

"Iraq on Simmer." *Impact International* 10, 8 (1980): 5–6.

Iraqi Islamic Association in America. *Nashra I'lamiya* (Information pamphlet). Dearborn, Mich.: Iraqi Islamic Association in America, 1987.

————. *Sayyid Mahdi al-Hakim.* (Arabic) Dearborn, Mich.: Iraqi Islamic Association in America, 1988.

Ireland, Philip. *Iraq.* New York: Russell and Russell, 1937.

Islamic Movement of Iraq (in Europe). *Al-Mujahidun* (The Freedom Fighters). Windsor, Berkshire, UK: Islamic Movement of Iraq (in Europe), 1980.

Islamic Task Organization. *The Voice of Iraqians* [sic] *to the Free People.* N.p., 1980.

Ismael, Tareq. *Iran and Iraq.* Syracuse: Syracuse University Press, 1982.

Issawi, Charles. *The Economic History of the Middle East, 1800–1914.* Chicago: University of Chicago Press, 1966.

Jamali, Fadil. "The Theological Colleges of Najaf." *Muslim World* 50, 3 (1960): 15–22.

Jansen, Godfrey. "Who Started the Gulf War?" *Middle East International*, May 15, 1987, 15–16.

————. "The Slow Return to Normality," *Middle East International*, December 16, 1988, 12–13.

Jawad, Sami Abd al-Rasul. "Min Mudhakarat Intifada Safar al-Khalid" (Memories of the glorious Safar *intifida*). *Sawt al-'Iraq al-Tha'ir*, November 4, 1987.

al-Jomard, Atheel. "Internal Migration in Iraq." In *The Integration of Modern Iraq*, ed. Abbas Kelidar, 111–122. London: Croom Helm, 1979.

Kaslow, Amy. "Oil Pays Iraq's Way Toward Big-Power Status." *Christian Science Monitor*, January 10, 1990, 1.

al-Katib, Ahmad. *Tajribat al-Thawra al-Islamiya fi al-'Iraq* (The Experience of the Islamic Revolution in Iraq). Tehran: Publishing House of Islamic Enlightenment, 1981.

Keddie, Nikki R. "Iranian Imbroglios: Who's Irrational?" *World Policy Journal* 5, 1 (1988): 29–54.

Kelidar, Abbas. "The Shii Imami Community and Politics in the Arab East." *Middle Eastern Studies* 19, 1 (1983): 3–16.

Khadduri, Majid. *Independent Iraq.* Oxford: Oxford University Press, 1951.

————. *The Gulf War.* New York: Oxford University Press, 1988.

Khadduri, Walid. "Social Background of Modern Iraqi Politics." Ph.D. thesis. Johns Hopkins University, 1970.

al-Khafaji, Isam. *Al-Dawla wa al-Tatawwur al-Rasmali fi al-'Iraq 1968–1979* (The State and Capitalistic Development in Iraq, 1968–1979). Cairo: Publishing House of the Arab Future, 1983.

————. "The Parasitic Base of the Ba'thist Regime." In *Saddam's Iraq*, ed. Committee Against Repression and for Democratic Rights in Iraq, 73–88. London: Zed, 1986.

————. "State Incubation of Iraqi Capitalism." *Middle East Report* 142 (1986): 4–9.

al-Khalil, Samir. *Republic of Fear.* Berkeley: University of California Press, 1989.

al-Khatib Ibn al-Najaf. *Tarikh al-Harakat al-Islamiya al-Mu'asira fi al-'Iraq*

(History of the Contemporary Islamic Movement in Iraq). Beirut: Dar al-Maqdasi, 1982.

Khomeini, Ruhullah. *Islam and Revolution.* Trans. Hamid Algar. London: KPI, 1985.

Klieman, Aaron S. *Foundations of British Policy in the Arab World: The Cairo Conference of 1921.* Baltimore: Johns Hopkins Press, 1970.

Lawless, R. I. "Iraq: Changing Population Patterns." In *Populations of the Middle East and North Africa,* eds. J. I. Clarke and W. F. Fisher, 97–129. London: University of London Press, 1972.

Litwak, Robert. *Security in the Persian Gulf: Sources of Interstate Conflict.* Montclair, N.J.: Allanheld, Osmun, 1981.

Longrigg, Stephen. *Four Centuries of Modern Iraq.* Oxford: Clarendon Press, 1925.

————. *Iraq, 1900–1950.* Oxford: Oxford University Press, 1953.

Lyell, Thomas. *The Ins and Outs of Mesopotamia.* London: A. M. Philpot, 1923.

McAdam, Doug. *Political Process and the Development of Black Insurgency, 1930–1970.* Chicago: University of Chicago Press, 1982.

Mallat, Chibli. "Iraq." In *The Politics of Islamic Revivalism,* ed. Shireen Hunter, 71–87. Bloomington: Indiana University Press, 1988.

————. "Religious Militancy in Contemporary Iraq: Muhammad Baqer al-Sadr and the Sunni-Shia Paradigm." *Third World Quarterly* 10, 2 (1988): 699–729.

Marr, Phebe. *The Modern History of Iraq.* Boulder: Westview Press, 1985.

Matar, Fuad. *Saddam Hussein.* London: Third World Centre, 1981.

Mawdudi, Maulana Abul 'Ala'. *The Islamic Movement.* Karachi: Islamic Foundation, 1984 (1945).

Mernissi, Fatima. *Beyond the Veil.* Rev. ed. Bloomington: Indiana University Press, 1987.

Miller, Judith, and Laurie Mylroie. *Saddam Hussein.* New York: Times Books, 1990.

Millward, W. G. "Aspects of Modernism in Shi'a Islam." *Studia Islamica* 37 (1973): 111–128.

Mirakhor, Abbas. "Economic Dependence a Denial of Islam." In *Issues in the Islamic Movement, 1982–1983,* ed. Kalim Siddiqui, 158–159. London: Open Press, 1984.

Mitchell, Richard P. *The Society of Muslim Brothers.* London: Oxford University Press, 1969.

Momen, Moojan. *An Introduction to Shi'i Islam.* New Haven: Yale University Press, 1985.

Morony, Michael. *Iraq After the Muslim Conquest.* Princeton: Princeton University Press, 1984.

Mottahedeh, Roy. *Loyalty and Leadership in an Early Islamic Community.* Princeton: Princeton University Press, 1980.

Mutahhari, Murtadha. *A Discourse on the Islamic Republic.* Tehran: Islamic Propagation Organization, 1985.

————. *Jihad.* Trans. Muhammad Salman Tawhidi. Tehran: Islamic Propagation Organization, 1985.

————. *Society and History.* Trans. Mahliqa Qara'i. Tehran: Islamic Propagation Organization, 1985.

al-Nafeesi, Abdullah Fahad. "The Role of the Shi'ah in the Political Development of Modern Iraq." Ph.D. thesis. Cambridge University, 1972.

Nelson, Joan M. *Access to Power.* Princeton: Princeton University Press, 1979.

Nieuwenhuis, Tom. *Politics and Society in Early Modern Iraq, 1802–1831*. The Hague: Martinus Nijhoff Publishers, 1982.

Nonneman, Gerd. *Iraq, the Gulf States and the War*. London: Ithaca Press, 1986.

Norton, Augustus Richard. *Amal and the Shi'a*. Austin: University of Texas Press, 1989.

Parsons, Talcott. *Essays in Sociological Theory*. Rev. ed. New York: The Free Press, 1954.

Penrose, Edith. "Industrial Policy and Performance in Iraq." In *The Integration of Modern Iraq*, ed. Abbas Kelidar, 150–170. London: Croom Helm, 1979.

Penrose, Edith, and E. F. Penrose. *Iraq: International Relations and National Development*. London: Ernest Benn, 1978.

Phillips, Doris G. "Rural-to-urban Migration in Iraq." *Economic Development and Cultural Change* 7, 4 (1959): 405–421.

"Plots Against Saddam Hussein." *Foreign Report*, July 23, 1981, 3–4.

Pool, David. "From Elite to Class: The Transformation of Iraqi Political Leadership." In *The Integration of Modern Iraq*, ed. Abbas Kelidar, 63–87. London: Croom Helm, 1979.

Quint, Malcolm. "The Idea of Progress in an Iraqi Village." *Middle East Journal* 12, 4 (1958): 369–384.

Qutb, Sayyid (Sayed Kotb). *Social Justice in Islam*. Trans. J. B. Hardie. Washington, D.C.: American Council of Learned Societies, 1953 (c. 1945).

Ramazani, R. K. *Revolutionary Iran: Challenge and Response in the Middle East*. Baltimore: Johns Hopkins University Press, 1986.

———. "Editorial." *Middle East Journal* 43, 2 (1989): 165–167.

———. "Iran's Foreign Policy." In *Iran's Revolution*, ed. R. K. Ramazani, 48–68. Washington, D.C.: Middle East Institute, 1990.

Rassam, Amal. "Al-Taba'iyya: Power, Patronage and Marginal Groups in Northern Iraq." In *Patrons and Clients in Mediterranean Society*, eds. Ernest Gellner and John Waterbury, 157–166. London: Gerald Duckworth, 1977.

"Reign of Terror Sweeps Iraq's Scientific Community." *New Scientist*, April 2, 1981, 3–4.

Renfrew, Nita. "Who Started the War?" *Foreign Policy* 66 (1987): 98–108.

al-Rihaimi, Abd al-Halim. *Tarikh al-Harakat al-Islamiya fi al-'Iraq 1900–1924* (History of the Islamic movement in Iraq, 1900–1924). Beirut: House of Scholarly Printing, Publication, and Distribution, 1985.

Riley, Peggy. "Letter from ath-Thagir." *Middle East International*, April 19, 1985, 20.

Rodenbeck, Max. "Saddam's Opponents Unite." *Middle East International*, January 11, 1991, 11.

Ross, Dennis. "Soviet Views Toward the Gulf War." *Orbis* 28, 3 (1984): 437–447.

Sachedina, Abdulaziz. *Islamic Messianism*. Albany: State University of New York Press, 1981.

al-Sadr, Muhammad Baqir. *Min Fikr al-Da'wa al-Islamiya* (Thoughts on the Islamic Call). Information Center of the Islamic Da'wa Party. N.p., n.d.

———. *Contemporary Man and the Social Problem*. Trans. Yasin al-Jibouri. Tehran: World Organization for Islamic Services, 1980.

———. *Islam and Schools of Economics*. Trans. M. A. Ansari. Karachi: Islamic Seminary Publications, 1980.

———. "Nida' al-Qa'id al-Shahid Ayatullah al-Sadr ila al-Sha'b al-'Iraqi al-Muslim" (Message of the Martyr Leader Ayatullah al-Sadr to the Muslim Iraqi

People). Tape-recorded by Ayatullah al-Sadr and circulated widely as his "Last
Message." 1980.

———. *The General Bases of Banking in the Muslim Society*. Trans. Yasin al-
Jibouri. Washington, D.C.: Islamic Revival Movement, 1981.

———. *A General Outlook* [sic] *at Rituals*. Trans. Yasin al-Jibouri. Washington,
D.C.: Islamic Revival Movement, 1981 (1977).

———. *Islamic Political System*. Trans. M. A. Ansari. Karachi: Islamic
Seminary, 1982.

———. *Our Philosophy*. Trans. Shams C. Inati. London: Muhammadi Trust, 1987
(1959).

———. *Iqtisaduna*. Excerpt trans. I. K. H. Howard. In *Expectation of the
Millennium*, eds. Seyyed Hossein Nasr, Hamid Dabashi, and Seyyed Vali Reza
Nasr, 117–125. Albany: State University of New York Press, 1989.

Sahliyeh, Emile F. "The West Bank and the Gaza Strip." In *The Politics of Islamic
Revivalism*, ed. Shireen Hunter, 88–100. Washington, D.C.: Center for
Strategic and International Studies, 1988.

Schahgaldian, Nikola B. *The Clerical Establishment in Iran*. Santa Monica: Rand
Corporation, 1989.

Shaban, M. A. *Islamic History*. Cambridge: Cambridge University Press, 1976.

Sherbiny, Naien. "Expatriate Labor Flows to the Arab Oil Countries in the
1980s." *Middle East Journal* 38, 4 (1984): 643–667.

Sick, Gary. "A Glimmer of Hope for Iran-Iraq Peace." *New York Times*, February
21, 1988. E23.

Siddiqui, Kalim, ed. *Issues in the Islamic Movement, 1980–1981*. London: Open
Press, 1981.

———. *Issues in the Islamic Movement, 1982–1983*. London: Open Press,
1984.

Sivan, Emmanuel. "Sunni Radicalism in the Middle East and the Iranian
Revolution." *International Journal of Middle East Studies* 21, 1 (1989): 1–30.

Sluglett, Peter. *Britain in Iraq*. London: Ithaca Press, 1976.

Springborg, Robert. "Baathism in Practice: Agriculture, Politics, and Political
Culture in Syria and Iraq." *Middle Eastern Studies* 17, 2 (1981): 191–209.

———. "Iraq's Agrarian Infitah." *Middle East Report* 145 (1987): 16–21.

Stowasser, Barbara, ed. *The Islamic Impulse*. London: Croom Helm, 1987.

Tamadonfar, Mehran. *The Islamic Polity and Political Leadership*. Boulder:
Westview Press, 1989.

Tarbush, M. A. *The Role of the Military in Politics*. London: Kegan Paul, 1982.

Thesiger, Wilfred. *The Marsh Arabs*. Harmondsworth, UK: Penguin Books, 1967
(1964).

Towler, Robert. "The Changing Status of the Ministry?" *Crucible*, May 1968:
73–78.

United Activists for a Democratic Iraq. "Appeal to Human Rights Organizations."
Socorro, N.M.: UAD Iraq, June 2, 1991.

U.S. Department of State. *Country Reports on Human Rights Practices for 1985*.
Washington, D.C.: Government Printing Office, 1986.

Vinogradov, Amal. "The 1920 Revolt in Iraq Reconsidered: The Role of Tribes in
National Politics." *International Journal of Middle East Studies* 3, 2 (1972):
123–139.

Weber, Max. *Economy and Society*. 3 vols. Eds. Guenther Roth and Claus
Wittich. Trans. Ephraim Fischoff et al. New York: Bedminster Press, 1968.

Whittleton, Celine, Jabr Muhsin, and Fran Hazelton. "Whither Iraq?" In *Saddam's*

Iraq, 2nd ed., ed. Committee Against Repression and for Democratic Rights in Iraq, 242–252. London: Zed, 1989.

Wilson, Arnold. "Mesopotamia, 1914–1921." *Journal of the Royal Central Asia Society* 8, 3 (1921): 144–161.

Wilson, Rodney. *The Arab World*. Boulder: Westview Press, 1984.

Wolf, Eric. "Peasant Rebellion and Revolution." In *National Liberation: Revolution in the Third World*, eds. Norman Miller and Roderick Aya, 48–67. New York: Free Press, 1971.

Index

Hakim, Ayatollah Muhsin al-, 15, 32,
42(n12), 46, 48, 49, 58, 62, 65,
69(n65), 76, 77, 78, 79(fig.), 81, 82;
and Ba'th government, 46, 47; political
activism of, 33–34, 36, 37, 40, 41, 107
Hakim, Sahib al-, 78
Hakim family, al-, 60, 62, 70(n71), 77, 84,
95
Halabja, 64
Hammadi, Sa'doun, 2, 90
Harakat al-Rabitat al-Islamiya fi Kurdistan,
al-, 62
Haras al-Istiqlal, 16
Hariri, Ghazi al-, 55
Hasan, Imam, 11
Hasan, Abu Thar al-, 63
Hasani, Baqir Ahmad al-, 20, 28(n45)
Hashim, Banu, 16
Hashimite monarchy, 4, 16, 22, 23, 33,
108
Hawza al-Imam al-Mahdi, 78
Hawza al-Zaynabia, 78
Hawza Hashimiya, 78
Higher Agricultural Council, 94
Hilla, 11, 37
Hizb al-Da'wa al-Islamiya, 2, 3, 32, 54–66,
83, 84, 92, 108, 124, 145; Hizbullah
cells and, 63–64; membership of, 86–
88(table), 91(table); opposition to, 39–
42; organization of, 55, 57, 82,
86(table); recruitment to, 38–39, 54–55
Hizb al-Fatimi, 40, 44(n43)
Hizb al-Tahrir al-Islami, 23, 28(n54), 36
Hizbullah, 62, 63–64, 92
Hotel Jundiyan, 64
Housing, 34, 50, 90, 111
Human rights, 112–113, 136–137, 147–
148
Husaini, Abu Baida' al-, 91(table)
Husaini, Muhammad Salih al-, 87(table)
Husainiya Al Mubaraka, 38
Husainiya Al Yasin, 38
Husainiya Tehraniya, 46
Husri, Sati al-, 18
Hussein, Imam, 10, 11, 24, 51, 54
Hussein, King, 39
Hussein, Saddam, 40, 49, 51, 64, 66(n2),
105, 106, 114, 117(n10), 146, 147,
153(n15); assassination attempts on,
58, 59–60, 63, 82, 94; as enemy, 54–
55; power of, 45, 53, 97, 115
Hussein, Sharif, 16–17, 19

Husseini, Ali al-, 77
Husseini, Muhsin al-, 83

ICP. See Iraqi Communist Party
ICP/CC. See Iraqi Communist Party/Central
Command
Ijtihad, 31–32, 121–122, 124, 128, 138
Ikha Party, 21
Ikhwan al-Muslimin, 23, 41, 145
Imam al-Jawad School, 76, 82
Imams, 11, 13, 83, 120–121, 125
Imperialism, 147
Independence, 14, 15, 17, 19, 20–21
Inheritance: laws of, 34, 35, 43(n24)
Insurance companies: nationalization of,
40
Intelligentsia: role of, 85–89, 105–
106
International Organization for the Defense
of Human Rights, 113
Intifada, 68(n32), 95; 1952, 23; Rajab, 52–
53, 88(table); Safar, 51–52, 78
Investment: foreign, 136
Iqta', 12
Iqtisaduna (al-Sadr), 4, 126, 129, 130
Iran, 5, 8, 27(n40), 41, 46, 50, 58, 60, 64,
78, 89, 91(table), 96, 136, 141(n56),
146, 149; exile in, 24, 144; expellees
to, 48–49, 92(table), 113; Islamic
government in, 1, 133, 134; rural
poverty in, 135–136; Shi'as in, 5(n2),
12; terrorism by, 2–3
Iranians, 50, 66; expelled, 46, 48–49,
59(table)
Iran-Iraq War, 2, 58, 60, 63, 78, 86(table),
91(table), 117(n17), 136; Ba'th
government in, 114, 146
Iraq: as Arab name, 7–8; as British mandate,
15, 16, 17–24; control of, 12–13;
Islamic government in, 143–144;
religioethnic composition of, 5, 8–9
Iraqi Communist Party (ICP), 22, 33, 39,
52, 65, 117(nn16, 21); opposition to,
36–37
Iraqi Communist Party/Central Command
(ICP/CC), 41
Iraqi National Action Committee, 65
Iraqi Petroleum Company, 21, 49
Irrigation system, 12
Isfahani, Abu al-Hasan, 19, 22, 23
Isfahani, Arbab, 122
Isfahani, Muhammad Riza al-, 78

Law 117, 48
Law number 188, 34
League of Muslim Women, 62
League of Nations, 21
Lebanon, 77, 83, 92, 148; Iraqis in, 50, 78;
   Shi'as in, 5(n2), 12
Legal system: Islamic, 120, 121–122
Legitimacy, 10; government, 22, 115;
   Islamic, 107, 108, 134; political, 106,
   109
Literacy, 15, 22, 101–102, 108
Liwas, 48
Loans, 114, 129–130
Lyell, Thomas, 18

Mada'in, 10
Madhab, 34
Madinat al-Hurriya, 60
Madinat al-Thawra, 40, 53, 63, 99(n28),
   105, 113, 117(n12); demonstrations in,
   53, 89–90
Madrasa Zahra', 82
Magianism, 9
Mahdi, 121
Mahmoud, Shakir, 16
Majlis al-A'la lil Thawra al Islamiya fi al-
   'Iraq, al-, 60, 62, 64, 145, 150;
   leadership of, 61(table), 78, 84;
   meetings of, 83, 165–166
Malnutrition, 15
Mandate period, 17–18
Mansuri, Abd al-Amir Hamid al-, 58,
   87(table)
Maraji', 76, 95, 122, 123(table), 134–135
Marriage, 124
Martial law, 22–23
Martyr al-Sadr Force. See Shahid al-Sadr
   Force
Martyrdom. See Shahada, Al-
Martyr Muhammad Jawad al-Jibouri Group,
   91(table)
Mashkur, Abd al-Amir, 87(table)
Maula, Muhammad Taki, 64
Mawdudi, Maulana, 2, 119
Mecca, 12
Media, 59
Merchants: in Islamic movement, 94–96
Mesopotamia, 7, 8, 10, 75
Middle class, 22, 33, 95, 96, 101–102
Midhat Pasha, 14
Migration: of peasants, 21, 25; rural-urban,
   90, 93–94, 103, 105, 149

Milani, Muhammad Hadi al-, 78
Military, 21, 22, 26(n17), 33, 55; Ba'th,
   51–52, 96–97, 111; coups by, 24, 39–
   40; Iraqi, 17, 42(n1); Islamic, 4, 54;
   Majlis, 61–62, 64
Military intelligence, 114
Ministry of Planning, 60
Miriya, 60
Modernization, 22, 33, 74, 108; economic,
   106, 130; under Ottoman Empire, 14–
   15, 101
Mongols, 12
Montezeri, Ayatullah, 134
Mosul, 13, 15, 24, 37, 63
Mubarqi', Qasim al-, 53, 90
Mudarrisi, Muhammad Hadi al-, 66, 83, 84,
   148
Mudarrisi, Muhammad Taqi al-, 66, 83
Mudirun, 18
Muhajirin, 49, 95
Muhammad (the Prophet), 1, 10, 11, 16, 25,
   34, 104, 106, 119, 120, 123, 124, 133
Muhammad, Aziz, 65
Muhammadi, Mustafa, 87(table)
Muhannad, Abu, 90
Mujahid, Abu, 63–64
Mujahidat, 62
Mujahidin, 15, 54, 57, 62, 68(n51),
   70(n82), 86(table); attack on Hussein
   by, 60, 94
Mujtahids, 14; power of, 18, 19–20, 122;
   role of, 31–32, 34, 128
Mullas, 14
Munazzamat al-'Amal al-Islami. See Islamic
   Task Organization
Musawi, Abu Aziz al-, 88(table)
Muslim Brotherhood, 23, 31, 34. See also
   Ikhwan al-Muslimin
Mutahhari, Murtaza, 128, 140(n43)

Nahda party, 20
Na'ini, Muhammad Hussein, 19, 28(n42)
Najaf, 11, 17, 38, 46, 47, 77, 78, 90, 113;
   intifada in, 52–53; pilgrimages to, 24,
   51; scholars in, 48, 74, 75(table), 84;
   schools in, 19, 20, 41, 76, 82
Napalm, 66
Naqib, Hasan, 65
Naqib, Talib, 15
Naqib, Nuqaba' 13
Nasriya, 90
Nasser, Gamal Abdul, 39, 40, 42(n1)

About the Book
and the Author

Beginning in the 1950s with an educational strategy and continuing today with a revolutionary strategy, the Iraqi clergy have issued a call to Iraqis to defend the cause of Islam, an alteration in the traditional Shi'i position of noninvolvement in politics. Wiley details the contemporary Islamic movement by means of which observant Shi'as and Sunnis are working for Islamic government in Iraq. She describes the philosophy of governing through Islamic law, a philosophy aimed at eliminating corruption and tyranny. In the process, she sheds light on the social bases of the movement and the political ideology of Islamic government.

JOYCE WILEY is a visiting assistant professor in the Departments of Government and International Studies, University of South Carolina at Spartanburg.